# Breaking Free

## from your past

### How To Create A Life Of Your Own

**CAROLYN FOSTER**

*Headway* · Hodder & Stoughton

*To my husband, Donald, and our daughters, Carrie and Alexa,*
*for their steadfast love, understanding, and humour*

*Cataloguing in Publication Data is available from the British Library*

ISBN 0 340 60278 3

First published in US by The Putnam Publishing Group, 1993
First published by Hodder Headline, 1994

Inpression number 10  9  8  7  6  5  4  3  2  1
Year               1998  1997  1996  1995  1994  1993

Typeset by Wearset, Boldon, Tyne and Wear.
Printed in Great Britain for Hodder & Stoughton Educational, a division of Hodder Headline Plc, 338 Euston Road, London NW1 3BH by Thomson Litho Ltd, Scotland

# CONTENTS

# A NOTE FROM CAROLYN FOSTER

A packet of letters written by members of my family living in San Francisco at the time of the 1906 earthquake and fire led me to this book. I had read these particular letters as an adolescent, enthralled by the dramatic narrative. A few years ago, rereading words written in that time of crisis by my great-grandmother, her sister, and her daughter, I realised that their attitudes, feelings and even style of expression mirrored those of my mother, my daughters and myself. The similarities I noticed between my ancestors and my current family fascinated me. These family patterns of shared attitudes and behaviour had to be powerful and deeply ingrained to carry through so many generations.

For example, I notice in myself and in my current family a strong tendency to be both extremely pessimistic and extremely optimistic. When faced with a potential crisis, a change in a relationship, or an upcoming work deadline, I am usually of two minds: I expect and prepare for the worst; I also believe in, hope for, and work towards the best. This strange blend allows me the illusion of feeling in control, because no matter what happens, I'll be ready.

In my family's earthquake letters, I recognised both extremes in the differing attitudes of those who experienced the tragedy. Camped on the hill outside their home, my great-gramdmother wrote to describe the inferno:

*To stand on 21st Street Hill and look down is just like looking into a blazing furnace three miles square.*

Devastated, she closed her letter:

*San Francisco is ruined – it can never recover.*

Her father, an entrepreneur whose business ventures took the family from wealth to poverty and back again many times, had only twenty dollars in cash at the time of the quake. His contracts, stock certificates and gold were in a safe in a downtown office. As my grandmother told it, when the family saw the Daniel Marker building, which housed Grandpa Wilbur's office, dynamited in an effort to stop the fire's progress, Grandpa threw back his head and laughed. He let the past go, assuming that the future would work out. His other daughter, my great-great-aunt Libbie, wrote to another family friend in one of her letters:

*Do not worry about the folks. . . . There will be no trouble as everybody will help us all.*

I find comfort in knowing that the mix of despair and bravado with which I approach life is part of my heritage. I can look at the family patterns that echo down the generations and make more sense of my own behaviour. When I can more clearly understand how I got to be the way I am, I increase my options to respond in the old way or to choose a different outlook.

All my life I have wanted to understand family relationships. An only child, I observed my parents and relatives closely. I listened as my grandmother told and re-told stories about ancestors who sometimes seemed more real to me than my classmates. My curiosity about how families work drew me to study for a master's degree in marriage, family and child counselling when my own children were still quite young.

My work with clients consistently led back to the roots of feelings and behaviour in the family attitudes we learn in early childhood. As I watched people struggle with the legacy of their family upbringings – poor self-esteem, unclear communication, unhappy relationships, unfulfilled ambitions – I wanted to apply the insights I had gained from my own family's letters and from the writing I had done about my own family's patterns.

Writing can be a powerful tool that illuminates and heals the way our families affected our behaviour. Expressing ourselves freely on paper sheds new light on situations, relieves our feelings and clarifies directions to take. Through courses, workshops and retreats over the years I came to believe in writing as a tool for personal growth. Out of my belief in writing's healing power, using principles I had learned that can help people change, I developed a course called 'Writing From Your Roots'. The core of this course, which is presented in this book, is a series of writing exercises that help identify growth-producing and painful family patterns and clarify actions to reinforce or change those patterns.

Having taught this course many times, I have seen how exploring family patterns through writing leads to insight and strategies for change that have benefited a wide range of people. The participants in the course come with differing expectations and agendas, including curiosity about family mysteries, recovery from traumatic family experiences, the desire to avoid replaying hurtful patterns and the wish to put positive family patterns to greater use in the present. Their comments after the course usually include these three responses:

'I'm surprised at how much I remembered, and I'm full of memories and feelings.'

'I can see how helpful it is to understand the influence of the past on the present.'

'I know it will take me a while to absorb all this and put it into action, but I now have tools for making changes in my life today.'

I often hear from participants in the weeks and months after the last class, and their responses show that the themes of the course and the insights of the writing process continue to help them make positive changes.

The development of the Writing From Your Roots course into this book began with another earthquake. For over six months, I delayed phoning an editor to whom a colleague had suggested I propose this book. Then, on October 17, 1989, came the Loma Prieta earthquake, a 7.1 shaker. Our family home escaped with almost no damage, although neighbours and friends were not so lucky. I spent six hours by the phone, trying to reach the retirement home near San Francisco where my grandmother, then 95 and the only family survivor of the 1906 quake, lives in the medical facility on the twenty-second floor. When I finally got through close to midnight, the nurse reported, 'She's fine, but we can't get her to bed; she's standing at the windows watching San Francisco burn'.

Family dramas, family patterns: the 1989 earthquake led me to call the editor my friend had recommended, who took time to listen to my quake-rattled outpouring of words and later saw the possibility of this book in a course outline and some impassioned pages.

Writing this book and continuing to teach the course are also part of my own ongoing work with my family patterns. It's a lifetime commitment, learning to enhance the qualities I'm delighted to have absorbed from my family and to change those that frustrate, limit or hurt me and others.

There are no short-cuts to these deep changes, but I have seen in my own life, as well as in the lives of others, that exploring and becoming aware of family patterns can yield rich rewards in greater self-worth and more fulfilling relationships. I offer *Breaking Free From Your Past* as a companion on this journey.

# CHAPTER 1

# YOUR PROBLEMS AND YOUR FAMILY PATTERNS

Many personal problems are like poison ivy; they keep growing back, and they signal their presence with discomfort and pain. In your daily life, these problems can erupt in different ways. Sometimes your body makes you aware of them with symptoms and illness. Sometimes persistent thoughts or unexpected emotions such as anger, fear and depression make you unhappy or confused. Perhaps you say or do something that doesn't reflect your usual behaviour. Perhaps conflicts with family, friends or colleagues develop at home or at work.

In all these cases, the chances are you don't know what to do at first. Yet because of the discomfort of the problem, you want it to go away, as fast as possible. People who come in to see counsellors almost always end their initial description of the problem by saying, 'Now what should I do?' They want the problem solved more than they want to understand why it happened. When you take your car to a mechanic, you don't want a history of the internal combustion engine; you want your carburettor fixed.

Yet our problems tend to repeat themselves in patterns, and part of the solution is understanding the history that set up those patterns. Perhaps your lover has betrayed you, your boss is impossibly demanding or your teenage child stays out too late. You can leave your lover, resign from your job and keep your child at home next weekend, but if you don't work out the underlying causes for these problems they will probably happen again, with new characters or in new ways.

Problems recur in patterns because people are likely to do what is familiar, even when it is clearly not working. Because it's familiar, you often don't realise that there is another possible course of action. The root of your old ways of doing things goes back to your family experiences from childhood and adolescence. If you look back over the development of a problem, you will come to the roots of it in your early family life.

You can move far from the places where you were born and brought up, and you can cut yourself off completely from all family members. However, your attitudes and behaviour are still primarily shaped by your family experiences from the past. These experiences created your psychological root system.

Your past experiences formed a pattern for your growth, shaping the way you perceived and responded to yourself, your family members and the world outside the family circle. You can't change those experiences, but through exploring your past you can better understand your life now and change your future.

Your family was the soil from which you were born, and from infancy through adolescence most families provide nourishment in the form of life-sustaining food, shelter and human contact. Since families are never perfect, as no soil is perfect, you probably received a combination of both nutrients and pollutants from your family ground. Perhaps your basic needs were met, but no one went out of his or her way to make you feel special. Or perhaps you were protected so much that you had a hard time becoming strong and self-sufficient.

Just as you can't predict how a plant will develop and guarantee that it will thrive, there is no magic formula for the growth of a happy human being. However, psychologists and family therapists study what conditions help children grow into healthy and fulfilled adults. Through learning from the diversity of family situations in their practices, they notice that for healthy development children need to receive these conditions:

- a stable foundation of responsible, caring adults;
- an environment where it is safe for children to discover and express themselves;
- the nourishment of love and the direction of parental guidance;
- a model of how to make a good life and how to cope with adversity.

You may have been forunate enough to grow up with *all* of the above conditions met. More likely, however, your family provided a complex mix of helpful and hurtful experiences; and to the degree that they are hurtful, they are probably harming your life today. You can't get rid of all your problems quickly but you can trace how current difficult or painful areas of your life developed in your family context and make specific plans for positive change.

By recalling and writing about the roots of your family memories from childhood and adolescence, you can understand more fully how you got to be the person you are today. Writing from your roots through the exercises in this book can help you become the person you want to be.

This book provides writing exercises that trace the patterns of your past, reveal their imprints on your present and point you in the direction of more fulfilling patterns for your future. As a foundation for the exercises to come, this opening chapter will explain the hows and whys of family patterns and suggest ways to use this book.

# HOW FAMILY PATTERNS AFFECT YOU

Family patterns are so powerful partly because they grow out of instinctual need. Sticking close to their parents ensures young animals' survival in the wild; human babies bond to the faces, voices and bodies of their parents as well. What you experience with and learn from your parents shapes your view of life and your participation in it in a multitude of ways. Three specific areas are:

- knowing yourself and feeling secure;
- handling pain and enjoying life;
- relating to others.

Examining each of these will help you understand the all-pervasive effect of family learning and identify areas that are strong influences in your life now.

## KNOWING YOURSELF AND FEELING SECURE

When you were only three months old, you didn't see yourself as separate from your mother. At around five months you began to develop your own identity, recognising that your mother was not a part of you and could go away. How your needs were met during the first year or two of life laid the foundation for your sense of self to evolve.

A strong sense of self grows from a firm foundation of trustworthy care, just as a tree thrives on good soil, water and sunlight. This first relationship of trust with whoever cared for you in your early years taught you to view the world as either safe or unsafe. If your family did not meet your needs well in this area, you may have problems with:

- feeling betrayed by those you care about;
- wondering why life is so unfair;
- doubting yourself and having poor self-esteem;
- getting stuck but being frightened to try something new;
- mistrusting authority figures in your life.

If you identify with these problems, you may say these kinds of things to yourself:

'I just don't feel comfortable with that person.'
'This place makes me nervous; I don't feel safe here.'
'Why can't I stand on my own two feet?'
'Don't take a chance. It's not worth the risk.'
'Nobody is ever really there for me.'
'If I don't do it myself, it won't happen.'

## HANDLING PAIN AND ENJOYING LIFE

When you were between two and five years old, you began exploring beyond the orbit of your parents' immediate protection. If your parents were comfortable with your zigzag path

3

between daring and needing help, you learned to manage the jolts that came with the adventures. A child whose efforts are supported and encouraged despite failures grows strong in initiative and learns to enjoy the process as well as the goal.

Parents negotiate this critical child-raising stage either helped or hampered by their own upbringings. They teach by example. If they can handle their own pain, they will be better able to teach you to handle yours. Casual acceptance of mistakes and emphasis on continuing progress are precious gifts for a growing child. Impatience, ignorance of the child's needs, overprotection and unrealistic expectations are a few of the ways that parents undermine their children's abilities. If your family had trouble with these issues, your problems may include:

- getting overwhelmed by life's ups and downs;
- wanting things *your* way;
- feeling worried or anxious much of the time;
- being afraid to fail;
- wanting someone to understand and take care of you.

If you identify with these problems, you may say these kinds of things to yourself:

'I hate feeling so vulnerable all the time.'
'Why don't things work out my way?'
'I know I'm a perfectionist but I can't help it.'
'How can I learn to let go?'
'I just want to relax and enjoy life more.'

## RELATING TO OTHERS

Your school-age years through to early adulthood immersed you in relationships with others. In the classroom, on the playing field and in friendships, first loves and first jobs, young people discover themselves through activity and interaction. If your parents spoke clearly and listened well, showed they had healthy values, earned your respect and showed respect for you, upheld standards but were understanding and flexible, you received excellent preparation for successful relationships.

If your family relationships were full of conflict and pain, you may have depended for your security on external activities, friendships and partners to love. You wanted to become good at something, to be recognised for it, to have an identity and to have someone who really loved you. However, if you tried to make up for your family's inability to fill these relationship needs, you may have found that new relationships were affected by old conflicts and pain. Your problems might include:

- trying many different jobs without feeling successful;
- believing that what you are is limited to who you know or what you own;

- alternately clinging to people and pushing them away;
- having trouble making friends or keeping friends;
- struggling to set and to achieve goals;
- longing for the approval of others.

If you identify with these problems, you may say these kinds of things to yourself:

'I suppose I haven't found my niche yet.'
'I've got to keep up a good front.'
'This person's the one for me, the love of my life.'
'We had such awful communication problems; it'd never have worked.'
'It's impossible to please other people, and I can't seem to please myself either.'
'I just want to be loved for myself.'

# HOW PAINFUL FAMILY PATTERNS CAN BE CHANGED

For most people, having the same kind of problems and saying the same things over and over again to themselves eventually becomes too painful, and they decide they really want to change. If patterns of thought and action are so ingrained from your childhood, what can you do to make it different in the future?

Changing an established pattern in your life is a cyclic process. First, you become more **aware** of what the problem is, gathering information about what's going on now. Next you trace your current problems to their roots in your family patterns and **assess** how changes now would affect you and the others in your life. Finally, you plan and create **change** that is gradual but definite. As you make changes, you need to be aware of your feelings and other people's reactions, so the cycle begins again.

To examine this cycle, let's focus on the three types of action that form a sequence for changing unproductive or destructive family patterns:

- **increasing your awareness;**
- **assessing the situation;**
- **changing your behaviour.**

This sequence forms a cycle of positive growth. Increasing your awareness of your problems and how they affect you and your family members gives you a clearer, broader picture of what's really going on. Being able to assess and describe the problems more precisely helps you decide exactly what changes you want to make. Positive change builds positive forward momentum, so that the future does not simply repeat the painful parts of the past. Some specific examples from one person's struggle to change family patterns may help you understand this progression.

Barbara, a 39-year-old administrative assistant, suspected that the problems she was having related to her childhood experiences. She was in danger of losing yet another job because of conflicts with her boss and she felt worn out from juggling work and her responsibilities at home with her two sons and her husband, Joe. 'I feel like I've been under so much pressure all my life, and I can't cope anymore.'

Because she was distressed by the situation with her boss, Barbara's situation may not seem to have much to do with family patterns. However, as she began to write about her history of feeling pressured, she started to see a pattern related both to the family she grew up with and the one in which she currently lived. Her responses to other people's needs and expectations created overwork, stress and a sense of not controlling her own life.

## INCREASING YOUR AWARENESS

People's pain often comes from the gap between how things currently are in their lives and how they wish they could be. Reflecting on how she wished things could be, Barbara wrote about a peaceful life in which she made everybody happy and felt fulfilled and free to relax. The more she detailed everything she would have to do to make her boss, husband, children and parents happy, the more she realised that her ideal situation would give her no time for herself, just as in her current situation. In one writing exercise, she scribbled, 'I never have had any time to go out and play,' and tears welled up in her eyes as she read these words.

The oldest child of four, Barbara grew up with a father who had trouble keeping a job and a mother who always rescued the family financially. Barbara took care of her younger siblings until she grew up and married Joe, a young businessman. She was sure she had found someone as different from her father as possible. Yet she now sees that she is working as hard and feeling as unsuccessful at pleasing everyone as she did with her parents and siblings. Realising this makes her sad, angry, and confused. 'What am I supposed to do now?' she wondered. 'It seems like writing about all this just shows me more ways in which I'm unhappy.'

## ASSESSING

Increasing awareness does not automatically change painful situations; in fact, the more clearly you see a painful pattern in your life, the more you may be aware of the negative emotions associated with it. So at first, positive action to change a painful situation involves becoming more aware of your true feelings – thinking, talking and writing about them. As you do so, you can assess the situation, tracing your problem to its roots.

The influence of family patterns is subtle and complex, touching all areas of your life in deep and often hidden ways. An illustration from the world of computers demonstrates how thoughts, feeling and behaviour are encoded in family patterns. Certain computers have a key marked 'REVEAL CODES'. Pressing this key displays on the screen, in brackets, all the programmed commands that structure how the words are arranged on the electronic screen. Just as the computer memory holds the encoding of decisions to paragraph or tabulate, you hold within your own memories a wealth of information that can help you understand your family patterns. Once the codes of your family structures are revealed, you can recognise when they start to operate, assess whether they're helpful or not, and substitute new codes, new information and new actions when appropriate.

For example, as she wrote about her family memories, Barbara discovered an encoded expectation to work hard and take care of everyone. She recognised that when others depended on her and made demands, she never questioned that she had to do what they wanted. Writing about her mother's influence, she saw a similarity between taking care of her brothers and sisters as the oldest child in the family and taking care of people at work and at home in her current situation.

In the past, if she complained, her mother lashed out angrily and her father became depressed. 'Now I'm afraid my boss will fire me, and my husband will be disappointed in me,' Barbara said, 'but they're not my parents. How can I approach this differently?' Using writing to sort out past messages from her present situation, Barbara started to assess and explore her options to respond creatively rather than automatically.

## CHANGING YOUR BEHAVIOUR

In assessment, you can see that changes will affect not only you but also everyone else involved in the problem. Family therapist Virginia Satir suggested that the family is like a mobile: each person is on a separate branch of the structure, but anything that touches one person makes the whole structure move in response. In planning for positive changes in your problems, you can't anticipate others' reactions. For that reason, reflection, writing and talking with an objective person provides ongoing support. By tracing a problem to its roots and understanding how you are repeating the past – or reacting against it – in your present situation, you're more equipped to make life-affirming changes.

Because family patterns are so influential, it's helpful to identify a theme that runs through the lives of different individuals in different generations. Barbara saw how her habit of working harder than anyone else was a repetition of her mother's working to compensate for her father's inability to stay with a job. The common theme, she realised, had to do with pleasing others. Barbara remembers her mother describing futile efforts to please her stepmother after her own mother's death. This multigenerational aspect of family themes is a potent tool for understanding and change. 'Underneath it all,' Barbara wrote, 'each one of us was just trying to get noticed and loved.'

Gradually, Barbara noticed the beginning of a healthier pattern with her boss. She initiated a discussion of her workload and duties and outlined a plan to satisfy them both. She started to anticipate his criticisms, recognising how much they reminded her of those of her mother. She was able to acknowledge his concerns without giving up on what she wanted. Her husband and sons cheered her success but also teased her about her newfound toughness. 'I think they're afraid I'll make them do some of the chores,' she commented ruefully.

A cycle of positive change had begun for Barbara – as always, tentative, gradual and far-reaching. Barbara's story illustrates four guidelines for planning and carrying out changes in family-based patterns:

- **go slowly;**
- **take small steps;**
- **expect resistance and surprises;**
- **remember that change is a process, not a product.**

Since the problems in your life have deep roots, rapid, radical solutions are too disruptive to produce lasting improvements. Also, an important question to ask yourself when planning a positive change is: What will I have to give up if I do this?

Barbara discovered that she was attached to her righteous anger at her boss. Complaining about how hard she tried to fulfil his unreasonable demands kept her feeling good about herself. As she planned something different, she had to deal with inner doubts and self-criticism. As you become familiar with your own patterns, making changes slowly and in small increments will build secure bridges to new behaviour.

Maintenance of the familiar will always be easier than establishment of a new pattern. Your resistance to change may surprise you, since you sincerely want your life to be better. Again, the familiarity of the old ways cannot be overestimated. A month later, Barbara remarked, 'This wasn't a one-time decision; I have to keep working out how to react every time I'm asked to do something.' As she began to be more honest about her feelings and less sacrificial in her behaviour, she encountered resistance from her husband, who felt threatened by this new Barbara, and from her sons, who discovered that Mum didn't bend over backwards for them anymore.

Everyone in a system of relationships is affected by the disruption of an old pattern. Everyone wants to feel secure, accepted and appreciated. As you, like Barbara, make changes in long-established patterns, keep asking yourself: What really matters here? Am I following my heart? As you guide yourself through this growth process, you'll be strengthened to respond to others in your life who are also feeling the pressures of change.

Remember that you are not creating a product but learning a process. The result of your efforts will be a new way of life in which you adapt creatively to your circumstances, enhancing the family patterns that work well and gradually changing those that don't. Throughout this process, writing can be a powerful tool for awareness, assessment and change.

# HOW WRITING PROMOTES POSITIVE CHANGE

Making changes in family patterns is difficult, partly because family interactions are so complicated. Family members express themselves in a wide variety of gestures, facial expressions, communication styles and behaviour. When family interactions go well, all the members feel good about themselves and about being part of the family, despite the complications. When the relationships are full of conflict and strain, family members become overwhelmed with the complications and experience frustration and stress.

Under stress, it is hard to think clearly and understand your problems. Your mind works in two different ways: seeing a whole picture and looking at the pieces that make up the whole. The whole-picture mind (often called the right brain) sees patterns; the little-pieces mind (often called the left brain) analyses the parts of the whole. When you are under stress or having problems and you write about it, you use both parts of your mind. Writing brings out hunches, connections, feelings and images from the right brain and helps your left brain make sense of them in logical ways to create strategies and solutions.

Writing is an ideal tool for dealing with the large-scale patterns and specific behaviour of families because it fulfils three functions:

- **expressing your emotions;**
- **broadening your perspective;**
- **applying insight to problem-solving.**

Writing as an expressive outlet helps you discover what you really feel, put your memories and present experience into a clearer context and design a creative new approach to old problems.

## EXPRESSING YOUR EMOTIONS

Writing facilitates two types of emotional expression: discovery and catharsis. Discovering what you really feel occurs through putting thoughts and vague emotions into words; catharsis, or expression that relieves strong emotion, occurs when you can air your feelings fully on paper. Research has shown that putting your feelings into words promotes both physical and mental health.

Kelly, who often felt overwhelmed by her emotions, describes the impact of writing about her feelings:

'I used to avoid dwelling on my feelings, but I ended up getting more and more confused. Pouring out some of that confusion helped me separate and understand the different emotions. In one situation, I discovered I was anxious, angry and excited all at once. By sorting out my feelings, I chose what to do *about each one – relieving my anxiety by writing, expressing my anger to my sister and channelling my excitement into my work.'*

## BROADENING YOUR PERSPECTIVE

Kelly's words point out another benefit of writing: it creates order out of chaos. Thoughts, feelings, memories and wishes float around in your field of awareness all the time, but it's hard to make sense of them all. Writing provides the perspective to understand the meaning behind the events of your life and to resolve problems.

Jim, a man with a history of divorces, suggests that writing gave him a wider view of his family life:

*'I really had tunnel vision before I started writing about my family. I understood why I couldn't get close to people as an adult when I was so close to my family growing up. Now I see that we – my parents and brothers – created such a comfortable world with each other that we never learned how to include other people in it. No wonder none of us has stayed married.'*

## APPLYING INSIGHT TO PROBLEM-SOLVING

Your painful past family experiences and your current problems hold you back from your goals and dreams; problem-solving through writing helps move you forward towards making those goals and dreams reality. Jim's dilemma illustrates how writing gives you a wide-angle lens through which you can see yourself, your family and your life experiences more clearly. With that sharper focus and broader view, you have insights to make your life more fulfilling.

Gail took my Writing From Your Roots course and concluded afterwards:

*'Before I started writing, I knew I had very mixed feelings about my parents and sister but didn't understand this was why my husband and I were fighting about how to raise the girls. Writing brought back painful memories, but it also helped me see how my childhood jealousy of my sister still gets in my way. I'm building a bridge to change by writing out my feelings and plans.'*

As you express your feelings, gain perspective and solve problems through writing, you reveal the coded patterns that shaped your past and reshape them to strengthen your self-worth and your relationships. The specific topics and exercises of this book will lead you through this journey of writing from your roots to promote healthy growth.

# ABOUT THE EXERCISES

The writing exercises in this book are designed to help you identify the underlying patterns behind many of the problems you are having as an adult and trace their roots to your family experiences. As you explore in writing your family past, you will discover how your family members interacted in close connection, like parts in a machine or cells in a biological organism. You will notice which aspects of your family's interactions caused bad feelings and conflict and which promoted good feelings and harmony. By doing the exercises, you will learn some family therapy techniques for observing, analysing and changing the patterns in your life that originated with your family.

Writing about these early family experiences has two advantages. First, writing allows you to re-create a past experience or to describe your current situations vividly, reproducing the atmosphere and feelings. Second, writing encourages you to observe closely what you have re-created and make conclusions about what you have learned.

You will start each set of exercises by re-creating a vivid scene from your early family life. Then you will step back from what you have written and analyse what you can learn from it. Each exercise will encourage you to re-enter your family experience and give voice to all aspects of it. This form of writing is far more powerful than a simple recounting of facts or events.

Once you have immersed yourself in the original family experience and described it fully in writing, you can get new perspectives by investigating the new information. Your perspective on a family member may change. 'I never realised,' one person stated, 'how my grandmother's unhappiness affected us all when she lived with us.'

You may be able to describe how you were affected by family situations with greater detail and accuracy. The same person went on: 'Grandmother's sadness was like a heaviness in the air, and I could hardly breathe because of the tension. I felt guilty each time I laughed or played loudly.'

You may also see more clearly how that past experience affects you now. The grown-up granddaughter concluded: 'I am still ultrasensitive to other people's moods and I try not to disturb anyone. Then I feel depressed. I see now that I am conforming to old constraints and I want to change that.' The writing exercises in this book are designed to lead you naturally to insights such as these and to help you plan the elements you want to strengthen and the changes you want to make in your life today.

You can benefit from the book whether or not you have written much before. Most people have little experience in writing, but they find that once they begin, the words sparked by memories and feelings flow easily. Your own life story, as you will discover, has the power to carry you into and through the writing exercises.

Style, grammar, punctuation and spelling do not matter in this type of writing. Your aim is to get to the heart of your own experiences, and writing with energy and momentum will do that. With each exercise, follow the threads of your memories and feelings. Feel free to modify exercise topics or techniques.

Two basic writing techniques that may help you if you find yourself stuck with a topic are freewriting and clustering.

**Freewriting** works best when you choose a time limit – perhaps five or ten minutes – and write steadily for that time about whatever comes to mind. You may start with the topic on which you have been attempting to write but allow yourself to wander freely wherever your thoughts go, writing whatever occurs to you.

When the time is up, reread what you have written to gain a clearer picture of yourself in the moment. You may discover the approach you need to take to your writing topic or the reason that you are having difficulty. You can then decide how to proceed, writing further on a specific exercise or setting this topic aside for a while. A student commented: 'When I freewrite, I always learn what's going on inside me right now. I feel as if I'm standing on firmer ground afterwards.'

**Clustering** is a brainstorming technique designed to allow the creative, intuitive part of your mind to generate new ideas about a subject. These are then organised into short written pieces, or word sketches. In clustering, you pick a topic or issue about which you want to learn more, such as 'anger in my family' or 'how I was affected by my parents' divorce'. Then you condense this topic into a single word ('anger' or 'divorce') and write it in a circle at the centre of a blank piece of paper. This becomes your nucleus word, around which your clustering will organise.

Next, start putting down all the associations you can make to the central word, circling each new word or phrase. Link the first idea you have to the nucleus word with a connecting line. You can branch out from your first idea to other related ideas in a string of associations. Each time you start a new train of thought, return to the nucleus word and branch out from there in a different direction. Keep adding to your cluster until you run out of associations.

Here is a portion of a cluster done by a woman who wanted to know more about how she was affected by her parents' divorce when she was nine:

After writing a passage starting from the word 'scared', the woman said, 'I never realised that I blamed myself for my parents' splitting up until I looked at that string of associations – scared, guilty, my fault. Through writing, I recognised that my guilt has hurt me and that I wasn't responsible for their breakup.' Powerful insights such as those often result from the clustering

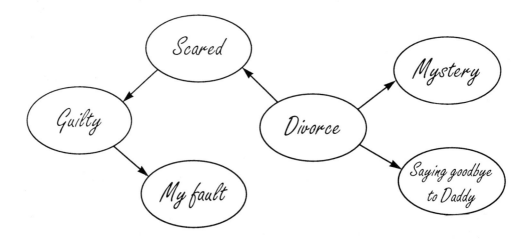

technique. By using it to tap your intuitive knowledge, you increase your problem-solving resources.

In addition to the two basic techniques of freewriting and clustering, which you can use at any time, you will also explore formative family patterns by writing responses to unfinished sentences, making lists and creating dialogues.

**Unfinished sentence** exercises supply some words about a topic to get you started. Examples of unfinished sentences include: 'One thing I would change about my relationship with my mother is . . .' and 'I show my anger at family members by . . .' The advantage of an unfinished sentence is that you can write the first thing that comes into your head without worrying about where you are heading with the topic. And this usually turns out to be closely related to your problem.

**Lists** help organise your thoughts and feelings about a large or unclear issue. Examples of topics for list-making include 'family members with whom I felt comfortable', 'things I do when I'm scared' and 'my problem-solving techniques'. Lists create a sense of order in which you can see the meanings in your experiences more clearly.

**Dialogues** portray events from more than one perspective at a time. You can write a dialogue between you and a family member (such as asking your father how he felt about having three daughters), between different parts of yourself (such as the part of you that wants to help and the independent part of you) or between you at a younger age and you now (such as asking the eight-year-old inside you what it was like when Grandma came to live with you). Written dialogues promote openness, as your responses on paper can be more honest than an actual conversation.

These writing techniques lead to insight and encourage taking action for positive change. To get the most benefit, you can follow up any exercise with written comments summarising what you learned. Here are some useful questions on which to base your comments:

**As I wrote, did I notice:**

- **any physical reactions?** (such as restlessness, twinges of discomfort, or relaxation or tension in face, neck or hands)

  'Putting down my three biggest problems made my stomach knot up. I carry a lot of body tension about these problems.'

- **any new thoughts or realisations?** (such as a different perspective or a previously unseen connection)

  'I saw that my biggest problem – not feeling self-confident – bothers me because my mother never seemed to feel good about herself either.'

- **any emotional responses?** (such as fear, relief, anger, depression or guilt)

  'When I wrote about my family when I was 14, this wave of anger came back, just as if I were still that rebellious adolescent.'

- **any wishes or longings?** such as unfulfilled hopes, ambitions, heartaches or deep desires)

  'I really hope my son feels differently towards me than I do towards my dad.'

Jot down reflections like these as the last step in any of the exercises. Further insight into the influence of your family's patterns on your own will come as you keep what you've written circulating in your mind. The problem-solving strategies you learn through the writing exercises will also continue to benefit your life long after you finish this book.

# HOW TO GET THE MOST FROM THIS BOOK

The chapter topics in this book explain different aspects of family patterns, calling on theory, research and clinical experience from psychology and family therapy. Each topic condenses a great deal of information about family patterns. The writing exercises will shed light on your family situations and suggest ways to move from problems to growth. The topics covered and their progression throughout the book follow a successful model from the Writing From Your Roots course.

**Chapter 2** explores the idea of the family as a system whose interactions shape your development from childhood into adulthood; you will discover how your family history lives on inside you and in your current relationships. **Chapter 3** addresses your family's life stance, their shared attitudes and approaches to life; you will learn how to shape that inherited stance in more positive ways. **Chapter 4** analyses family language, both verbal and nonverbal styles of relating; you will learn how to shape the language you inherited for clearer, more direct communication. **Chapter 5** investigates the four components of your sense of self – body, mind, emotions and spirit – which are shaped by the family you grew up with, and how you can learn to expand your own sense of identity and range of expression. **Chapter 6** examines the development of your personal power – which includes your self-esteem, independence and initiative – in your family; you will find ways to enhance self-worth and counter self-defeating behaviour patterns. **Chapter 7** concentrates on family stories, secrets and silences; you will clarify your memories of family experiences, discovering the truth of your own perceptions. **Chapter 8** summarises what you have learned from this journey through your family past. You will begin integrating what you have learned and mobilising your healing resources to put your insights into action.

The chapter topics and exercises are designed to build on each other in sequence; however, feel free to skip around. Adapting the book to your own needs will give you freedom and flexibility. As you sort out the roots of family patterns, you may find topics or memories that evoke especially strong feelings. Painful experiences in the family context have had a strong effect on your life, so proceed with respect for your own sense of timing. You can defer writing about these experiences or talk them through with a trusted friend or a professional counsellor or psychotherapist. Writing's healing power is always available, now or in the future.

When you complete this workbook, you will be more firmly anchored in the present, with plans to continue growth in your relationships. The process of reshaping your family patterns encompasses a lifetime. Because family members are interconnected as if on a mobile, the positive changes you make affect others in the family, rippling through the generations. As you recall and recount past events and feelings, you will understand how your family roots have both restricted and enabled your growth. Planning for and establishing new patterns will lead you towards fuller self-development and more rewarding relationships. You will write a new story from your roots that moves forward into the future.

# CHAPTER 2

# SURVEYING YOUR FAMILY SYSTEM

All of us find it difficult to view our own family clearly. From birth on, we are adapted to the context and conditions of our own particular family group. Children take for granted that their family's patterns are 'the way families are', and that even extreme or destructive patterns of behaviour are not unusual.

As adults, we still have difficulty seeing our own family clearly. Clarity requires perspective, which requires distance. Though we no longer live with the people who brought us up, we may not have much psychological distance from them.

We internalise our parents' voices and behaviour patterns throughout childhood and adolescence – encouraging and criticising voices, loving and hurtful ways of behaving. Those internalised family experiences colour our adult expectations of family life as potentially healthy or destructive patterns. You can live a thousand miles from your mother but if you still criticise yourself for mistakes in the same harsh way she used to, you do not have distance from her influence on you. By surveying the family system of your childhood, you will begin to gain the clarity and perspective to recognise and emphasise the healthy patterns and change the destructive ones.

The three sections of this chapter focus on ways to help you see your family realities more clearly by describing them in writing. In the first section, you will look at your family and your role in it at various times throughout your childhood. Our family memories are often stored in **snapshot glimpses:** you and Grandpa digging in the garden, you holding your little sisters' hands, you in front of the new house when you were six.

Writing about these snapshot glimpses can tell you a great deal about the feelings and relationships of the people involved, if you look at them carefully and describe them thoroughly. For instance, a written snapshot may show you how you viewed your grandfather as a protective, safe person, or how jealous you were of your sisters. These written psychological snapshots tend to prime the pump of memory, so that your recollections of how it felt to be growing up in your family become more accessible and clear.

Another dimension of family memories comes alive when we look at interaction patterns or **home videos** rather than static snapshots. In the second section of the chapter, you will write about your family's behaviour patterns and interactions that shaped both your past and your present. When you describe the motion of a family scene, you can more clearly see how people are doing things in response to one another. You see Grandpa taking you out to the garden because your parents are fighting; you notice your sisters hogging all the adults' attention at the dinner table.

Repeating familiar patterns can be helpful, because they provide a sense of belonging and security. Some patterns of interaction are simply convenient and comforting, just as some home video scenes are traditional. Mother always holds Susie on her lap in the car because she's the youngest. Grandpa always has the children helping him in the garden.

But if you have unhappy memories of repeating patterns of family interaction, these scenes can help you understand how you were affected in painful ways. Perhaps when Grandpa hurried you away from your parents' fights, you learned that conflict was frightening and now you have trouble expressing your anger with your spouse. Perhaps when you complained about your sisters, your parents sided with them. Perhaps you learned that no amount of effort got you attention, an attitude that is affecting your job performance now.

To understand how your childhood family's patterns of interaction contributed to your present problems, you need to write your memories of early scenes with special attention to detail and feelings. These elements from the past will often stir connections with present-day circumstances. Making the connections between past memories and present pain is the first step in addressing your current problems.

Recounting how your father fell silent and walked away when you disappointed him, you may connect this experience with your sadness today when you try to please another important person in your life who withdraws from you. Writing about angrily picking up broken dishes your father smashed at dinner when he was drunk, you might understand better the anger you feel when you pick up after your messy teenager.

In the third section, your lens of observation focuses on your parents' relationship as a determining factor in your family life and your own development. Even if your biological parents never married and you were brought up by a single parent, the ghost of their relationship haunted your childhood. All of us as children acutely observed whatever marital drama was played out in our family. Yet as children, we could not understand adult dilemmas:

'I hit my sister and now Mummy and Daddy are fighting. It's my fault Daddy is so angry.'
'If Mother hadn't become pregnant with me, my daddy would've stayed around. He was too young to take care of a family. My being born was a mistake.'

Statements such as these, typical of our childhood logic, harm our sense of worth and damage our ability to grow up happy and secure. Many parents aren't aware that children think this way, and some are so confused by the family dramas that they don't know how to help themselves, much less their children.

Yet as an adult you can help yourself to understand intimate marriage and family relationships better. By looking at your past through your adult perspective, you can:

- see the characteristics of your parents' relationship;
- remember your responses to their interactions;
- understand how some of your current problems can be traced back to your observation of their partnership.

The child who believed she caused her parents' fights by hitting her sister may be an adult who holds herself back from aggression. The child who felt his being born was a mistake may be an adult whose self-doubt holds him back. No matter what you learn from writing about your parents' relationship, your insights will give you greater opportunity for choice and change.

In the final section, you will make a preliminary assessment of harmful and helpful patterns in your family. Your impressions of how the family patterns formed and how they shaped you will probably change with more information and insight as you write your way through the book's exercises. At the end of the book, you will have an opportunity to take another overview and write your conclusions from that vantage point. Here, you will put your opening observations to work by describing which family patterns you now want to keep and which ones you want to change.

You can begin to survey your family system with some opening 'word snapshots'.

# YOUR FAMILY SNAPSHOTS

*I*f a photograph could be made that showed not only your family members' faces, bodies, clothes and hairstyles but also their personalities and their effects on you, that psychological snapshot would come close to capturing how you view your family. Then, if you placed yourself in the picture, describing whom you were next to and what you were thinking, feeling, and doing, you would have a snapshot of your role in the family as you experienced it. Finally, if you could accumulate a series of such snapshots over a period of years, you would see how your family make-up changed and how you and others were affected.

You'll be creating these three types of family snapshots with words as you do the following exercises. These initial psychological pictures will help you gather information about how you have viewed yourself and your relatives from your early memories through to the present. Once your memories start accumulating, you will start to see the roots of your current problems in your family past. Understanding how your family system worked is the first step towards healthier family relationships now.

## EXERCISE

## GATHERING BASIC INFORMATION

The sentences that follow focus on snapshots of your family through your eyes at different ages and as you see them now. Completing unfinished sentences is a wonderful way to find out what you really think and know. The opening part of the sentence acts as a prompting device, getting your thoughts flowing into words. Use the words supplied for you as questions in an interview, and respond with whatever words come to your mind first. Unlike in an interview, you are speaking only to yourself, so you can scribble down whatever comes into your head without worrying about an audience.

*Copy the unfinished sentence onto another piece of paper; then complete the sentences with whatever responses come first to mind. Use one sentence or many.*

When I was 7 years old, I described my family as ......................................................................

When I was 14 years old, I described my family as ..................................................................

When I was 21 years old, I described my family as ..................................................................

Today, I describe my family as ..............................................................................................

Thinking about my family, I want to understand ...................................................................

The emotions I most often feel about my family are ..............................................................

Jackie, a nurse in her forties, responded this way:

'When I was 7 years old, I described my family as noisy, sometimes fun, sometimes frightening.

'When I was 14, I described my family as hypocritical, because we were all covering up for my Mum's drinking.

'When I was 21, I described my family as too much of a mess to be involved with.

'Today, I describe my family as dysfunctional and codependent. It frightens me that I keep taking care of people like I used to with my mother.

'Thinking about my family, I want to understand how we contributed to Mum's drinking through her worrying about looking after us. Also, how can I stop responding like that now?

'The emotions I most often feel about my family are anger and regret. We can't get back what we missed. I wish we had been able to be close.'

Jackie summed up by writing: 'I see how my life was so shaped by this one fact – Mum drank – and I want a life shaped around something positive.'

This exercise's snapshots gave you some general impressions of how you saw your family and felt about them in the past and what you wish for in relation to your family today. These impressions will help you begin remembering and considering other events and feelings associated with your family. Each new snapshot contributes to a fuller perspective on your past and a clearer view of your hopes for healing and change.

## EXERCISE

## YOUR ROLE IN YOUR FAMILY

Now focus on your place in the family picture. Each family member tends to play a distinctive role, contributing to the continuation of either helpful or harmful family patterns. Through the technique of clustering in this exercise, you'll be exploring what your role was in the family you grew up with.

A 1 Put the words MY ROLE in a circle in the centre of a blank page.

   2 Then allow yourself to start making associations to your place or role in your family – whatever words or phrases come into your mind. For example, 'the rebel' might be your first thought. Write your word on the page with a circle around it and a line connecting it back to the words MY ROLE.

   3 The new word or phrase may trigger a string of other words. From 'the rebel', you might generate 'troublemaker at school', 'always angry' and 'long-haired defiance'.

   4 When one string is complete, begin another train of thought branching out from the nucleus phrase.

   5 Keep clustering until you feel a shift in your attention, as if you've emptied out your thoughts for now.

B 1 Look over your clustered associations. One may stir a number of feelings or memories, a clue that you may have more to discover and express in this area.

   2 Identify which portion of the cluster affects you most strongly and use that part as a departure point to write a 'word sketch', a short passage that expands on the associations triggered for you.

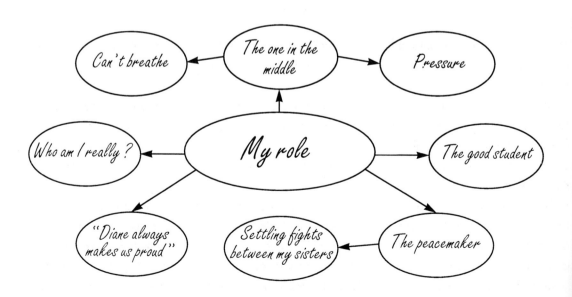

The central portion of a clustering done by Diane, an editorial assistant in her late twenties, is included here. Notice, in Diane's word sketch, how she started with the association 'can't breathe' and then brought in some of the other items from the cluster.

*'I felt squashed in my role, as if I couldn't take a breath without considering how it would affect the others. In the middle with everyone – keeping people happy – but what would make ME happy? I just wanted to be alone, to think things out on my own. But then I feel guilty. I must get out of this trap.'*

In speaking about her word sketch, Diane added, 'I wrote about what I experienced in the past but I can tell that I'm still trying to please others. That's why I wrote the last sentence: I'm still in a pattern that feels like a trap.'

On reflection, Diane wrote how her pattern of being in the middle played itself out differently with her parents and an influential uncle. She acted as mediator in her parents' fights and placated her rich uncle when he was offended by her father. Reflecting on the present – 'still in a pattern that feels like a trap' – Diane noticed how patterns persist through the years. She is more motivated now to get out of that trap, because putting memories and feelings into words focuses and intensifies the need for change.

After completing your own cluster and writing a word sketch, you will have a series of snapshots that connect the roles you played in your family to the variety of roles that you play in relationships today. Seeing these connections more clearly will help you assess whether and how to change your current patterns.

## EXERCISE

## TIMELINE: YOUR FAMILY ACROSS THE YEARS

This three-part exercise looks at how your family make-up varied as you grew up and how you were affected by the changes. Identifying who lived with you at different times sharpens the focus of your snapshots.

Most of us think of 'my family' as being an individual entity. Yet every family is actually a series of families, changing as people come into or leave the family home. Each change means adjustment for all family members. Some problems go away; other problems arise. However, when you are in the midst of these changes, you are too involved to understand how arrivals, departures and the personalities of those who come and go affect you.

Perhaps you were an only child until your brother was born, or your parents adopted a fourth child from another country. Then, your oldest brother went into the army. Your parents may have divorced and perhaps your father moved away. Or possibly your grandmother died and your grandfather moved in with you. Or your uncle who was out of work came for a month and stayed three years.

By creating a timeline and writing about the people who appear on it, you will generate a set of snapshots of the families within your family, identify the people most central to your upbringing and sketch your impressions of the character of those people.

As the clustering of the previous exercise focused on your role to help you see yourself more clearly, this timeline focuses on the family members around you, clarifying the personal qualities of those who shaped your early years. Blood relatives may or may not have been the only people you lived with; recall and list long-term visitors, new partners of a divorced or widowed parent and live-in au-pairs or nannies who may have been part of your family make-up.

A 1 On a piece of paper, draw a timeline to represent the years from your birth to the time you moved out on your own. If you still live with your family of origin or have moved back in with them, your timeline will go up to the present. The timeline can be a straight line, a spiral or even a graph line with ups and downs.

 2 Mark the beginning of the line with a dot to represent your birth. Next to that dot, write the name or names of the family members you lived with right after your birth.

 3 As you move along the timeline, put another dot and a revised list of names whenever the births or deaths or arrivals or departures of family members changed the make-up of your household.

Here is the timeline done by Mike, a 35-year-old building contractor:

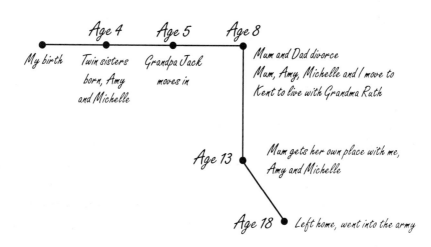

B When your timeline is complete up to the time you left home, answer the following questions in short passages about the various family groups, much like the word sketches of the previous exercise.

Which family grouping is the one you think of when someone asks, 'Who was in your family?' Which family grouping is vague in your memories?

Which family grouping was the most comfortable; the least comfortable?

Mike wrote:

*I don't remember much before my twin sisters were born but I know I was jealous of all the attention they got. My favourite time had to be those years with Grandpa Jack in the house. When my parents fought, he'd take me out in the garage and show me how to build things. I hated being in Kent with Grandma Ruth, Mum, and my sisers. It was a little better when Mum got her own house but I escaped to the army as soon as I could.*

You may find, as Mike did, that you didn't get all your influence from the people you view as your 'real family'; others seem important to you because of the impact of their personal qualities or character and the role they played in your life. For instance, Grandpa Jack's influence was great because his attentiveness made Mike feel special and because he provided stability when Mike's parents couldn't. In only three years, Mike and his grandfather created a 'real-family' bond. You will have more opportunities to look at the people who shared deep kinship bonds with you in Chapter 8, *Living from your roots.*

C  1  List the names of those people on your timeline who had the most impact on you, either in a positive or a negative way.
2  Next to each person's name, jot down three words that describe that person.
3  To complete this exercise, sum up what you have noticed in a few sentences.

For example, for his mother, Mike wrote, 'tired, resentful, a fighter', and for his Grandpa Jack, 'patient, giving, expert'.

Through a child's eyes, Mike saw his mother's fatigue, heard her resentful comments about his father's lack of support, and admired her strength bringing up three children alone. In choosing those three qualities to describe her from his adult perspective, Mike called on many years of observations.

You too will find that writing some qualities of these central family members gives dimension and colour to the snapshots of your timeline. Your descriptions will reflect the complexity of your view of these important people in your family story.

As he wrote all this down, Mike came to a new perspective. 'I suppose I admire Mum for moving out on her own – that took courage. Maybe I went into the building trade because of all that Grandpa Jack meant to me. I certainly don't feel I ever knew my father well – the family shadow, slipping in and out of my life.'

The word-picture snapshots from these exercises focused in on you and your family members as individuals. Writing about how you saw your family at various times, what your family role was, and who lived with and influenced you, you have probably gained greater clarity and perspective in your view of the separate people who made up your family group. From this perspective, you can now survey and observe the patterns of interaction that took place among them as family members.

# HOME VIDEOS: YOUR FAMILY IN ACTION

Snapshots give brief glimpses of family members, but video-tapes convey the complexity of a family. Seeing how the family members talk together, move around and touch or avoid touching each other can give you an effective look at the characteristic interactions among them.

An actual home video might show how Mum took charge and lined everybody up to be filmed while Dad tried to keep everybody happy by chattering away and patting people. The written counterpart of a home video focuses on patterns of interaction. A written home video describes how this pattern of Mum-the-commander and Dad-the-comforter played out in daily life, affecting you and the others.

Details such as Mum's loud voice and pointing finger and Dad's tense forehead and waving hands are vital in helping you write about old home scenes. You responded emotionally to those details as a child and your feelings will become clearer and stronger as you write down your memories. The home-video exercises in this section are designed to help you use details and feelings to capture the impact of past repeating interactions and see their effects on you then and now. Some of those interactive patterns brought out the best in you and others; some limited your own or someone else's growth.

Each family has a balance of helpful and harmful patterns, and you can gauge more clearly the balance in your family through the exercises that follow. One measure of the balance between helpful and harmful factors is to ask how **open** or **closed** your family system was. If your family was a really open system, you and other family members tended to:

- feel good about yourselves;
- function well independently or in co-operation;
- feel free to speak clearly, directly, and honestly;
- disgree and argue yet feel safe and cared for;
- participate in neighbourhood or community as well as family activities.

If your family was a really closed system, you and other family members tended to:

- feel bad about yourselves;
- be over-dependent on each other and/or be unable to co-operate;
- communicate indirectly and unclearly, keeping secrets;
- fear and avoid conflict or experience frequent, unresolved conflict;
- be isolated from the world beyond the family.

Most families fall somewhere between the two extremes of very open and very closed. These brief passages describe two people's experiences of their families. The family of the first, Sandy, was remarkably open:

*My parents were very open about my sister's having Down's syndrome. We were taught to believe we were capable and she wasn't a special case. People in shops sometimes stared or said stupid things about my sister, and my parents told us how to be respectful but blunt. People can change for the better, they'd say.*

Ray's family, on the other hand, had many of the characteristics of a closed system:

*I was always careful of what I said. My dad had a temper and all hell'd break loose if he got going. If I needed money for school, my mum had to take it out of the grocery money. When he was drinking, we'd keep the windows closed, no matter how hot it was, so the neighbours wouldn't hear him. I never brought friends home; I kept to myself.*

Sandy's and Ray's family home videos illustrate how different patterns of interaction can be in open and closed systems. You can probably guess where your family might fall on a continuum from open to closed but you may have a hard time saying why.

To change the harmful repeating patterns of a more closed system, you need to identify where the problems were and how they affected you. To help you do this, the following exercises examine the four aspects of family life that therapist Virginia Satir, in her book *Peoplemaking*, identified as key markers of open or closed systems – **self-worth**, **rules**, **connections to society** and **responses to change**.

## SELF-WORTH

This survey begins with self-worth because it is the basis of personal and family stability. Virginia Satir called self-worth 'the source of personal energy'. Families who value and promote self-worth provide fuel for healthy actions and relationships.

Even though they want their children to have high-esteem, parents who were not raised to feel good about themselves may lack the power of belief within themselves to give the encouragement they did not receive. The topic of self-worth is so central to family health and personal problems that it will be the focus of Chapter 6.

When peple lack self-worth, the power to believe in themselves, their behaviour reflects their low opinion of their abilities. One extreme of such behaviour is represented by those who lack initiative, are unwilling to take risk and undermine their own efforts. These people are self-critical and may suffer from depression. Another extreme is represented by those who demand obedience from others and radiate inflated and aggressive self-confidence. These people are also self-critical and prone to depression. No matter what public face we show to the world, if we don't feel good about ourselves, we lack vital energy for work and relationships.

Virginia Satir sums up the importance of self-worth this way:

Good human relations and appropriate and loving behaviour stem from persons who have strong feelings of self-worth. Simply stated, persons who love and value themselves are able to love and value others.

## EXERCISE

## SELF-WORTH IN YOUR FAMILY

In this exercise, you will focus on capturing memories of common actions within families that either promote or inhibit self-worth. You may recall instances in which your own ability to value yourself was encouraged by someone else. By remembering and writing any positive self-esteem message you received, you strengthen your current levels of worth and confidence. Building on strong patterns of valuing yourself and others will help you become a more open and healthy individual and a constructive force for change in your present family.

The actions in the column on the left are typical of people with high self-worth, while those in the right column exemplify people with low-esteem. Read through the lists and respond in writing to the questions that follow.

| | |
|---|---|
| praising; encouraging; giving appreciation; being consistent and reliable; expecting success trusting; showing respect for all | criticising or blaming; making sarcastic comments; apologising; being untrustworthy; predicting failure; mistrusting; belittling others |

When you were growing up, who in your family had high self-worth? Whose was low?
Which column is more typical of the responses you received from the adults in your family?
Write any memory that comes through strongly about these self-worth themes, noting both positive and negative influences by family members.

Michelle, a graphic artist, wrote:

*The only person in my family who seemed to feel good about her life was my Aunt Viv, who owned a flower shop. I remember her smiling, smelling wonderful, responding excitedly to our plans and dreams. My mother's responses fell in the right column. Maybe she felt bad about herself because my dad left, but she never had a good word to say about herself or us children. 'What makes you think you're so great?' she'd say, frowning. My Aunt Viv made the difference. I can still hear her soft voice repeating, 'You have a lot of talent, darling, and you're going to find your way.'*

Michelle found that her Aunt Viv's belief in her was an ongoing source of good memories and feelings. She decided to compile a list of Aunt Viv's sayings and keep it on her refrigerator.

Like Michelle, you may discover that writing some of your family members' helpful sayings and actions will tap that positive source once again. While it can be painful to remember and write about the critical messages, they too bring clarity when examined with some distance. In Chapter 4, on family language, and Chapter 6, which discusses self-esteem, you will build on these realisations about family sources of discouragement or encouragement to create healthier relationships in the present.

## RULES

The second aspect of family life that shows whether your family was more open or more closed concerns the sets of rules you lived by. These rules might not have been consciously thought out by your parents. Virginia Satir wrote that rules 'form a kind of shorthand, which becomes important as soon as two or more people live together.' Before you were born, your family had created some rules about living together, based on their experiences growing up.

The clash of unconscious rule legacies from the past often causes uncomfortable adjustments in early marriage. When your mother's 'Everyone eats breakfast alone, without talking' marries your father's, 'The wife calls the family to the table so that we can discuss the day', their expectations clash and they must find new rules.

By the time you were born, your family had evolved a set of rules, some consciously chosen, some unconsciously functioning. Adults can communicate the family rules to the children either directly or indirectly, but they often expect children to obey all rules, whether expressed or implied.

Rules do provide necessary stability. You know what you can do and what you had better not do by the family rules, both those that are spoken ('Don't talk back to your parents') and those that are not (everyone's table manners improve when company comes).

In a more open family, rules are helpful guidelines, subject to discussion and change. If a rule outgrows its usefulness – as when teenagers' participation in school sports make it impossible for all family members to eat dinner together every night – anyone can point out the problem and open up discussion about it. After considering many solutions, everyone agrees to try one option, with the understanding that they can make changes later. Of course, this idealistic scenario usually involves noise and conflict in reality, but an open family can handle the stress of adpating rules to individuals.

In a more closed family, people must adapt to the rules. Rules are rigid demands, the property and tool of those who hold the power. Anyone who challenges a rule risks criticism or punishment by others in the family who have a strong investment in the status quo. Keeping family life predictable, even when the rules are severely limiting, is valued highly in a closed family.

## EXERCISE

## RULES IN YOUR FAMILY

In this exercise, you can survey how rules functioned in your family's life.

A  Make a list of five rules, spoken or unspoken, that you remember from your childhood and adolescence.

B  Write your responses to these questions, giving examples or recounting vivid incidents:
Who made the rules in your family?
How were the rules enforced?
How easy or hard was it to change the rules?
How were you affected by your family's rules as a child? How have you either kept them or changed them as an adult?

Sam, who introduced himself as 'age 31, still stuck at 17', describes how he continues to rebel against his father's militaristic rules, even though he no longer lives with his family. These rules include:

1  *No cheek.*
2  *Don't ask why; just do it.*
3  *Work hard and you'll stay out of trouble.*
4  *The family sticks together.*
5  *No complaining.*

*Good rules for an army battalion, but life certainly felt grim. My dad didn't allow us to question his rules. We acted up anyway: I talked back, my sister complained, and my brother got into trouble. We were determined to rebel, but I think we're still tring to please Dad. Each one of us is stubborn, hard-working and loyal. I wish we could have had more fun.*

Sam realised that he is still 'talking back' to the authorities in his life. While he doesn't complain directly as his sister used to or get into trouble as his brother did, he challenges his boss and colleagues through sharp-tongued comments. 'I've defined myself by my sharp tongue,' Sam commented. 'Now I wonder if the sense of freedom it gives me is outweighed by its effects.'

You may find that you are still living by or rebelling against certain of your family's rules. If those rules suit your current habits and goals, you will be comfortable with this aspect of your past. If, however, you find that you are trying to follow internalised rules that hold you back or cause pain in work or personal relationships, you might consider dropping your allegiance to those demands from the past. By keeping in mind that rules exist to serve people, not the other way around, you can design fitting guidelines. Chapter 6, on personal power, will offer more opportunities to explore growth and healing this area.

# SOCIETY

The third aspect that determines openness and closedness in families is how your family relates to friends, neighbours, strangers and community members and organisations. 'Every family teaches something about how to deal with the outside world,' Satir states, believing that openness between family life and the larger community is healthy and vital.

From an open family, energy flows out to others and returns in a comfortable interchange. Perhaps you mow your neighbours' lawn when they're away; a friend from work brings food over when your mother has surgery; you participate in a school fête to raise money for a local charity. Strong and varied connections to neighbours and community bring new ideas into the family and give everyone a wider circle of people to trust and enjoy.

In a closed family, energy is held in out of fear, mistrust and secrecy. You may be encouraged to play with your siblings rather than to bring friends home; your parents may tell you all people with a different skin colour are dangerous; or perhaps you can't tell your teacher that your mother never comes to parents' evenings because she drinks. Children who lack connections outside the family are less likely to grow intellectually and emotionally.

## EXERCISE

## YOUR FAMILY IN SOCIETY

This exercise will re-create the patterns of interaction between your family and the outside world.

A Thinking back to your childhood and adolescence, write down as may of the following as you can think of:

- close friends of your parents;
- godmothers or godfathers to you and your siblings;
- neighbours with whom your family was friendly;
- colleagues of your parents whom you also knew;
- clubs to which your parents belonged;
- religious or political affiliation groups with which your family was involved;
- regular local functions in which your family participated.

B Consider these questions and write a passage about your family's involvement with the outside world.

Looking at the list you have just made, how involved was your family with people other than family members?

Did you move a lot and did that isolate you or just mean that you knew more people in more places?

How has your family's style of involvement with the outside world affected you as an adult?

Lynn, a publicist for an ecological organisation, responded: 'My parents were complete opposites, with Mother involved in everything and Daddy wishing that everyone would go away. He'd mutter, "You help out every stray lamb, and they turn out to be spongers and scroungers. What's wrong with staying at home?" She'd say, "You just want me to keep you company in this stuffy house." I agreed with her, but I felt sorry for him. Now I go back and forth, sometimes overinvolved, sometimes hibernating.'

Lynn has trouble limiting her work schedule. Every time she starts to turn down an appeal, she hears her parents' old arguments and feels torn. She usually agrees to the request but then feels pressured or guilty. Since her husband's retirement, he has wanted her to be more available. 'I hate replaying my folks' conflicts with my husband,' Lynn wrote, 'and I need to sort out my past so that I can talk with him about our lives now and our future plans.'

Your family's style of relating to friends, neighbours and community may work well for you today. But if your adult experiences mirror isolation, loneliness, suspicion or overcommitment from your childhood, you can create a different style of being involved with others. Chapter 10 will present ways to strengthen your sense of belonging, your connection with the world.

## CHANGE

Virginia Satir maintains that what most distinguishes a closed family system, where interaction is unhealthy, from a healthy, open family system, is how members respond to change. In a closed system, people resist change; in a more open family, it is permitted and encouraged.

A certain amount of resistance to change is a natural human protest against disruption. However, a bad familiar situation may actually feel safer or more comfortable than any kind of change. When the overall family attitude works against flexiblity and growth, family members are forced to conform or rebel. Both options inhibit free choice and adaptation. Families demonstrate resistance to change by:

- parents refusing permission for children's activities;
- children wanting family routines to stay the same;
- grandparents or other relatives interferring with plans;
- conflict between parents over a job change or move;
- unwillingness to recognise one person's growth leap.

In an open family system, changes are expected, the difficulties are acknowledged and feelings and decisions are discussed regularly. No solution to the routines of daily life is expected to work forever and each person's right to grow is respected. Some instances of family openness to change that students have written about include:

- a parent helping a graduate look for a flat;
- children making breakfast for their stepmother on Mother's Day;

- everyone taking turns doing the chores of a family member who has a long illness;
- a family which often has to move sharing a ritual of decorating their new home in the holidays.

There is no such thing as isolated individual change in families. As on a mobile, the impact of one person's change disrupts everyone's equilibrium. 'Since our oldest started going out with boys,' one parent moans, 'we never see her at weekends.' 'It's great that John got his driver's licence,' another parent exults. 'I'm no longer a chauffeur.'

Yet we usually react to change in complex ways: the first parent worries about her daughter's socialising, and the second enjoys her son's new freedom. How well each of these families copes with the consequences of their young people's maturing is related to how they have learned to work together to meet changing circumstances.

As healthy and necessary as change is, it brings disruption that all of us occasionally resist. Writing about transitions, William Bridges suggests:

Few people stop to reflect . . . on the radiating waves of change in their lives. When they do, they may find that apparently minor events have had major impacts. They may find that some puzzling and hard-to-identify distress that they are feeling can be traced back to incidents or situations that set off the transition process in their lives.

Both minor and major changes in your childhood family affected you then and may still affect you now, for you learned your ability to flow with change or resist it in those early experiences.

## EXERCISE

## YOUR FAMILY CHANGES

In this exercise, you can survey various types of changes and capture memories of your family's pattern of dealing with change. You will learn how your ability to deal with change as an individual or family member today has been shaped by your early experiences.

A Read through the survey below, and underline any example that has a strong memory or feeling associated with it.
B Pick one or more of the changes you've underlined and write a short passage describing an incident or pattern.

How did your family react to changes in their schedule?

- What happened when someone was late? When someone arrived unexpectedly? When the weather forced a change in plans? When the times for getting up or going to bed changed?

31

How did your family react to age-related changes?

- What happened when a child wanted more freedom? How did you get permission to drive? What was it like when you or another family member moved away from home?
- How did your family feel about children? (Should be encouraged or seen and not heard?) How did your family feel about old people? (Were they considered sources of wisdom or a bother?)

How did your family react to changes in status?

- What happened when you moved to a more affluent neighbourhood or a less affluent one?
- What happened when a family member lost his or her job? Got promoted? How did the family react to a dramatic change in financial status?
- What happened when a child started doing worse at school?
- What happened when someone experienced illness or health-related changes?

Mark, a restaurant owner who described himself as 'perpetually frantic', wrote:

*Changes in schedule! In my family, dinner was at 6.00, bedtime was at 9.00, we all got up at 6.30. There was NO deviation allowed. My parents ran their lives by the clock. I tried to conform but I just wanted to lie on the grass and daydream. In many ways, my family was pretty open, but their rigidity about scheduling closed down some parts of me that I'm only now exploring at 48.*

Like Mark, who acknowledges that rigidity about scheduling has been useful in his restaurant business even though it has inhibited his creativity, you may notice that your family's reaction to change has had both helpful and harmful effects. For caution and stability, you can call on family patterns of resistance to change; for risk taking or response to disruption, you can emphasise positive responses you learned.

# HOW YOUR PARENTS' RELATIONSHIP AFFECTED YOU

By capturing in writing the memories and feelings stirred by each of the four aspects of family life – self-worth, rules, relating to the outside world, and response to change – you created your home videos of various patterns of interaction in your family. Your parents' role in setting those patterns is central; their relationship has affected you from your roots to the present.

As a child, you imitated the adults in your family. When you were a week old, you could imitate your mother's facial expressions. Because your physical and emotional security was so linked to your parents' care, they were your world in your earliest days.

As you grew, your understanding of yourself was primarily determined by your parents' actions. How they spoke to, held, fed, played with and guided you laid a foundation upon which your sense of self grew. In addition, you watched the behaviour and listened to the communication between your parents or between your parent and any other adult who lived with you. The relationship of these primary adults gave you a model for imagining an intimate partnership for yourself someday.

This model of partnership had its own foundation. In the case of your biological parents, the foundation was laid before you were born. From their first meeting, your parents created a blueprint for your family's relationships. In *Peoplemaking*, Virginia Satir called the couple 'the architects of the family'. The qualities of your parents' relationship affected the shape of your family once you and any siblings were born. Family therapists agree that a strong, healthy relationship between parents can contribute significantly to children's strength and health.

Whatever their relationship was like in the time before your parents had children, the arrival of you or your oldest sibling involved change and stress. Many couples experience changes in their feelings about each other as well as in their self-images. How your parents worked out these stresses with each other, how they talked about them with their friends (in conversations you may have overheard) and how they talked to you directly about each other all shaped your view of their partnership.

Whether your parents stayed together or split up, you have been affected by the qualities in their character that generated both attraction and conflict. You inherited some of those qualities genetically and you absorbed some of them from the family environment.

One student wrote that his mother used to shout at him, 'You're lazy! Just like your father! I fell in love with him because he was so easygoing, but I didn't know he'd never help me'. Qualities that you and your siblings received from your parents' blueprint contributed to your character and your past family experiences. Those same qualities are probably still affecting your family life and relationships.

From your parents' relationship, you observed and learned a wide range of attitudes and behaviour. The list below conveys the scope of how you may have been affected by your parents' relationship. Following each factor are examples that I have heard from clients and students. Your parents' style of relating strongly influenced you in the following areas:

- how you view the opposite sex;
  ('Mother always insisted, "Men are so helpless – you have to do everything for them." ')
- how you touch and like to be touched;
  ('I hear myself saying to my wife: "Why are you always clinging? Couples don't have to do that." I never saw my parents hug.')
- how you express your thoughts and feelings;
  ('Should I have to tell you every little thing on my mind? A man's entitled to some peace and quiet at home, just like my dad got.')

- how you identify and solve problems;
  ('I was brought up to believe that you just jumped in and did things. My husband always wants to wait and discuss everything.')
- how you bring up, or plan to bring up, your own children;
  ('My wife wants to do everything for our kids. I grew up strong because my parents didn't mollycoddle me.')
- how you relate to in-laws and extended family;
  ('Every damn Sunday we go to his mother's house for dinner. In my family we only saw our grandparents on holidays.')
- how you handle money;
  ('My husband is so mean. My dad gave Mother a free rein with money and I never thought I'd have to fight about finances.')
- how you handle issues of power and control;
  ('When I grew up, the husband went to work and the wife dealt with the children's problems. Why can't my wife take care of the children's arguments herself?')

Your family experiences shape your expectations of family life and your experiences of your parents' partnership shape your expectations of intimacy and marriage. Yet because of the all-pervasive nature of our parents' influence, many of us have difficulty looking clearly at their relationship and understanding its effects.

## EXERCISE

## YOUR PARENTS' RELATIONSHIP

The purpose of this exercise is to help you see how the qualities and characteristics of your parents' relationship appear in your own personality and interactions. By understanding the influence of their relationship blueprint you can trace the roots of current problems and choose which attitudes and behaviour patterns from the past you want to change.

For this exercise, focus on the partnership that shaped your family the most – possibly that between your biological mother and father, your adoptive parents, or a parent and step-parent. If you lived with only one parent and never knew your other parent, create the voice and personality of the unknown parent through whatever information you have as well as your intuitive hunches.

A 1 Choose the parent you were closer to and imagine that you are able to speak with that parent's voice. Write a short monologue as if that parent were speaking about his or her partner. A good opening line is: 'When I first met your father, he seemed so . . .'

   2 Include what drew that parent to the other and write whatever other information the parent wants to share. Or you might explore how your parents' relationship changed by starting a sentence, 'Then, later, he seemed . . .'

3  Switch to the other parent, and write a similar monologue from his or her point of view.

Joan, wife and mother of three, wrote in her father's voice:

*When I first met your mother, she had the sweetest disposition. She was always smiling, never cross. After we were married and had children, it seemed as if her sweetness was only for neighbours and friends. In public, all smiles, fake sweetness. At home, it was 'Don't talk to me, don't touch me, I'm too tired.'*

Writing in her mother's voice, Joan discovered that she was overwhelmed by the demands of home and children and felt that she had to pretend or she might explode. Seeing both sides of her parents' dilemma, Joan began to ask herself what it was like to be caught between them. Writing in her parents' voices prepared her for memories of her own responses to them as a child.

## EXERCISE

## YOUR RELATIONSHIP LEGACY

A 1  Read through the monologues you wrote, asking yourself: so what happened to me when my parents felt and did these things?
  2  Write a short passage from your point of view as an observer and participant in your parents' relationship.

You may find memories or feelings that take you back to when you were young, observing your parents. You may have been drawn in to support one parent or the other, a common pattern in families. Whatever happened affected you then and affects you now.

Joan wrote:

*I especially hated Mum's fake sweetness when I was a teenager. I sided with my dad and criticised her. The trouble was, by watching her, I learned how to do it too. I suppose it's a way of protecting myself from people, being nice and polite. It's too much of a strain and then I blow up at my husband or the children and feel guilty.*

As Joan discovered, we tend to repeat the same patterns of handling intimacy that we observed our parents using. When qualities that you learned from your parents' relationships cause problems now, you can target them as patterns to watch for and work on. To complete this exercise, you can use your awareness of your parents' harmful relationship patterns to identify the qualities that you need in a healthy partnership.

B 1 Make a list of five qualities that you want to characterise your marriage or intimate relationship. Choose the qualities that speak most to your unique longings for love and companionship.

Here is Fred's list:

*passion*
*forgiveness*
*kindness*
*spontaneity*
*honesty*

2 For each of the five qualities, write a sentence or two beginning with the phrase 'I want . . .' explaining how this quality relates to the legacy of your parents' relationship.

Fred wrote:

*I want kindness as a valued quality in a partnership because I saw how destructive, deliberate, and even unconscious, cruelty can be between married people.*

*I want passion because my parents never seemed to care deeply about each other or about anything, really.*

*I want spontaneity because I loved the way my aunt and uncle would swoop down unexpectedly and take us children off on a picnic. My parents always had to plan everything.*

Examining and writing about your parents' relationship from these three perspectives – your parents' viewpoint, the effects of the legacy on you and your own relationship longings – helps reveal some of the underpinnings of your family structure and what you have built on the foundation your parents established. As you link the qualities that nurture a good relationship for you with the pleasures and difficulties you saw in your parents' relationship, you clarify and strengthen their positive legacy in your current relationship. You may also be more prepared to challenge the destructive qualities you absorbed from them that threaten your hopes for healthy intimacy today. Although the blueprint of relationship patterns lives within you, you now have the power to adjust it. In this final section, you will use the insights from this chapter's exercises to determine which family patterns enhance your life now and which block your growth and need to be changed.

# FAMILY PATTERNS: WHAT TO KEEP? WHAT TO CHANGE?

You can keep from automatically repeating the patterns of the past if you use clarity and perspective to define who you are and what you want. In *The Dance of Intimacy* (Harper & Row, New York, 1989), Harriet Lerner stresses the importance of personal clarity about self and others:

Changing any relationship problem rests directly on our ability to work on bringing more of a self to that relationship.

You gain a stronger sense of who you are by sorting out the people and events in your original family. Your identity is a unique mixture of your genetic inheritance, the influences from your family environment and your individual responses to the important people and events in your past.

Sharpening your view of past people and events brings other people into focus. In your written snapshot glimpses, you gathered information about your family members, revealing your feelings and your roles. In your written home-video scenes of family interactions, you clarified how people felt about themselves, what the rules were, and how your family related to the outside world and reacted to change. Examining your parents' relationship showed you the legacy of expectations about intimacy that you received from observing their partnership.

## EXERCISE

## IDENTIFYING HARMFUL AND HELPFUL PATTERNS

With every new insight you gain about your family members, you sharpen the lens on your own individuality. As the details and feelings from the past illuminate your current experiences, you become more aware of how you have internalised your family experiences into a code of expectations or a blueprint. The code can be changed, the blueprint altered.

Identifying healthy and fulfilling changes now inaugurates the slow cyclic process of awareness, assessment and change. Family patterns do not change quickly, like the rapid flashing of colours in a kaleidoscope. They change as a result of your decisions to make things different every day, slowly altering your response to the environment, much as an ecological clean-up begins through individuals changing their habits that pollute the system.

In *The Dance of Intimacy*, Harriet Lerner writes of the thoughtfulness that deep changes require:

Substantive change in important relationships rarely comes about through intense confrontation. Rather, it more frequently results from careful thinking and from planning for small manageable moves based on a solid understanding of the problem, including our own part in it.

Sorting out what helped you from what affected you negatively is part of moving from awareness to assessment to change. Using the information and insight from this chapter's previous exercises, you can assess the broad scope of your family's patterns through the following exercise. You will look separately at what helped you and is worth strengthening and what harmed you and is worth changing. Finally, you will identify and plan for some 'small, manageable moves' to put your insights into action.

A 1  Make a list of three to five harmful patterns that you experienced in the family you grew up with. These can be either major or minor concerns – whatever memories or feelings are currently in your awareness.

  2  Use three statements to describe each pattern.

    a  First, write a general statement of how the pattern functioned in the whole family.

    b  Write specifically how the pattern affected your attitudes and behaviour.

    c  State how the pattern blocks your growth or harms your relationships now.

---

George, a businessman in his forties, wrote a list that included these patterns:

- Our family communicated with hints and generalisations. I didn't learn how to say what I really meant. Today, my wife complains that I expect her to be a mind-reader, and we argue about my indirectness.
- We all blamed each other; nobody took responsibility. As a result, I find it difficult to admit that I have made a mistake. Now my teenage son and I flare up at each other daily and I know I contribute to the problem.
- We grew up dreading my father's humiliating criticisms. Now if I'm afraid of being wrong, I don't take the risk to say or do something. This pattern is holding me back at work, where I need forcefulness to get my next promotion.
- My family was very materialistic. I rebelled from that outlook at university, but now I'm ashamed to admit how much money means to me. My shame keeps me from making sensible plans for our financial future.

George described writing the list of negative patterns as a difficult task. 'It was easy to come up with the negative influences from the family,' he said, 'but owning up to how I've been affected made me feel embarrassed. I can see why you stress that changing these takes time.'

If you, like George, find it difficult to identify how your life has been hurt by your response to family patterns, it is because you adapted to the conditions in your family as needed in order to survive and thrive in that environment. The more destructive the environment was, the more internalised negative self-images you will have.

We will explore techniques to heal those harmful family dynamics further throughout the book. For now, appreciate your willingness to bring painful patterns to awareness and know that your assessment of those patterns' effects on your life will lead to positive change.

B 1 Make a list of three to five helpful patterns that you experienced in the family you grew up with. These can be qualities that nurtured you, habits that helped you or actions that modelled healthy behaviour.

2 Write three statements about each pattern:

a a general statement about the pattern and your whole family;

b a specific description of the pattern's effects on your attitudes and behaviour;

c a conclusion about how the pattern has a constructive influence on your current growth and relationship.

Jenny, a scientific researcher in her twenties, described these private patterns:

- My family believed in finding solutions to problems. I earned their respect if I came up with an innovative idea. In my work now, I solve problems by being resourceful and determined.
- My grandmother made me feel loved just as I was. I developed a strong sense of self-worth from her attention and praise. I call on that now when I run into problems with my friends or colleagues.
- I listed my family's rigid rules as a negative influence but they also had a positive effect. Their insistence on doing things logically made me very organised. I can quickly get through some of the paperwork involved in scientific research.

Jenny commented that describing the positive patterns made her more aware of strengths she usually takes for granted: 'My family didn't like boasting, so I had to work to be as direct about these positive statements as I was about the critical ones. But I know these things about me are true and I feel stronger for having written them down.'

C 1 Choose three to five new attitudes or behaviour patterns that you want to develop over the next year. These attitudes or behaviours are your contribution to changing painful or destructive patterns in the family with whom you're currently living.

2 If the first statement you write is general, write another sentence or two to make what you mean more explicit and direct. If you list 'a better relationship with my spouse', go on to 'speaking more honestly and directly to him' or, even more specific, 'try going out for coffee at the weekend and catching up on what we've been thinking and feeling'.

3 Connect the new behaviour with an old pattern if possible: 'I want to stop confiding in the children when I'm angry with my husband; when my mother did that with me, I felt as if I had to take care of her.'

Here is a sampling of responses to give you a look at the wide range of possible areas for change:

*'I want to stop apologising automatically for everything. I always took the blame for my sister. When I hear myself saying "I'm sorry" now, I'll stop and ask if I really need to apologise.'*

*'I need to show my daughter that I care by listening more and talking less. I should know parental lecturing doesn't help, since my own parents did it enough. When she starts to talk at dinner, I'll watch my automatic habit of saying what I think and try asking her a question instead.'*

*'This sounds minor, but it's not for me. I have to get more sleep so I'm not always short-tempered. My mother seemed to equate exhaustion with saintliness and I keep trying to prove how good I am by going nonstop.'*

One student referred to these three lists – of what helped, what hurt and how you hope to change – as 'The Good, the Bad and the Possible'. By surveying your family patterns and how they have affected you as you have done in this chapter's exercises, you can begin to strengthen the good, bring healing to the bad and make what is possible a reality in your daily life.

In the next chapter, you'll investigate how your family's approach to daily life influenced your growth as a child and your development as an adult. This 'family life stance' grew out of your parents' attitudes and influenced your approach to life. Writing about the roots of this life stance will enable you to plan for positive changes you may want to make in your approach to life.

# CHAPTER 3

# YOUR FAMILY'S LIFE STANCE

By surveying your family system, you have already accumulated valuable information and insights. You might imagine that you now have a box labelled 'family patterns' that is stuffed with snapshots, video cassettes, memories, feelings and scraps of paper on which you have scribbled clues to the workings of your family system.

In addition, this large box contains a smaller one that you have not yet opened. This box is labelled 'family life stance'. As you open it, you will discover how your family shared an approach to daily life through attitudes and behaviour. You will explore how your family met the challenges of daily life – with optimism or pessimism, passively or actively. This box contains many clues to your own character and life history.

Every family has a particular shared approach to daily living that shapes family members' attitudes and behaviour. All family patterns evolve from this life stance, and it is played out through the attitudes and behaviour of family members.

You and your relatives were probably not aware of how your shared approach to life affected your thoughts and actions. However, you may have noticed such a life stance while spending time with families other than your own. When people are asked to write about a family they loved to be with when they were young, they recall at first a general atmosphere.

'It was so exciting being with my friend Rina's family,' one of my students remembered. 'I felt alive and bubbly walking in their house to the noise of music and laughing voices.' Asked about the family's attitudes, she replied, 'Her mum and dad made it seem as if anything was possible.' They supported trying new things: 'We could dream up a crazy, fun activity and they'd immediately tell us to go for it. My parents worried so much about every consequence that it wasn't worth trying new things.'

Out of these memories, this student concluded that her family's life stance had been 'anxious caution'. She then spoke up and said, 'But that's *my* worst fault! I hate my indecisive side, always afraid to take a risk. I'm still looking for people like Rina's family to release my inhibitions and encourage me.'

Sometimes, these same questions reveal that a family life stance has had positive effects previously unnoticed. Asked to remember a family that he did not enjoy visiting, another student wrote about 'my distant cousin's family, where I would feel stifled in their stuffy, quiet house. My aunt's attitude was that children were inferior and uncivilised and she behaved coldly towards us. In contrast, my family seemed so free, because we were treated warmly and with respect. My family's life stance was "strict permissiveness" but I only appreciated the permissiveness after I'd visited Aunt Myrtle.'

Like these students, you will find both limiting and enabling qualities of your shared approach to life. We can change aspects of our inherited stance that keep us from what we want in our lives today. The following list of common positive and negative life-stance qualities will illustrate the limiting and enabling extremes, and the subsequent sketches of three different families will show you some of the ways that life stances can act themselves out.

If your family had a strong constructive life stance, these qualities were noticeable about your family's approach to life:

- **zest for life** – an energetic vitality and awareness;
- **confidence** – a hopeful outlook;
- **resourcefulness** – a creative attitude towards problem-solving;
- **mobility** – the freedom to take risks and make changes.

If you family had a strongly destructive life stance, these qualities were noticeable about your family's approach to life:

- **coldness or flatness** – a lack of interest and energy;
- **anxiety, doubts or fear** – a belief that life is dangerous and resources are scarce;
- **limitation or helplessness** – tunnel vision that can't conceive of hopeful possibilities;
- **rigidity** – control, unwillingness to alter the status quo.

The following three families are composites of individuals I've known through counselling and teaching. You can make your own guesses about each family's life stance from the following introductory paragraphs; different characteristics of each family's stance are examined afterwards.

John and Miranda Dobbs have two children: Bill, 11, and Eileen, 7. John is a computer programmer and Miranda is a nurse. John's parents and brother live far away but Miranda's widowed mother and brothers are within an hour's drive. Bill, the son of John's first marriage, lives with his mother, Carol, in the summer. Eileen is John and Miranda's daughter. They say that their problems are not having enough money, arguments between Bill and Eileen and the pressure of busy lives. Their family motto is 'If at first you don't succeed, try, try again'.

Anna Fortune, a secretary, is the divorced mother of Shelley, 13, and Maria, 10. Her first marriage broke up eight years ago and her former husband is no longer in contact. Anna relies on her close, large family for child care and support. Now she has invited Dick, an electrician she has been going out with for three years, to move in with them. Anna's daughters like Dick but he often feels like an outsider and wishes the extended family weren't so ever-present. Anna's motto with her family has always been 'You and me against the world'. Dick wants her to form a new family with him; each of them says that their biggest problem is communication.

Charles and Teresa Jordan have three children, Tessie, 12, Robbie, 8, and Molly, 2. Charles is a successful lawyer; Teresa worked part-time in his office until Molly's birth. Charles is a favoured son in his family's eyes, while Teresa has no relatives nearby. Tessie is starting to challenge Charles's rigid rules. Looking good to the outside world is the important family value. Charles says the family has no problems; Teresa and the children don't say anything. The unspoken family motto is 'Just don't talk about it'.

The first two families exhibit some of the positive characteristics of a healthy family life stance, while the third family has turned towards the negative characteristics. Each family struggles with unhappiness resulting from the absence or blockage of positive life-stance traits.

The dominant characteristics of the Dobbs family is resourcefulness. They have made many adaptations to blend two families and juggle their activities. Their life stance of persistence ('try, try again') requires mobility in generating new solutions to their dilemmas of time, money and access to family attention and affection. At best, family members radiate zest for life and confidence. When fatigue and conflict take a toll, John and Miranda worry that they're not doing enough for Bill and Eileen and the rest of the family.

The large Fortune family demonstrates abundant resources of confidence and resourcefulness, helping each other out generously. Their collective presence is formidable. Individually, however, their mobility or freedom is somewhat constrained. When someone gets a little too independent, he or she is reminded that 'family comes first'. Personal confidence is less important than family agreement. Anna was attracted to Dick's strength and independence, but now he threatens her family solidarity. She doesn't want to have to choose and wishes he could just blend in. As a new family, Anna and Dick must dance between conforming to the family stance and challenging it.

The Jordans' family stance of obedience and silence is dangerous. When one family member dominates and dictates to the others, resourcefulness and mobility are blocked for everyone. Charles's energy and confidence have brought him professional success. At home, his need to control the family and their acquiescence to his dominance have led to the worst aspects of the closed family system – shaky self-worth, rigid rules, fear of change and avoidance of the world beyond the family ('Just don't talk about it'). Because of self-doubts and unresolved conflicts inside and between family members, this life stance creates an unhealthy atmosphere in which addictions and abuse can flourish.

While life-stance characteristics may sometimes be easier to recognise in a family other than your own, you can become aware of both healthy and harmful aspects of your past through the writing exercises in the four sections of this chapter. They focus on breaking the family trance that keeps us unaware of our family's life stance; the stance itself; trust; how trust is expressed; and assessing and building on your family's life stance.

The first section describes the necessity to break what has been called the **family trance**. The family trance is an often unconsciously agreed-upon view of who a family is and how its members live together. Children are naturally prone to bond with their parents, feeling as they feel and doing as they do. The parents thus create and maintain the family trance by their attitudes about and behaviour towards each other and the children.

The more you write about your family, the more you may be challenging your own or your family's belief that you shouldn't bring to light its unhealthy or unflattering aspects. You can now give yourself permission to explore and describe your family's attitudes and behaviour. As you internalise that permission and write with greater freedom, you will be mobilising positive forces for change in your life.

The second section addresses the specific **life-stance characteristics** of the family you grew up with. Through writing about common family sayings, values and behaviour – all reflecting shared attitudes and beliefs – you will define your family's life stance more precisely.

Clarifying positive and negative life-stance characteristics will give you a broader perspective on the forces that shaped you and that may still influence your life. Defining your family's shared approach to life will prepare you to look at the foundation of trust underneath the attitudes and behaviour.

The third section focuses on the **trust** that is at the core of a family life stance. The major factor that keeps people from changing their own life stance, inherited from their family's patterns, is fear, rooted in a lack of trust. This lack of trust results from an absence of care and attention in early life.

Some psychologists call the first stage of development a young child goes through 'basic trust vs. basic mistrust'. In their first few years, children learn from their parents whether the world is a trustworthy place. The comfort of parental care and attention, warmth, food, dryness and cuddling creates a stable foundation of trust. If those comforts are significantly absent, the child's pain turns to anxiety, fear and mistrust.

When people lack trust, they are unable to feel secure. Our instincts tell us to run away, to hide or to freeze if a big threat comes along. Changing the way you and your family have always done things is a big threat. Even if your family's legacy of patterns has created a painful life stance, your fear and lack of trust will make it harder to change. Family situations tend to stay the same because each individual fears adding more stress, being the one to topple the existing family structure. Even as an adult separate from the family you grew up with, you may be hampered by old fears, by the lack of trust your family taught you. Trying to develop a sense of trust as an adult is like trying to build on an unstable foundation.

Beginning to trace your family life stance towards trust will help you become aware of how your foundation was laid and what shape it is in now. You can strengthen your own personal foundation in order to increase your sense of trust in yourself, others, and the world around you. Then, when you want to make changes, you will act confidently, increasing your chances of success.

The fourth section addresses two major ways that a family's level of trust is expressed, in

**attitudes** and **behaviour**. Your basic attitudes about trust learned from your family in early childhood influence your level of optimism. The product of a strong foundation of trust is the ability to have hope. Similarly, your family's beliefs about the effectiveness of action contributed to their passive or active life stance. If your family believed that life was generally out to get you and that the world was corrupt, you may have grown up in an environment of passive, hopeless behaviour. However, once you identify how your family's relationship to hope and action affected you, you can work on and change these attitudes and behaviour patterns from your family past.

In the fifth and final section, you use the information you have gathered about your family's life stance and your core of trust to assess their **influence** on your life and plan for **future changes**. Even if you experienced a lack of warmth in your early life, you can establish a stronger foundation now by caring responsibly for yourself and seeking out the care of trustworthy others. Your creativity, problem-solving ability and enjoyment of life will increase as you develop a more positive and healthy life stance.

# BREAKING YOUR FAMILY TRANCE

You will only become aware of the need to make changes in your life patterns when you break free of the family trance.

Of course, this is not a simple process. It is important to note that what needs to be broken is not necessarily your bond with your family, but with implanted beliefs, such as that you are not very intelligent. When you can say to yourself, 'I value my mind – I *am* intelligent', you have broken that part of the family trance and your parent's negative message.

Nor is breaking the family trance a once-and-forever achievement. The shared view of reality from your formative years may still exert a powerful pull. Each time a situation arises that challenges your chosen belief that you are intelligent (for example, if your boss questions a decision you made), you will need to reinforce that bond by rejecting the trance response ('You see, you are thick') and choosing to believe in yourself ('I made that decision with the information I had at the time; it was a wise move').

The family trance is the inner counterpart to the family life stance, a view of reality that each person accepts unquestioningly. When someone breaks the trance by expressing thoughts or feelings strongly at variance with those of the rest of the family, that person will be pressured to return to the consensus view of reality. In your family you may have heard:

'How dare you question our authority?'
'You shouldn't feel hurt by our teasing.'
'You can't trust these people.'
'If you know what's good for you, you'll listen to your family.'

The power of the familiar tends to compel agreement. For instance, in the Jordan family, Tessie's adolescent rebellion against Charles's rigid rules threatens the status quo of silence and submission. Questioning and breaking the family trance are actions appropriate to the stages of adolescence and early adulthood. To the degree that you have not questioned your family's ways, you carry the family trance into any new relationship. The clash of competing trances characterises the early stages of couple relationships, as with Anna Fortune and Dick, or of step-families, as with the Dobbses ('My family always believed . . .'; 'We always celebrated the holiday by . . .').

Most of us carry conflicting feelings about breaking the family trance in adult life. To say or write how you really feel about family members and your past family can be very difficult. Some of my students have described their difficulties writing about their family attitudes and behaviour:

*I feel disloyal talking about my parents that way.*

*What do I really know? I'm not that intelligent.*

*Maybe I just remembered it this way because I want to make excuses for the problems I have.*

Most students find that acknowledging these conflicting feelings helps them keep writing. A number of people have told me that if they had not written about their feelings of discomfort or disloyalty for digging into their family past, they would not have been able to complete the course.

The more open your family was, the easier it is to break the trance. In *Peoplemaking*, Virginia Satir adopts this point of view when she writes:

Members of a nurturing family feel free to tell each other how they feel. Anything can be talked about – the disappointments, fears, hurts, angers, criticisms, as well as the joys and achievements. If Father happens to be bad-tempered for some reason, his child can say frankly, 'You're in a bad mood tonight, Dad.' The child isn't afraid that Father will bark back, 'How dare you talk to your father that way!' Instead, Father can be frank, too: 'I know I'm in a bad mood. I had a terrible day today!'

Satir described this freedom to break trance as 'permission to comment' and the more you had this freedom, the easier will be the task of exploring your family life stance.

## EXERCISE

## YOU CAN WRITE WHAT YOU KNOW

In the following exercise, you will address concerns you may have about opening up undiscussed areas of your family life and taking a position different from the family viewpoint. You will go on to imagine a 'permission to comment' that offers encouragement to trust your own attitudes and beliefs. This permission to deviate from the family trance will help you carry out whatever changes you decide to make in your inherited life stance.

A Describe any concerns or fears you have about breaking the family trance by writing about your family. You can start with the words 'I'm afraid that . . .' or 'It bothers me that . . .' or 'I'm uncomfortable about . . .'

Many of us imagine some disaster should we try to challenge an established family pattern ('My family won't ever speak to me again' or perhaps 'I'll make our family problems worse and everyone will blame me'). If your mind supplies a horrible consequence for disagreeing with your family, you can deflate the power of that scenario by describing it.

B Imagine the worst that could happen and recount it in detail. Write until you feel finished and then notice and write comments about your feelings when you imagined the worst.

Jeremy, who was about to be married, wrote:

*I'm uncomfortable writing about my parents' fighting, since we never talked about it. I am betraying the picture of our family we always tried to project. I'm afraid of hurting them, but my worst fear is that I'm somehow to blame for what went wrong between them. I was educated privately, draining the family finances. I remember lying in bed and crying as I heard my parents argue over the school fees. My real worst fear is that I'll get married now and then have money problems. We'll get divorced and it'll be my fault. Thinking about all this, I feel anxious and depressed.*

C Once you have written your fears, imagine that someone you trust is handing you a piece of paper on which is written a sentence giving you permission to challenge your discomfort and fears over breaking the family trance. Write what you see on that piece of paper.

Write the sentence that comes into your mind, stick it by your desk or mirror, or say it to yourself whenever you need permission to explore unknown family issues or to acknowledge what you do know.

The title of this exercise is taken from what one person described as her 'permission to comment': **you can write what you know**. Here is the permission statement Jeremy discovered:

*I saw this friend approaching. She handed me a note on which she had written, **You can go ahead – it wasn't your fault**.*

Several weeks later, Jeremy reported that the warmth and confidence he felt when he imagined this permission returned whenever he thought of the words. 'I've written more freely recently,' he went on, 'and it's also helping with my nervousness about getting married.'

You can use the acknowledgement of your fears and the encouragement of your 'permission to comment' statement to keep exploring your family's life stance. As you break free of the family trance, you will be better able to decide what life stance is right for you now and in the future.

# YOUR FAMILY'S LIFE-STANCE CHARACTERISTICS

Your family may have approached daily life with some of the zest, confidence, resourcefulness and mobility that promote health, but chances are they demonstrated many negative characteristics as well. Recognising and describing the central characteristics of your family's approach to life will help you choose those you want to preserve as well as those you want to change. Here are some students' descriptions of the central characteristics of their families' life stances:

- **resentful resignation** – 'We were stuck with our circumstances, but we didn't like anything about them.'
- **defence of family honour** – 'Our family name had to be preserved; you didn't dare disgrace our reputation.'
- **approval-seeking** – 'Pleasing other people and being co-operative and well-liked were our most important goals.'
- **confused helplessness** – 'We were in debt, had trouble with the landlord and the neighbours. My dad was always being fired "for no reason", and he and my mum would shrug and say, "Why do these things always happen to us?" '
- **confident rigidity** – 'We know the right way to do things, and we *will* succeed. Don't bother arguing; we will do it *our* way.'

Life-stance characteristics are endlessly varied, as fascinating and complex as the individuals and families who display them. Identifying your family's characteristics gives you some perspective on them. From a distance, you can claim the characteristics for yourself or imagine ones that better express a healthy life stance. You can clarify that stance and its characteristics by remembering and writing about **attitudes, mottoes** and **behaviour**.

**Attitudes** translate feelings into thoughts and beliefs. For example, the student whose central family value was honour identified pride and shame as the most important feelings in her family. Sharing pride in family achievements created order and meaning in their world. When an event threatened the family honour, as when a teenager got in trouble, the whole family felt shamed and let down.

This feeling of family pride led to thoughts such as 'We really give a lot to this community; we're important'. The feeling of family shame led to thoughts such as 'Everybody must be talking about us; we can't hold our heads up until we sort this out'. These thoughts structured the family's beliefs, which included 'We are important people' and 'We must maintain our reputation'. Attitudes, as feelings put into thoughts and beliefs, thus reveal the psychological origins of family life-stance characteristics.

**Mottoes** are family sayings that sum up shared attitudes. As words to live by, they are a shorthand way to remind family members of what they feel, think and believe. For instance, the student whose family sought approval cited, 'If it's worth doing, it's worth doing well' and 'We just want everybody to be happy' as frequent remarks. Mottoes can be rallying cries or demands for compliance. Whether they are encouraging or guilt-producing depends on how much freedom the family allows its members to create their own motto or to change old ones.

**Behaviour** is the outer result of attitudes, the result of the mottoes. Behaviour doesn't always match attitudes and mottoes. The family members who projected confused helplessness were capable of acting quickly and sensibly on occasion, but their preferred style was to claim they were powerless. They usually behaved as if they had no idea why a situation had become so critical or how to improve it.

Shared behaviour is powerfully reinforcing, as the common experience of people being in a lift together shows. The appropriate shared behaviour is to stand facing forward and keep eyes focused on the doors or the numbers of the floors.

In a family, individuals behave in ways that are more subtle but no less structured and they demonstrate correct and appropriate behaviour through their manners with each other, their style of speaking and their expectations.

Of course, family attitudes, mottoes and behaviour work together and are not usually noticed separately. A family's central characteristic will come out in each area. For example, the Dobbs family's central characteristic is persistence. John and Miranda share attitudes that a happy family runs smoothly and that work is valuable. They want to make their family life orderly and rewarding, and they believe that they will achieve their goal with concentrated effort.

This attitude is reflected in mottoes such as 'If at first you don't succeed, try, try again' and 'We can do anything if we put our minds to it'. Each family member's behaviour also reflects the family's shared persistence. John persists in the way he fights for promotion and increases in salary; Miranda persists in the way she juggles nursing jobs so she can lead Eileen's girl guide troop; Bill and Eileen persist in drawing attention to themselves by their constant bickering. This family goes at life with energy and an intention to succeed. Their overall confidence and optimism are challenged daily by the pace of their lives and the complications of being a harmonious family.

In looking for the central characteristics of your family's approach to life, you will need to examine the attitudes, mottoes and behaviour you held in common. Remembering family mottoes and sayings is an easy way to get in touch with the life stance that was important to your family.

When you can more clearly see what life-stance characteristics you inherited, your own values become more available for assessment and change.

## EXERCISE

### YOUR FAMILY'S LIFE-STANCE MOTTOES

In my Writing From Your Roots classes, students occasionally swap family sayings, and the shared groans and laughter indicate how much parental language influences us and how common these sayings are. Together, the students and I devised this exercise.

A  Make a list of ten expressions you heard often in your family. These can be:

- **maxims** – 'The early bird gets the worm.'
- **advice** – 'Never tell anybody anything you wouldn't want to swear to in court.'
- **philosophy** – 'What they don't know won't hurt them.'
- **cursing** – 'Someday when you have a child of your own, I hope he gives you as much trouble as you've given me.'
- **religious sayings** – 'God loves unselfish people.'
- **warnings** – 'If you keep making that face, it'll stick that way.'

B  From your list of ten expressions, pick the one that holds the strongest memories for you.
C  Write a short passage that includes the expression as it was used in your past and how you feel about it now. What kind of approach to life does this saying demonstrate? What does your current reaction to the motto make you want to do?

Tom, a self-employed consultant, wrote:

*Remembering those words – **Who do you think you are?** – I see the morning sun across the breakfast table and smell coffee and cigarettes. I'm eating my cereal and trying to tell my dad my latest great idea, a plan to get the bike I want by selling a neighbourhood newsletter. Over his newspaper, he shoots a look at me, shoots me down: 'Who do you think you are, son, Richard Branson? That'll never work.' I've heard it all before, but my cornflakes taste like sawdust.*
*I can taste the deflation right now, feel the hopelessness in my muscles. Today, that forget-it attitude enrages me. I want to go out and prove to the old man that I'm capable and successful. I'd really like to do it just for myself.*

Tom read what he wrote to the class with marked anger in his voice.

*Writing those words – **who do you think you are?** – brought back resentment. If he'd only noticed me, I thought, and then I felt sad as well as angry. I still feel that anger when someone resists one of my* *business ideas. I feel awful when someone turns my services down. I'm still trying to get noticed and to prove how good I can be.*

Like Tom, you may find strong memories and feelings associated with family mottoes that still affect your approach to life. You will gain a fuller picture of your family's characteristic way of life and its continuing influence on you when you explore their attitudes and behaviour in the following exercise.

## EXERCISE

## YOUR FAMILY'S LIFE-STANCE ATTITUDES AND BEHAVIOUR

Attitudes and behaviour are shaped by values, the ideals that people hold as important, believe in and act on. Sometimes family attitudes and behaviour are at variance ('Do as I say, not as I do'); sometimes the behaviour grows out of the attitudes (valuing honesty, a parent allows a child to speak frankly within the family).

Two questions will clarify your family's ideals and actions. The first question is: **What did your family value?** The second question follows: **How did your family demonstrate their values?**

A  To address the first question, tick on the list below, any of the items that you feel were of great importance to your family. You may add other items that aren't on the list.

.................. work and achievement          .................. approval by others
.................. money and possessions          .................. creativity
.................. control                        .................. independence
.................. intelligence                   .................. service to others
.................. political beliefs              .................. religious beliefs
.................. emotions                       .................. humour
.................. honesty                        .................. leisure and play
.................. physical strength, skill       .................. authority
.................. stability                      .................. seriousness
.................. togetherness                   .................. self-respect
.................. conformity                      .................. change

B  Read over the items you ticked and pick the three that were most strongly valued by your family. Start writing with the words, 'My family mainly valued . . .'
C  To address the second question, ask yourself how those values appeared in attitudes and behaviour. Did your family preach one thing but practise another? Or did their actions, whether creative or destructive, follow on naturally from their beliefs?

51

D Write a sketch of memories and feelings based on your family's values and how they were demonstrated.

E Close by taking note of your reactions today to your family's life-stance attitudes and behaviour. In the final section of this chapter, you will return to this list to choose what you now value and want to practise.

Phyllis, a computer specialist in her mid-thirties, wrote:

*My family mainly valued intelligence, money and leisure. If you used your intelligence, you'd make money with which you could buy leisure. 'Living well is the best revenge' was our family motto. My dad loved being a wheeler-dealer, and I loved the drama and admired his guts and drive. It worked for him – he made a lot of money and now he's living well. I've experienced some business success myself by now, but I'm thinking of having a child and I'm questioning what kind of life stance I want to pass on.*

Phyllis described herself as 'ambivalent' about her family's life-stance characteristics: 'As an adult, I see a ruthless quality that I don't want to perpetuate. But I also really like living well. I need to think more about all this.'

In exploring some of your family's sayings, beliefs and behaviour, you have also described the contours of your family's life stance, their approach to the world. The core of a family life stance is the ability to trust and to be trustworthy. To the extent that your family could trust, you and other family members were free to be yourselves. To the extent that your family's core of trust was damaged, you lived with fear and the need for control. This next section looks at your family's experiences with trust.

# WHAT YOU LEARNED ABOUT TRUST IN YOUR FAMILY

In your first few years, you learned about trust through your parents' care. The way they met your basic needs for food, warmth and dryness, holding, and interacting with sounds and facial expressions shaped your earliest experience of the world. If they were reliable in taking good care of you, you came to trust that the world was safe for you, even if your parents were not there with you a lot of the time. Psychologist Erik Erikson noted this aspect of trust when he wrote:

The infant's first social achievement, then, is his willingness to let his mother out of sight without undue anxiety or rage, because she has become an inner certainty as well as an outer predictability.

If you grew up with the inner certainty that you would be taken care of, you had a firm foundation of trust that life was okay from which to launch into the world. If the adults who took care of you in your earliest years were not able to give you that stability (often because they had not experienced it themselves and were trying to create what was not familiar), you may have grown up with a lack of trust in yourself and life.

Approaching adulthood with a lack of trust can cause serious problems. If your basic needs for affection and nurture were not met in early childhood, you may:

- expect disappointment;
- fear taking risks;
- feel you have no right to exist;
- feel that something is always missing;
- feel powerless or hopeless.

If you expect disappointment, you will have difficulty forming intimate adult relationships. If you fear taking risks, you will find it hard to make plans and follow your goals. If you feel you have no right to exist, you may seek affirmation from others to prove your worth and value. If you feel something is always missing, you may try to fill your loneliness with addictive substances, relationships or activities. If you feel powerless or hopeless, you may question how worthwhile life itself is.

Problems such as those caused by lack of trust can shape a whole family's way of life. Families who expect disappointment don't trust each other or the outside world. Families who fear risk avoid confronting each other and taking action. Families whose members lack self-worth seek approval but often pull each other down. Lonely family members long to have their needs met through the family but often feel rejected and isolated. Powerless and hopeless families struggle with frustration and despair, wanting a different life but doubting that change is possible.

To illustrate how lack of trust causes family problems, let's examine the effects of mistrust on each of the three families profiled in this chapter. In the Dobbs family, for instance, Miranda grew up with an alcoholic father, and much of her mother's energy went to him. The family's life stance of scarce resources was communicated as 'We're all in this together, but you'll have to take care of yourself'. Miranda wants to give Eileen a different experience but she feels frantic about doing it right. John grew up in a more stable home and his more relaxed parenting style, learned from his family, helps balance Miranda's intense concern.

Anna Fortune's two daughters experienced the chaos of her marriage during their infancy but they were buffered by the availability of Anna's parents, grandparents, aunts and uncles. The loud fights and their mother's distress were predictable but so were the waiting arms and warm laps of their many relatives. The life stance of Shelley and Maria adopted was 'The world may knock you around, but you can always come home to your family'.

Charles Jordan grew up with an abusive father who set impossible standards for his sons and then beat them when they failed to measure up to them. Charles learned to control his pain and fear and to succeed competitively but he never allowed anyone to get close to him. Teresa Jordan watched her mother struggle to support the family when her father was unemployed and she swore she would choose a strong man who would take care of her. Charles and Teresa brought the cumulative effects of their malfunctioning families into their marriage, with some very negative results. Charles's strength has turned into tyranny and Teresa cannot allow herself to acknowledge that he has sexually abused Tessie and now Molly. The family stance that they all share says 'You can't trust anyone; look good in public and keep your mouth shut'.

As the Jordan family shows, the more that trust is lacking in a family, the more their life stance will focus on dominance and control. If you grew up in such a family, you may still be attempting to control the people and events in your daily life to create predictability and order. These attempts at control can be internal attitudes ('I expected this disappointment, so it doesn't really bother me') or external behaviour (living by rigid rules and masking loneliness or emptiness with overwork or compulsive spending).

The trouble with control as a coping strategy is that it creates more problems than it solves. Besides suppressing your natural creativity and spontaneity, excessively controlling attitudes and behaviour alienate the very people who might get close to you and help you begin to trust. A self-defeating cycle leads from mistrust to fear to attempts to control to rejection to more mistrust. You can begin to break that cycle by exploring your family history with trust and by laying the groundwork for building on it.

## EXERCISE

## YOUR FAMILY'S ATTITUDES ABOUT TRUST

You need to remember specific attitudes, sayings and behaviour patterns in order to see how trusting or nontrusting your family was. The exercise below helps survey your family's attitudes about trust, while the second exercise weighs the influence on your life of your family's need to control each other's thoughts, feelings and behaviour. If you find losses or lacks in that area, the last exercise encourages you to explore what a firmer foundation of trust would feel like in your everyday life.

As you respond to the list of attitudes below, notice your emotional reaction and any connections you can see to your current attitudes. You may trace some of your present problems to compliance with or resistance to old family attitudes. Once you understand how the present links with the past, you can start to change what no longer works.

A Of the possibilities below, tick those that were characteristic of one or more members of your family.

B Write a short passage in which you expand on a particular memory of a family attitude, exploring also whether that attitude still shapes your behaviour.

Did your family attitudes include the following?

.................... constant worrying ('What if . . . ?')

.................... immobilising self-doubt ('I won't be able to . . .')

.................... realistic confidence ('I'm going to do the best I can.')

.................... doubting others' abilities to care for themselves ('If I didn't look after you . . .')

.................... belief in others' ability to care for themselves ('I know you can do it.')

.................... fear of external dangers ('Lock the door. . . . Take your umbrella. . . . Don't sit on the toilet seat. . . . Don't eat that; it might be off. . . .')

.................... trust in the external world ('People are usually friendly. . . . You'll find the help you need. . . . Things generally work out for the best.')

.................... dreading the risk in new situations ('This is going to be a disaster.')

.................... anticipating positive results from a new situation ('We'll learn some new things from this.')

.................... trying to minimise the risk in new situations ('If I worry enough and work hard enough, this will probably turn out all right.')

Genevieve, who was caring for her ageing mother and bringing up two teenagers after a divorce, responded this way:

*That unfinished sentence – 'If I didn't look after you . . .' – really got me going. I was a forgetful child, always daydreaming. I don't know if I really would have forgotten my head if it wasn't attached to my neck, but I heard that expression from my mother a million times. The irony is, even now that she's ill and I'm the adult taking care of her, she still says those things and they still bother me. I'm coping so well with everything going on in my life that I can't be that helpless. But in my heart, I still wonder if I can trust myself. Self-doubt paralyses me at times.*

Genevieve's situation illustrates how we can both demonstrate and doubt our competence and trustworthiness. The inability to believe in our own abilities is a negative consequence of a poor foundation of trust. If the typical family responses you ticked and wrote about showed lack of trust that continues to get in your way, you will find help to begin changing that in the trust exercise at the end of this section and in the final section's writings.

## EXERCISE

## WHAT YOU LEARNED ABOUT CONTROL

This exercise will help you investigate how your family may have used control as a coping strategy and how you may have been shaped by the need for predictability and order.

Even the best foundation of trust doesn't protect us from accidents, job loss, illness, ageing and death, so we all attempt to control our circumstances to some degree. But if your family foundation taught mistrust about life's perils, you probably dealt with your fear by learning coping strategies that overemphasised control.

Write a short answer to each of the questions below. You can respond to each question separately or weave the questions together in a passage of memories, current situations and reflections.

- How important is control to you?
- Was your family life chaotic and out-of-control, fairly stable and orderly or over controlled and rigid?
- Did you learn as a child that keeping control of a situation was one way to be safe?
- Has your family life stance about control worked well for you? If that approach to control has not worked well, what negative effects do you see?

Debbie, a sales representative for a pharmaceuticals company, found that her family stance on control had influenced most of her adult decisions:

*My mother had a chronic mental illness. She would disappear to be treated and then come back quiet and strange. My dad's message to us was 'Don't worry – I've got things under control'. In some ways that helped us, because life felt so frightening and unpredictable. But in other ways, it wasn't the truth. Neither he nor my mother nor the doctors could control when she was 'herself'. Now I've sought control through excelling in a precise, demanding profession. But I pour all of myself into work so there's no time for relationships.*

Debbie felt her need for control as 'a constant tightness in my head'. If you too can relax only when everything is in order, you may be attempting to solve old issues of trust and anxiety through control. Creating a new, more trusting life stance requires time as well as willingness to risk, but it is possible, and it begins, as all positive change does, with an inner leap of the imagination. If you find yourself wishing for another approach to life, you can experiment with imagining an experience of trust in the following exercise.

## EXERCISE

## CREATING AN EXPERIENCE OF TRUST

Because we first learn about trust when we don't yet use language and logic, we often experience it as feeling safe in our bodies, comforted and content. Contrast your body's response to walking down a dark street at night in an unfamiliar part of town to your body's response to settling down cosily in a secure, familiar environment. You have probably already experienced trust as security and comfort in several different types of situation.

A For this exercise, write a short passage about one or more of the trust experiences below:

- **Describe a time of trusting yourself** (believing in yourself, having confidence about a decision, following your intuition or dream).
- **Describe a trustworthy place in which you feel comfortable** (an actual environment that you know or any place you can imagine).
- **Describe a trusting encounter between you and another person** (someone you know or an imagined ally or friend).

Or combine elements of the three choices in what you write. You can draw on positive memories or your imagination. Use vivid, descriptive language and write in the present tense. Don't just write 'The room makes me feel safe'; write 'The soft blue colour on the walls soothes my eyes. The window looks out onto an oak tree and I pile up the soft cushions on the window seat to sit down and read.'

B When you have described an experience of trust, ask yourself whether you could adapt any of the elements to your current situation. For instance, if you wrote about talking openly with a friend about something that was bothering you without feeling pressure or judgement, ask yourself whether there is someone in your life now with whom you can feel at ease. Could you seek that person out in a new way, offering as well as asking for trust and friendship? If so, write this down. Then try to take a small step by, say, phoning that person to catch up on news and then suggesting a future lunch.

If you find you're not ready to adapt elements of your imagined trust experience to real life, acknowledge that building trust takes time and encourage yourself to continue writing about it. This commitment in itself will create positive momentum, as the woman in the following example discovered.

Dana described herself as 'recovering from a friend's recent betrayal', so at first she resisted writing about an experience of trust. She chose to write about the unconditional love she received from her pets, crying as she read what she wrote: 'It's too bad humans don't have kind hearts like cats and dogs do.' The next week she reported dreams and memories of childhood betrayals of trust by her distant father and alcoholic mother. She heard echoes of the past in the recent event and wondered how to break the pattern of mistrust. A colleague suggested volunteering to work at an animal shelter or at a vet's surgery. Some months later Dana wrote to me:

*I wasn't ready to imagine an experience of trust with a person back then, but I kept writing about my pain and my hopes. I've discovered that I can build a bridge to people through my love of animals. People who love animals like I do seem pretty safe, and I'm feeling more trust than ever before by helping out here at the animal rescue sanctuary.*

Putting trust into practice is like planning and caring for a multitude of seeds, knowing that some will not come up and others will sprout and grow. Trust asks you to be a patient gardener, working land that your family has also tended. Your willingness to develop a healthy harvest of trusting attitudes and behaviour will gradually begin to change your approach to life and show you as well as others that the pain of the past does not have to keep recurring in the present.

In the next section you can explore in what ways your family style works for you now or causes unnecessary problems.

# YOUR FAMILY'S RELATIONSHIP TO HOPE AND ACTION

Most families' attitudes fall somewhere between the opposite poles of extreme optimism and extreme pessimism and their behaviour between being extremely active and extremely passive. Each of the four styles – optimism, pessimism, passivity and activity – has problems and benefits, although a more optimistic and active life stance is often identified as healthier both psychologically and physically. Hopeful people oriented towards taking action are less likely to become stuck in destructive behaviour.

However, blind hopefulness and unthinking action are not helpful, since they can mask unresolved aspects of a situation. If your family achieved a middle ground of 'reasonable optimism', that is of clear-sighted hope, and well-thought-out action, you learned a good balance of these qualities that grow out of a family's orientation to trust.

## OPTIMISM

If you grew up in a strongly **optimistic** family, you may have learned to seek out positive results. The benefit of optimism is that expectations do affect outcomes.

An optimistic family tends to:

- look for positive potential in most situations;
- trust themselves and others;
- pursue interests and goals with the expectation that the activity is worthwhile in itself and that success is possible.

Your family, if it was oriented towards optimism, probably believed that mistakes were simply part of the learning process. In an optimistic family, you might hear these words of explanation: 'Well, it's too bad it didn't work out, but we can sort it out and we'll know not to do it again.'

On the other hand, if you grew up in a strongly pessimistic family, you were surrounded with suggestions that it was unwise to expect good outcomes. The pessimistic style can be expressed in many ways, from resigned hopelessness to warnings of doom. In general, a pessimistic family tends to:

- look for and fear the negative potential in most situations;
- distrust themselves and others;
- pursue interests and goals with the expectation that their efforts may be thwarted and that failure is a threat.

Your family, if it was oriented towards pessimism, probably believed that mistakes and setbacks were a sign of failure. They were prepared to expect the worst. In a pessimistic family, you might hear these words of explanation: 'What did we expect? We tried hard, but you just can't win these days. We should have known better; it's not worth the effort.'

You can characterise your family's stance towards hope in this exercise. If your family experiences were extremely slanted towards one style, your current life stance may be in compliance with or in rebellion against that style. If your current stance causes problems, you can assess what changes you want to make.

## EXERCISE

## OPTIMISM VS. PESSIMISM IN YOUR FAMILY

This exercise will help you understand more clearly the balance of optimism and pessimism in your family's outlook, how you have responded to that style and how effectively your current beliefs about hope serve your present life. In the process, notice your family's beliefs about the general probability of failure and success. The failures can be as minor as a rained-off picnic or as major as a family member's bankruptcy or arrest. The successes can be as small as one peaceful family dinner or as big as the resolution of a long-standing family feud.

A  Write about two occasions when you were growing up when your family experienced a minor or major failure or setback.

B  Write about two occasions when your family experienced a minor or major success.

C  Write about each of the four events as if you were overhearing the family talking about it. Focus on one at a time, and write out what you hear, the spoken dialogue, and what you sense, the unspoken, underlying feelings and messages. For example, this description conveys both the words and the emotions underneath them: 'Mum quickly looked over at Dad, her mouth tight and her eyes angry, and said in a deliberately even voice, "Your father isn't at all worried about being out of work." '

D  When you have written what happened and who said what in all four instances, reread the four passages, putting an *O* by the more optimistic statements or feelings and a *P* by the more pessimistic ones. Surveying the four instances, write a short passage describing your family's overall orientation towards optimism, pessimism, or a mix of both.

E  To close the exercise, answer these questions:

- How has your family's optimism or pessimism affected you in the past?
- How has their orientation towards hope carried over into your present approach to life?
- Does your present stance of optimism and/or pessimism work well for you? If so, what are the benefits? If not, what are the problems?

Serena, a single mother in her late twenties, wrote her reflections on the four scenarios she had written:

*My parents were complete opposites here – all the optimism from my mother, all the pessimism from my father. We were poor, and Mum always said, 'God will take care of us.' Dad got mad and said there was no God, only hard work for people like us who never got a lucky break. Mum's faith was the strong influence in my childhood, but the difficulties I face bringing up my children alone make me talk and think like Dad. I feel angry and pessimistic, then guilty that I don't have faith. My parents' attitudes are at war inside me and I want to feel more peaceful.*

Like Serena, you may find that your family's ingrained attitudes have influenced your perceptions and responses. In the final section of this chapter, you can assess whether you want to clarify or change your orientation towards hope.

# ACTIVITY

Very active families attempt to solve problems by making things happen. The benefit of an active life stance is that experimenting with options and trying new ways does increase the possibilities for success. Activity that results from reflection on the possibilities is the most constructive style.

An active family tends to:

- tranlsate beliefs into practice;
- find self-worth in the good results of taking action;
- believe that doing the action is worthwhile in itself.

Your family, if it was oriented towards activity, liked to initiate projects, plans and experiments. A typical discussion in an active family will include a statement such as: 'We won't get anywhere just sitting here talking about it, so let's give it a try'.

On the other hand, if you grew up in a very passive family, you were surrounded by actions that reflected beliefs in the hopelessness of action. This stance grows out of the parents' early life experiences that discouraged them from taking initiative. Parents who hold their children back from being active out of protectiveness are unknowingly encouraging passive dependency that will not be healthy later on. At the extreme, some children develop a passive orientation because of family violence or abuse; fighting back put them in greater danger of harm.

In general, a passive family tends to:

- hold back from putting beliefs into action;
- encourage observation rather than participation, adaptation rather than change;
- believe that it is more risky to initiate action than to withdraw.

Your family, if it was oriented towards passivity, waited for others to take action and valued caution rather than boldness. In a strongly passive family, you might hear this statement: 'Let's just wait and see what happens. No point in sticking our necks out'.

## EXERCISE

## ACTIVITY VS. PASSIVITY IN YOUR FAMILY

In this exercise, you can discover the balance of active and passive forces in your family's life stance. You will discern the roots of your current activity level, equipping you to assess whether you need to learn how to take more initiative.

Three situations – holidays, crises and social activities – tend to call for responses from family members, who react either in an active or passive way.

A  Recall specific examples of these three situations:

- A holiday is coming up and plans need to be made.
- One family member is in a crisis (physical or emotional illness, school, job or relationship problems).
- Your family is asked to participate in some neighbourhood activity.

B  Choose the most vivid one and write an account of what happened, focusing on these questions:

Who took action? Who avoided action?
What was said to explain why action was or was not taken?
How did you feel then about what took place?
How do you feel now writing about it?
What connections do you make between your family's active or passive responses and your current orientation towards action now?
Does your current orientation work well for you?

Gary, a probation officer, wrote about his father's alcoholism:

*During Dad's periodic binges, Mum just put up with it. She wasn't exactly inactive because she was always cleaning up after him, making excuses to his boss, protecting us from his anger. But she did passively accept that these drinking bouts were going to happen and that she had to take the consequences. Now I notice that I avoid conflict with my boss and my wife, so I think I'm still responding out of that passive acceptance of bad circumstances. I don't like seeing that in myself at all.*

Our orientations towards hope or action have complex effects and we may change some hopeless or passive behaviour in one area of our lives only to find that we fall back into it in another. For Gary, it came as an unpleasant surprise to recognise that he was passive about problems with his boss and wife when he had learned to respond actively to the problems of his clients. Gary found it helpful to put his new responses and old habits in perspective and evaluate his overall life stance. Making positive changes in your life-stance characteristics like this is possible and will enhance your self-esteem and enable you to solve problems more effectively.

# CHANGING YOUR LIFE STANCE

With the information, memories and feelings that you have brought to the surface, you now have a clearer picture of your family's life stance, how it was built on the family's foundation of trust and how it played out in attitudes and behaviour. In the following two exercises, you will sum up what you have learned about you and your family's life stances and how you might benefit if you change your approach to life.

## EXERCISE

### SUMMING UP AND EVALUATING LIFE STANCES

Even though you inherited many of the qualities of your life stance from your family, your current stance and your family's are not exactly the same. In order to choose the way you want to approach your life in the future, it's helpful to differentiate what aspects of your life stance relate to family patterns and what aspects relate to who you are now.

A Using the impressions and memories from this chapter's exercises, write a brief definition of your family's life stance. Such examples as 'resentful resignation', 'anxious caution', and 'confident rigidity', mentioned earlier, illustrate others' definitions of their family's approach to daily life.

B Looking over your present circumstances and feelings, write a similar definition of what you think your life stance is now. 'Determined to change but confused and scared' was one man's definition. You will be following your intuitions about yourself and you may need to scribble possibilities or write a few sentences of explanation before settling on what applies to you now.

C Imagine and write down a description of a future life stance that would help you meet each day with confidence and enjoyment. By creating a statement of your intended life stance, you use the power of definition – if you can name it, you can claim it – to begin the process of change. Your future life stance might focus on such qualities as creativity, intimacy, independence, intelligence, service, faith, humour, honesty, stability, self-respect, flexibility, pleasure, courage, peacefulness, strength, freedom, joy, clarity and wisdom.

D Brainstorm a list of what you might do to bring those life-stance characteristics more fully into your life. These activities might include a range from the practical or easily achieved (for the student who wrote 'courage and directness', these included 'speak up more in the class I'm taking' and 'notice when I feel nervous') to the wildly imaginative or extremely demanding ('climb Mount Everest' or 'tell my mother how I feel about her intrusions in my children's lives').

E Choose one item from your list that you would feel comfortable taking action on now and plan it out in small, achievable steps ('When I write in my journal every evening before bed, I can note times during the day I felt nervous and times I felt courageous. I'll try that for two weeks and maybe I'll see a pattern that will help me understand why I get nervous and what helps me feel more confident.') Since all your life stances – in the past, the present and the future – build on your foundation of trust, this step helps you strengthen that base from which your life stance developed.

## EXERCISE

## STRENGTHENING TRUST, HOPE AND ACTION

When you created an experience of trust in the earlier exercise, you used memories or imagination to describe vividly comfort and security. We all lack trust to some degree, we all lose hope at times and we all have some difficulty taking necessary action. While you cannot rework those first years of your life when your foundation of trust was laid, you can strengthen your ability to trust, hope and act now by writing a brief letter to the child that you were then.

By writing to yourself as a young child, you bring your current wisdom and confidence to the self within you who has not fully grown up, who still fears and mistrusts as in early life. No matter how much you feel you still lack confidence, you now have an adult's awareness and abilities, and you can offer care to the young self within you who is frightened or hopeless.

Diarist Anaïs Nin comforted herself when confronting difficult childhood memories by writing a letter in her diary to her therapist:

By evoking her therapist as the audience for this introspective entry Nin feels safe, as if she were in her doctor's office. Actually her unsent letter is a way for Nin to evoke her own inner therapist in a time of emotional need.

A Write directly and simply whatever message you most want to convey about trust, hope and possibility to the child you were somewhere between birth and three.

B Notice and express whatever you feel as you write, and finish with some comments and reflections about the short letter you've written.

Debbie, whose mother's emotional breakdowns had kept her from being with her children, wrote this brief letter:

*Debbie, you don't have to be scared. You will grow up to be clever and strong and safe. I will take care of you, and you won't have to be alone.*

As she wrote this to her younger self, Debbie realised that she no longer has to go it alone as an adult either. She concluded: 'I've hidden behind my work long enough. I want real friends, not just colleagues and acquaintances. I can see how far I've come from that little girl in the past, but if I can help myself to develop some closer ties now, maybe some of her pain will heal too.'

By adapting the life stance that grew out of your family's circumstances to your own needs and characteristics, you build a strong bond between your past and your present selves. Developing a healthier and more trusting approach to life is a long-term proposition, but the good feelings of identifying your needs and values, taking care of yourself and putting your plans in action will keep you moving forward.

The next chapter examines family language, the styles and stances of communication that taught you how to respond to other people. In verbal and nonverbal communication, families use language in ways that are as unique as their life stances; your communication today reflects your particular family language history. No matter how your family communicated, you can learn the patterns of clearer and more direct language.

# CHAPTER 4

# COMMUNICATION IN YOUR FAMILY

*F*amily life centres around the ability to communicate. Further, how well you communicate today is linked to the clarity and directness of your family's communication patterns. Any problems with communication that you have now – an almost universal complaint in personal and professional relationships – go back to the communication patterns you learned from your family. However, by examining the patterns of communication that your family taught, you can reshape the way you approach conversation and improve your ability to communicate from now on.

Long before you could understand the meaning of the words spoken to you by your family, you were learning about communication. Even when you were an infant, your parents communicated with you in the way they held you, looked at you and made faces and noises in response to the expressions and sounds you made. Your earliest sense of safety and belonging came from that communication. Your sense of human connection was being established. If you were lucky, you experienced a strong bond with a parent, and you received this message at a deep level: I belong – it's okay to be me.

As a toddler, you began to use words to communicate your needs. You took your first steps towards independence by asserting what you wanted, whether or not it was what your parents wanted. 'No!' was probably your favourite word. In ideal circumstances, if the adults who took care of you encouraged your independence while giving you safe limits and responsive caring, your communication skills and your feelings of self-worth grew and matured as you did.

By adolescence, your thinking abilities were developing to a full adult level and your need to communicate with your peers and explore the world beyond your family was intense. Your communication with your parents was probably difficult, because you were trying to separate yourself from your family. If your parents kept communication lines open with you and conveyed both love and limits through this stage, you came into adulthood knowing that people can differ strongly and still communicate.

Most of us did not experience this ideal scenario when we were children, just as most of our parents did not experience it when *they* were children. All parents face not only the usual stresses of bringing up children but also their own unfulfilled childhood needs and unresolved feelings.

Your parents' ability to communicate with you was affected by the family environment in which they learned about caring and communication.

If your parents were not able to provide you with a secure environment and responsive caring, your communication experiences in infancy were probably of frustration and anxiety. If your parents were not able to tolerate your independence at toddlerhood, your communication with them was a battleground of wills. The communication problems probably escalated in adolescence, when your needs and your parents' were often in conflict.

To the extent that you and your parents struggled over what you said, how you said it, and what you wanted, you learned that communication was painful. If you learned that your parents were not interested in responding to you or would punish you for trying to express yourself, you learned that it was hopeless or dangerous.

However, when your relationship or your job is threatened today by communication difficulties, you usually don't understand why it's happening and how it is connected to your childhood. You know only that you want the frustration and hurt to stop. Being unable to solve a communication problem through communication is exasperating and painful. Examples of these problems include:

- **misunderstandings** that arise because you, the other person, or both of you didn't say what you really meant ('But I thought you said . . .' – 'That's not what I meant.');
- **insincere agreement**, when you try to say what the other person wants to hear instead of what you really think ('Of course, you're right' or 'No, I don't mind at all.');
- **destructive blaming**, when communication is a form of mutual attack ('If only you hadn't . . .' or 'I just did that because you . . .');
- **blocked expression**, when you can't express your feelings either verbally or nonverbally ('What's going on?' – 'I don't know; nothing, I suppose.');
- **confusion**, when you get distracted by double messages, differing assumptions, and indirect statements ('What do you mean . . . ?' or 'So you are saying . . . ?' or 'Oh, never mind . . .').

These unproductive patterns of communication build on each other until it seems unsafe to say anything. You feel misunderstood, misjudged or hurt by what others say. Your attempts to clarify the communication may make it worse. You can't escape, because your interactions with others depend on your ability to communicate. It can be argued that communication is the greatest single factor affecting a person's health and relationship to others.

You came into adulthood with a fully internalised set of communication habits and expectations learned from your family. Your family influenced your communication patterns in both verbal and nonverbal dimensions, including:

- the type of words you use and the way you put them together into statements, questions, requests or commands;
- how much and how fast or slowly you talk;

- what kind of regional accent, slang or family saying you use;
- the facial expressions, gestures and body movements that are the unspoken part of communication.

The way your family taught you to communicate reflects the mini-culture in which you grew up. How open or closed your family was, what kinds of life stances they adopted and how strong a foundation of trust they had are all revealed by your shared patterns of communication.

Since you learned about communication from your family, you can begin to take action to change any current communication problems by tracing them back to their roots in your family language system. This chapter explores five ways to do this: discovering your family's communication style and the emotional honesty of their communication responses; defining harmful communication patterns; and finally, learning new ways to communicate clearly and honestly.

In the first section, you will explore your family's verbal and nonverbal **communication styles**. You can evaluate how healthy your family's **verbal** style was by examining whether people talked to one another directly, clearly and specifically.

For instance, a parent might say to a child, 'Are you and your friends planning to go out this weekend?' If this question were asked out of pure curiosity, it would be direct, clear and specific enough. However, if the parent had an idea of what might be happening and wanted to offer some support and ask for co-operation, the communication would be indirect, unclear and unspecific. 'I would be glad to drive you and your friends to the game Saturday if you will be ready to go by six, since your mother and I are going out to dinner at seven' is a more complicated statement, but it is direct, clear and specific.

Another factor in your family's communication style involves the **nonverbal** dimension of communication.

The nonverbal portion of your family's communication comprises bodylanguage responses such as posture, gait, gestures, facial expressions, characteristic stances while standing or sitting, and signature movements like a toss of the head. Research shows that people take in the nonverbal portion of communication more than they hear the spoken words, probably because we responded to body language in early life before we could understand and use words. As adults, we interpret others' body language based on our family experience, so our current communication is affected by early learnings.

One man described his annoyance with his wife's habit of nodding her head while he talked. He interpreted that as fake interest, since his mother had done that while she read a book and pretended to listen to him. His wife protested that she was absolutely sincere, that her family had used nods and small remarks like 'Uh-huh' and 'Mmmm' to encourage each other.

Sometimes the body postures, facial expressions and gestures speak louder than the words. Some of the messages communicated by body language include:

- how comfortable the other person is in the situation;
- what inner feelings the other person has in response to you;
- how receptive the other person is to what you are saying;
- how involved the other person is in what you are saying.

One student contrasted her family's body-language habits with those of her husband's family: 'Both my parents were very expressive – big wide-open eyes, big wide-open arms, big smiles and laughs. When I married Len, I thought his family hated me because they were always so stiff and still, but that's just the way they act with everyone.'

Each family creates a body-language mini-culture in which certain expressions and gestures mean certain things. Len's family members showed strong interest by attentive silence, leaning slightly forward with a serious expression; his wife couldn't read those signals until she had known them for some years.

If a family's body-language communication is clear and direct among family members, it supports the words that are said. Sometimes body language and words don't match; the effect is confusing and results in communication difficulties. The reason that so few families use verbal or nonverbal communication that is direct, clear and specific is that being honest can reveal differences and lead to **confrontation**. Families differ according to how much **conflict** they tolerate, how much **agreement** they demand and how much **emotional honesty** they display. Your family's ability to handle the confrontations that arise in a shared household is the final measurement of a family's communication style. Each family practises a unique blend of these three styles.

Inability to reach agreement tends to produce conflict; what families see as too much conflict tends to generate pressure for agreement.

A family that is experiencing too much conflict might try to force agreement among the members ('If you children would just get on better, your dad wouldn't get so upset'). If everyone is pretending to agree but feeling in conflict, that conflict might erupt through some family member's remark or behaviour ('Joey, stop picking on your brother – Jeanne, why haven't you taught this boy to behave decently?').

If neither conflict not agreement is working, some emotional honesty on one family member's part might turn the situation towards clearer communication ('I hate bickering at meals. I don't like to keep shouting, but I come home tense and tired from work and I can't unwind and enjoy this family time if you are picking on each other').

**Emotional honesty** is central to healthy communication and in the second section of this chapter, you will examine this honesty and other communication responses. If your family members were emotionally honest with each other, their words and feelings matched, as in the father's example above when he admitted how coming home tense from work affected his behaviour at home. Honest responses lead to direct communication, a healthy pattern in which you clearly understand what the other person means and you clearly say what you mean. When you understand the interplay of conflict, agreement and emotional honesty in your family's communication style, you can more easily alter remnants of that style that give you problems today.

In the next section, which focuses on three harmful communication habits, other ideas for improving communication are addressed. If your family gave a lot of **double messages, punished each other with silent withdrawal** or **used words to belittle each other**, some of the painful effects of these types of communication may still be causing you problems.

In the final section, you will use your insights about your family communication patterns to develop new ways to communicate with clarity, directness and honesty. You can build on whatever communication strengths your family displayed – such as caring humour, flashes of honesty or a commitment to understanding each other.

As language researcher Deborah Tannen writes, 'By becoming aware of our ways of talking and how effective they are, we can override our automatic impulses and adapt our habitual styles when they are not serving us well'. No matter how poorly you felt your family communicated, you can learn new patterns based on emotional honesty and caring directness. The rewards of this kind of communication will spread into all areas of your life.

# YOUR FAMILY'S COMMUNICATION STYLE

Just as the attitudes and behaviour of individuals in your family characterised its general approach to life – its life stance – the speech patterns of the individuals in your family made up its general approach to language – its communication style. The clearer, more direct and more specific the speech patterns were, the fewer the misunderstandings and confusion in your family communication.

## INTERNAL CONVERSATIONS AND NOT SPEAKING CLEARLY

Two factors may have kept your family from establishing effective ways of talking to each other. First, we all carry on **internal conversations** with ourselves that are the inner counterpart of spoken dialogues. All misunderstanding and confusion start in our individual interpretations of what other people mean. For instance, the following exchange between a husband and wife sounds simple and matter-of-fact, but the communication breaks down because of what they are saying to themselves silently.

**Arnold:** *Are you coming to watch this programme?*

**Martha:** *As soon as I finish washing-up.*

As he walks into the kitchen to speak to Martha, Arnold is saying to himself, 'Why is she still in here? She's been acting strange. I hope she's not getting in one of those moods where she doesn't like anything I do.' As she hears Arnold approaching, Martha thinks, 'Well, it's about time. I've been here for ages clearing up. He can finish drying for me.' Then she realises Arnold isn't volunteering to help but wants her to watch TV with him. To herself, she thinks, 'How rude!' and makes her remark about finishing the dishes abrupt and emphatic. Arnold, missing the point that she wanted his help, walks out of the kitchen feeling rejected and saying to himself, 'Why did I bother? She just snapped at me'. As Martha walks into the living room and sits down with a sigh, they are thinking:

**Arnold:** *She never wants to do anything with me.*

**Martha:** *He never helps me.*

The problem with these internal conversations is that people assume others know what they mean, so they rarely think to mention these inner thoughts and feelings. They make conclusions ('She's cold' – 'He's selfish') that contaminate and confuse their communication from then on.

If your family kept their inner thoughts to themselves, misunderstandings and confusion resulted. If you keep your real thoughts to yourself, your family's indirect communication style from the past may still be causing you problems.

The second factor that may have hampered good communication in your family is **not speaking clearly and specifically** to one another. Since family members share so much personal history, any one statement can be taken a number of ways, based on what the hearer is remembering or assuming from years of past conversations. Often the speaker means a number of things by the statement as well, but doesn't state them clearly and specifically. For instance, a mother's question to her teenage son – 'Are you going to the school dance?' – may sound innocuous to an outsider, but the son may hear one or more of the following implications:

- You're too shy – get out there and mix.
- Will there be drugs or alcohol at the dance?
- Are we going to have to fight again about what time you get in?
- With exam results like yours, you shouldn't go to a dance.
- Are you going to want an expensive new shirt?
- I want you to go and have a good time.

The mother has not been clear and specific – possibly because she has mixed feelings about the dance but possibly because she assumes her son will know what she means. The son may get angry and say, 'Why are you always nagging me?' Or he might shrug and walk away.

If your family members, like the mother and son, had an unclear and unspecific communication style, they probably ended up frustrated or angry frequently. To the degree that you were influenced by this pattern, you may still find yourself wondering why other people don't seem to know what you mean.

In the following three-part exercise, you can describe how your family language looked and sounded, what you learned from your family about clear, direct and specific communication and how this history influences your current communication strengths and struggles. This will stir your memories and help you define your family's unique conversational style.

## EXERCISE

## HOW DID YOUR FAMILY COMMUNICATE?

A 1 Imagine that you are back in your childhood years, listening to your family talk at a meal or gathering.
  2 Write a brief description of the following aspects of their communication.

- the noise level (Was your family loud or quiet?)
- the amount of body language (Was your family expressive or subtle in their gestures, posture, facial expressions and movements?)
- the tones of voice (How did the adults' voices sound? The children's voices?)

Frances, a librarian in her fifties, responded:

*My family was quiet, as my parents insisted that only one person at a time could speak – no interrupting. My relatives had erect posture, restrained gestures, clipped speech and careful control of their facial reactions. We children were supposed to enunciate our words clearly when asked to speak.*

B   Amplify your description of your family communication by using the unfinished sentence 'My family communicated .................. by ..................'. Fill in one or more of the common family messages suggested below, showing how they communicated it. This time, write even more specifically, focusing both on the words that family members would typically use and the body language that would accompany the words. Choose from these messages:

- **acceptance** (caring affirmation of you and your feelings, thoughts and actions);
- **judgement** (critical evaluation of you and your feelings, thoughts and actions);
- **interest** (curious, attentive enthusiasm for each other's opinions and activities);
- **boredom** (emotional flatness or inattentive withdrawal from others);
- **calmness** (meeting events with serenity and steadiness);
- **anxiety** (meeting events with worry, agitation or fear).

Frances chose to write about how her family communicated 'acceptance and judgement, the two opposites. I watched for subtle signs, since the adults were reserved. My father showed acceptance by a twinkle in his eyes, a nod of approval but a matter-of-fact tone – "Now, that's fine." My mother showed acceptance by bending the rules without telling my father, but she never put her approval in words. They both showed judgement the same way: their manner got stiffer, their lips were tight and they said, "We don't do that. You know better." '

C    Finally, describe how clear, direct and specific you think your family's communication style was. Use these questions as guidelines:

- Did your family state directly what they were thinking and feeling or did they keep their thoughts to themselves and speak indirectly, assuming or hoping that others would understand what they really meant?
- Did your family talk clearly and specifically so that others knew the full range of what was meant or did they hint, leave things out or speak vaguely?

Close the exercise by noting how you were affected by this style and what specific habits you may still use that don't work well for you.

In writing the series of descriptions in this exercise, you have sketched the outlines and filled in some of the details of your family's communication style. In the chapter's last section, you will define some communication changes you can work towards to clear up the negative influences of your family's style.

Frances rounded out her family's portrait:

*My relatives were direct about their opinions but indirect about their feelings. They might state their political views very directly, while suppressing their emotions. They gave their children clear specifics only when we had somehow disappointed them. I grew up able to read subtle communications signals well. I know how to communicate in a polite, reserved manner but I long for a more expressive style. I still can't express myself freely and people comment that I seem stuffy or unemotional in the way I talk and act.*

Frances concluded that she hoped to change some of her inherited restraint. By enumerating the ways in which your current communication patterns reflect your family's style, you too are more prepared to evaluate how to make changes in it.

## CONFLICT, AGREEMENT AND EMOTIONAL HONESTY

Another way to characterise your family's communication style focuses on the balance of **conflict**, **agreement** and **emotional honesty** in their conversations.

Because individuals living together in families will always have different personalities, needs and preferences, conflict is inevitable. Conflict includes all disagreements, from the subtle, in which raised eyebrows or a muttered comment show disapproval, to the obvious, in which raised voices and agitated behaviour express differing opinions and needs. For example, in a family in which half the people like to go to bed early and half like to stay up late, one conflict will centre on what is the 'right' bedtime and how to manage people's differences.

Such a family **conflict** over sleep schedules might result in battling to come up with one solution. Or they might be inclined to manage the conflict by **agreement**, with the most authoritative or persuasive person choosing a solution and demanding everyone else's compliance. The demand for agreement can come in an unspoken rule (no one challenges Dad's need for a quiet house) or in a direct edict ('We will not have the TV on after 10 P.M., and that's final').

A healthy and clear communication style confronts differences within families by using **emotional honesty** as a valuable tool for balancing the extremes of unresolvable conflict and inflexible forced agreement. When family members are free to express what they feel directly, clearly and specifically, they can more easily resolve confrontational issues. Holding feelings in builds up anxiety and resentment; expressing feelings about difficult issues releases energy for positive problem-solving.

## EXERCISE

## CONFLICT, AGREEMENT AND EMOTIONAL HONESTY IN YOUR FAMILY'S COMMUNICATION

Every family has components of conflict, agreement and emotional honesty in their communication style. You can survey the way your family handled conflict when you were growing up and how you handle it now in this three-part exercise.

For each of the parts, you will bring back a memory of how your family handled confrontation resulting from differences or difficult issues.

By writing about how your body and emotions reacted, you immerse yourself in that past family atmosphere. By choosing a metaphor, an image of comparison, to describe how you were affected, you can create a vivid description of your internal reactions to an external situation. The metaphor will help you decide whether you are living with healthy or harmful past ways of handling confrontation that you learned while growing up.

A 1 Write about a time when you were surrounded by family conflict. Focus on family members' words and actions. Use these questions as guidelines:

- What did you want to do as the conflict appeared and grew?
  (run away – take charge – speak up – withdraw)
- How did you body react?
  (tense muscles – shallow breathing – stomach knots)

- What were your feelings?
  (panic – excitement – anger – numbness)

2  Let your imagination offer you a metaphor for what your family was like in that situation by comparing it to something else. You might encourage your imagination by writing 'My family in conflict was a ....................' then responding with whatever picture emerges, (a volcano – slapstick comedy – a war zone).

B 1  Write about a time when you were surrounded by family pressure for agreement. Guided by these questions, remember what was said and how people behaved when trying to get agreement about a difficult issue.

- What was it like to hide what you truly felt?
  (overwhelming pressure – like I might explode)
- If you kept silent, what didn't you say?
  (Stop pretending! – I don't agree!)
- If you spoke up, what was it like to go against the pressure for agreement?
  (I felt ignored and alone – I felt brave.)

2  Again, use your memories to create a written metaphor for this component of family communication, by taking off from the words 'Under pressure to agree or conform, my family was a ....................' (sardine tin – dark basement – set of plastic dolls).

C 1  Write a paragraph about a time when your family confronted a difficult issue with **emotional honesty**. Maybe all the members of the family said what they felt; maybe only one person dared to do so. If you cannot remember any instance of this with your family, recall feeling free to be honest with a friend or teacher. Focus on these questions:

- How did your body react when hearing emotional honesty, from yourself or someone else?
  (deep breaths – light-headed – muscles relaxed)
- What were your feelings?
  (wanted to cry – admired the person – felt frightened)
- What happened after the emotionally honest response?
  (The situation got better – I felt more in touch with my real feelings – My parents got even angrier.)

2  Describe the past situation of emotional honesty in a metaphor, taking off from these words: 'Experiencing emotional honesty in that situation was like ....................' (hearing a clear chime ring – coming out from behind a mask)

D  Describe your current responses to what you have written about the three components of conflict, agreement and emotional honesty. Write whatever you notice, including how these past responses remind you of present patterns. Identify which ones you'd like to change.

Tom, who described his own style as 'combative', wrote this about family conflict:

*When one of our constant disagreements started to escalate, I wanted to stand behind my father. He couldn't see me there and I'd be safe from his wrath. I could also let him be the spokesman for my anger. I felt out of control. My family in conflict was a time bomb ticking, until my father exploded and somebody got hit or hurt.*

Tom went on to describe how his mother would try to force agreement among her four sons, so the father would not get angry. However, he compared that pressure for agreement to 'a failed diplomatic effort when the troops were already marching'. His memories of emotional honesty are that it was not safe: 'That person was in danger by being emotionally honest, because it was like laying down your arms. The others might go ahead and shoot you anyway.'

Tom struggled to read aloud what he had written about the family conflicts, explaining, 'I hate those memories. Now I hide from my anger like I used to hide behind my violent father. Yet conflict is unavoidable and I need some new tools, not the old weapons.'

As you, like Tom, put words and images to the memories of your family's history with conflict, agreement and emotional honesty, you will fill out your picture of your family's communication style. You probably now have some clues about how your current communication style evolved from the past and some feelings about problematic or troublesome areas that you hope to change. You'll develop these hopes into concrete plans for change more fully at the end of the chapter.

In the next section, you will compare your family's communication responses with five that family therapists have identified – the emotionally evasive: blaming, placating, computing and distracting; and the emotionally honest: levelling. To the extent that your family used the first four, you adapted to family situations with automatic, fear-driven responses rather than authentic honesty. You can develop your communication abilities by learning to use the honesty of the levelling response more frequently.

# MATCHING WORDS AND FEELINGS IN FAMILY COMMUNICATION

Most of us have difficulty communicating in ways that reflect our true feelings. It has been estimated that only about 4½ per cent of us consistently use the emotionally honest levelling response, while 50 per cent placate, 30 per cent try to escape by blaming others, 15 per cent intellectualise by hiding their feelings in computing and ½ per cent try to distract others from the situation by hiding their feelings in irrelevant actions.

Levelling is honest communication because in it, words and feelings match. In the four incongruent responses, they don't. Everyone tends to use the incongruent responses when they are under stress and feel bad about themselves but don't feel they can freely say what is really going on. Each of the four responses covers up what the speaker is feeling inside with a contradictory communication posture. These cover-ups are due to anxiety about confrontation, criticism or rejection.

For example, when people in your family responded in a placating way, they were avoiding someone's anger or rejection. They put others' needs first and agreed with everything to avoid conflict. When someone was upset, they tried to make that person happy, even if they felt resentful underneath ('Whatever you say, Mum, of course, I'll be glad to do it').

When family members responded in a blaming way, they avoided being blamed themselves for a situation that felt threatening or out of control. They disagreed and made accusations, implying that anything that was wrong was not their fault. Despite their outward anger, they probably felt alone and anxious underneath ('You always ruin our weekends – if it weren't for your nagging, this family would be happy').

When people in your family used the computing response, they avoided the threat of vulnerability by intellectualisation and unemotional detachment. They asserted control by fact-finding and insistence on a rational, logical approach. Despite their outward restraint, they were probably tense and worried underneath ('I don't know what you're so hysterical about, I have the situation organised and under control').

And when they used the distracting response, family members tried to avoid danger by changing the subject in discussions and taking irrelevant actions. They may have appeared carefree, scatterbrained or energetic, but their distractions covered empty and scared feelings ('Does anybody know where the cat is? Mum! Dad! Stop arguing! Listen, listen! I have a report due tomorrow I need help with').

You will probably find that your family did not often communicate honestly over stressful issues. At those times, their words rarely matched their feelings. Instead, you and your family members probably learned and practised the four unhealthy responses because of one or more of these factors:

- **low self-worth** ('Nobody cares what I really feel.');
- **high stress** ('I can't stop to work out what I feel.');
- **basic mistrust** ('It's not safe for me to be honest.');
- **fear of rejection** ('If I show what I feel, they won't like me.').

The four unhealthy reponses – placating, blaming, computing and distracting – are nothing more than our attempts to adapt safely to an unsafe environment. In this way, our family communication habits are linked to the foundation of trust that the family had. If your parents grew up feeling bad about themselves, highly stressed and mistrustful, and fearing rejection, their communication habits sought verbal concealment in an attempt to compensate for their lack of trust in life and in other people. You learned your responses by observing them and by reacting to their behaviour.

In contrast to the four unhealthy responses, in which the words you speak do not correspond to how you really feel, in the levelling response we make a conscious choice to notice what we feel and to convey that in what we say. You can still exercise restraint or politeness to adapt levelling to social situations (for instance, by consciously choosing to praise your hostess's soup but not tell her that her stew is too salty for your taste). However, feeling free to reflect your feelings accurately and consciously choosing to do so is critical to healing and changing family patterns.

Levelling takes courage, but the rewards of clearer communication and more productive action are worth it. These rewards include:

- **learning you can survive confrontation** ('I stood up to my mother about the holiday plans, and I survived.');
- **connecting in a genuine way with others** ('It was hard to tell her my feelings about our relationship but she hugged me and said, "If you can't be honest with me, we can't be happy together." ');
- **relieving stress on your body and mind** ('After I told them how I felt, I went home and slept like a baby. Why did I wait so long to feel this good?');
- **increasing your sense of self-worth** ('Being honest about what I feel builds up my self-respect. I'm not a helpless little mouse; I can speak up and make a difference.').

In the following exercises, you'll focus on each of the communication responses in turn, discovering how your family used each one, to what extent you copied their responses and in what ways each helped or harmed your present communication patterns. In the final exercise on levelling, you'll learn how to improve communication by generating ideas for your own positive changes.

## EXERCISE

## YOUR FAMILY PATTERNS OF PLACATING

You can recognise **placating** – being agreeable in order to avoid conflict – in yourself or someone in your family by body language: a huddled, tense or cringing posture, an apologetic or pleading face and a whiny, self-critical or sugary voice. While placating, a person appears outwardly compliant but may feel resentful inside. You can determine how much impact placating had in your family by using these questions to explore the link between your family past and your present responses.

A Write a paragraph or more answering the following questions:

- Who did the placating in your family and what percentage of your family communication involved placating?

- What did the person who placated others the most look, sound and act like while placating?
- Imagine that you could talk to the placater (yourself or someone else) when that person was feeling secure and willing to be honest. Ask him or her: What would happen if you didn't placate? What does your placating cost you?
- Reflecting on your present life, is there someone you placate frequently or some situation in which you feel compelled to be a placater?

B Pay attention to your body responses as you write about this. Ask yourself what would happen if you stopped placating and what the placating costs you.

An additional benefit of this exercise is that you will notice any placating you do more frequently after writing about your family history with it, as did Georgie:

*My mother did the most placating, although it was a response my sister and I copied. Probably 50 per cent of our family communication was placating, directed at appeasing my father, who would feel hurt and subtly blame us.*

*'Your old dad is just in the way,' he'd say, and then my mother, looking anxious and whispering frantically, would urge us to go and apologise and restore his good mood with sweet talk.*

*When I imagined my mother's honest feelings, this is what she said: 'Keeping your father happy was my life. I thought that if I didn't keep reassuring him, he'd get really depressed and do something drastic.'*

*When I wrote that as my mother, I was chilled by her response. I placate my daughters, trying to make up for being divorced. I'm afraid if I stopped, they wouldn't love me. If I could learn to be more honest with them, I might get over my fear.*

If your family did a lot of placating, you are probably also familiar with the blaming response, as the two often go together in emotional confrontations.

## EXERCISE

## YOUR FAMILY PATTERNS OF BLAMING

**Blaming** occurs when we accuse others in order to avoid blame ourselves. Blaming can range from subtle guilt-producing remarks, such as Georgie's father's self-pitying ones, to raging tirades. Classic blaming body language includes a person leaning forward and shouting, one hand on hip, the other pointing in accusation. The blamer appears to be taking charge but inside he or she feels frightened.

A You can explore your family's blaming patterns by answering these questions:

- Who did the blaming in your family and what percentage of your family communication involved blaming?
- What did the person who blamed the most look, sound and act like while blaming?
- Imagine that you could talk to the blamer (yourself or someone else) when that person was feeling calm and safe. Ask him or her: What would happen if you didn't do your blaming? What does it cost you to do it?
- In your life today, is there someone you blame frequently or some situation that provokes a blaming response in you? Notice how your body feels about blaming as you write.

B  Describe what you think would happen if you stopped blaming, and what the cost of continuing to do it might be.

Tom, whose writing about family conflict appeared earlier in this chapter, wrote:

*My father was the five-star general of blaming. Only my mother placated, but her efforts were no more than 10 per cent of our total communication. My father in one of his rages looked larger than life.*

*I can't quite imagine him calm for long, but in one of his quieter moments, he might say: 'If I didn't keep those boys in line, they'd go completely wild. My father beat me to teach me a lesson and I turned out decent. The cost is there's not a moment's peace for me and nobody appreciates that without me this family'd fall apart.'*

Tom concluded:

*Writing in my father's voice made me aware of how trapped he felt and I feel trapped myself at times now. I'm afraid if I let go I'd fly off the handle like him. How can I be honest and not go up in smoke or hurt somebody?*

## EXERCISE

## YOUR FAMILY PATTERNS OF COMPUTING

If your family tried to avoid the emotional abuses of the blaming–placating dance, they may have adopted the unemotional computing response style. **Computing** occurs when we try to avoid an emotionally difficult situation by relating to it solely from our rational half in order to escape the pain it causes.

You can recognise the computing response in the body language of a rigid posture, an expressionless face and a flat, mechanical tone of voice. While the computing response appears to be very rational, the person assuming it may in fact feel extremely vulnerable.

A  To survey your family's use of the computing response, write your answers to the following questions:

- Who did the computing in your family and what percentage of your family communication involved computing?
- What did the person who emphasised rational fact-finding look, sound and act like while computing?

B Imagine that you could talk to this person when his or her life was under control. Ask these questions, and write down the answers:

- What would happen if you didn't respond by computing? What does computing cost you?
- In your current relationships, do you find yourself acting as a computer with anyone? What is the effect when you respond that way? Is there a cost to you or to the relationship?

Robert, a science teacher, wrote:

*My father and my uncle who lived with us liked very intellectual discussions about science and philosophy, so probably three-quarters of our family communication involved listening or responding to their talk. They sounded so convincing and confident that I wanted to be just like them. My dad might say this: 'My brother keeps me focused on the things that really matter, the life of the mind. If I didn't act reasonably, I would be drawn in your mother's emotional objections about supporting your uncle financially.'*

*When I write in my dad's voice, I notice that I agree with him completely. Yet it does seem to have cost him something, as he was always closer to his brother than to his wife. I've certainly modelled my life on my father's. However, one of my problems is not having met the right woman for me. I want a companion but communicating with someone when it's not about ideas is so messy.*

## EXERCISE

## YOUR FAMILY PATTERNS OF DISTRACTING

If you or someone in your family found your communication particularly threatening, you may be familiar with the **distracting** response, in which the aim is to avoid the tension-filled subjects or feelings by directing attention away from them. Distracting occurs when we say or do irrelevant things in order to avoid confrontation. A person expressing distraction may move around unpredictably, interrupt or change the subject.

Explore how your family used the distracting response in communication by writing your responses to these questions:

- Who did the distracting in your family and what percentage of your family communication involved distraction?

- What did the person who distracted look, sound and act like while trying to get people off a subject?
- Write in the voice of the distracter, as if that person were feeling safe enough to settle down and address these questions: What would happen if you didn't distract? What does your distracting cost you?
- When a situation gets tense today, do you use the distracting response? What do you feel like inside before, during and after your distracting behaviour? What effects or problems does distracting cause for you today?

Tina, a young mother of two preschool children, wrote:

*My little sister Amy was the family distracter. It seemed as if over 50 per cent of our communication involved responding to Amy's irrelevant remarks. She was a genius at getting us to laugh away our tension. Or she would ask question after question and get everyone involved in explaining. When I imagined her response about it now, she said, 'When people were upset or hurt, I would feel it in my stomach. A voice in my head would start shouting, Wait, wait, wait! I'd immediately say or do whatever popped in. I was always too busy clowning around to do what I wanted. The distracting thoughts continue now, even if I stop myself from acting on them.'*

Tina mentioned that she feels guilty for letting Amy carry the burden of handling family tension, noting, 'I never was a distracter, but I notice that I can't stand it when my kids interrupt, demand attention and show off. Are they just being normal kids or are they reacting to family tension like Amy? I snap at them and then feel guilty.'

## EXERCISE

## YOUR FAMILY PATTERNS OF LEVELLING

Despite the prevalence of placating, blaming, computing and distracting, all of us have some past experience with the emotionally honest levelling response and we can build on what we know to strengthen and clarify our communication.

**Levelling** occurs when our words match our feelings. When we level with another, we are being emotionally honest, speaking and acting with self-respect and integrity. In the body landuage of levelling, your body posture, facial expressions, tone of voice and words match what you are feeling inside. Through writing you can imagine some of your typical patterns of response and discover your own levelling responses as alternatives.

1 Write what you feel when you are tempted to use one of your typical incongruent responses. (How do you feel when your aunt gets angry with you and you're tempted to placate? Tight jaw – jumpy stomach – strong resentment?)

2  Write a response that conveys your inner feelings more directly and honestly in words. Keep writing different versions until you find one that matches just what you feel. (For example, 'Auntie, when I hear that you're angry, I feel tense. I think you want me to sort out what you're angry about and I'm not sure I can do that. I really don't know whether you want my help or just a listening ear. Could you say some more about what you'd like to see happen in this situation?') This levelling response gives the responsibility back to your aunt to be clearer; she may or may not offer any levelling in return but you will feel lighter and clearer yourself. She may be offended because you haven't placated her, but you didn't blame her either. Perhaps she might feel safe enough to be honest in return.

3  Write your reflections about the experiment. How easy or hard is it for you to come up with levelling responses? Notice who might be the easiest person in your life now to practise more levelling with and write some thoughts about how you might proceed.

Here are the responses to this last portion of the exercise from the four students discussed earlier:

Georgie wrote about how she might level more with her daughters, whom she usually placates:

*I play into their hands when they complain about wanting to spend more on clothes by not setting clear limits. I can level with them and say, 'We have this much to spend on clothes for each of you each month.' I'll need to tell the worried placater inside me, 'You're doing a good job with them. They have what they need from you.' Then if they come back with more complaints, I can be calmer. If I level with myself first, I'll do better with them.*

Tom wrote about levelling when he is angry, an important but frightening prospect:

*I'm trying to imagine an alternative to flying off the handle. I might say, 'I am really fed up because you haven't done the washing-up. I am so angry that I can hardly think straight, so I'm not going to try to work out a solution now but we will talk about this later tonight.' I feel better about setting limits on my anger by saying I'll discuss what to do later.*

Robert wrote about a past relationship in which his girlfriend broke up with him because he intellectualised so much and wouldn't show his feelings:

*I wanted to tell her I would miss her and I wanted us to keep trying but instead I talked about how we would divide up some of the things we'd bought together. If I were to level with her or someone new, I'd say, 'I want to spend time with you and I care about you. I'll always value my work very highly but I'd be lonely without you in my life.' That's probably more feelings than I ever put together at once but I think it's an honest attempt.*

Tina wrote about how she might approach her children's distractions with a more honest response:

*First, I'd have to talk to the young girl inside me who was tense about her parents' fights too but let her sister Amy do the distracting. I'd tell her she could speak up now and be honest. Then, I could talk honestly to a close friend and tell her how much the boys' interruptions drive me crazy. Then, I could just say, 'Boys, that's enough. I'll come and play with you when I finish this phone call.'*

The art of honest communication requires lifelong practise, and you will probably find it difficult to respond to every situation with emotionally honest remarks and behaviour. However, such honesty brings rich rewards in self-respect and has a persistent power to reach across communication barriers.

# HARMFUL COMMUNICATION HABITS

You can increase your ability to be honest and trustworthy by recognising and clearing away the three harmful communication habits – double messages, silent withdrawal, and hurtful, belittling remarks. Double messages offer the protection of confusion; silent withdrawal offers the protection of retreating from confrontation; belittling remarks offer the protection of feeling powerful by directing negative attention towards someone other than you.

However, these forms of family language are extremely damaging. They confuse, upset and hurt the people at whom they are directed. They damage your self-worth and keep you trapped in habits that destroy rather then build bridges between people.

**Double messages** mix two or more contradictory meanings, such as when a parent tells a child, 'I *am* paying attention, I'm interested in what you're saying,' while continuing to read the newspaper. Often words are contradicted by behaviour, facial expressions or body language. If you grew up with a lot of double messages, you may not trust what other people say and you may have trouble communicating honestly.

**Silence** as a deliberate refusal to communicate is a way to withdraw from direct interaction. No matter what the person giving the silent treatment intends, the person who is shut out from communication may translate it as 'You're not worth speaking to'. Just as babies or toddlers fear separation, as adults we are powerfully affected when someone we care about withdraws from us. If your family members used silent withdrawal to cut off communication, you may have stored-up fear or anger about that kind of treatment, although you may resort to it at times yourself when you don't know what else to do.

**Belittling** remarks can be delivered directly or disguised as humour. Name-calling or putting people down by labelling them – as in 'Hey, stupid!' or 'God, this child never does anything right!' – can be very overt and direct. Humour that is used to communicate ridicule or judgement is less direct but still wounding. If you heard, 'We're not laughing *at* you, we're laughing *with* you,' you probably didn't believe it. You felt laughed at and ridiculed.

While brothers and sisters and neighbourhood children may use belittling remarks directly or humorously as part of establishing status and hierarchy, the most wounding use of hurtful humour comes from adults' ignoring children's feelings about teasing or ridicule. If adults can model a caring approach to what's off limits because it hurts someone, children are strengthened to respond to humorous give-and-take with their peers.

But if family members called you names or made you the butt of jokes, you may have painful memories, like those of this young woman: 'I was tall and clumsy, and the adults roared every time I tripped over my chair or the cat. They'd keep going until I cried and then say that they were just teasing. I act seriously now because funny doesn't mean fun to me. I'm still really angry about the way I was treated.'

Whether you focus on how your parents learned to use these harmful habits or look at how your current communication has been harmed by them, these hurtful responses have roots in your past feelings. For your parents or yourself, these things are true: If being clear is too frightening, you learn double messages. If sharing how you feel seems unsafe and impossible, you retreat into silence. If you are hurt or threatened yourself, you may lash out with belittling remarks. By writing about the past, you can ease its painful effects and learn more creative and positive ways to respond now.

The following exercises survey the impact on your family of these harmful communication habits and help you work on your own communication problems in this area.

## EXERCISE

## CLARIFYING DOUBLE MESSAGES

Double messages occur when we give two contradictory verbal messages together. A father might remark, 'I'm so proud of your school report. Why did you get a B in Algebra?' The double message is 'I'm proud of you but I'm dissatisfied with you'.

Double messages can also occur when the body language you notice contradicts the words being spoken to you, as when you drop in on your aunt and she says, 'I'm glad to see you; come on in,' while standing in front of the doorway and looking agitated and annoyed.

A Think back over your family experiences and look for instances in which you received double messages. Notice who gave you the most such messages.

B Try writing about your communication with that person.

C Examine the effects of double messages in your present life, starting by filling in the blanks in this sequence:

When my .................. gave me a double message, he or she said .................. while also saying or doing .................. I felt .................. when this happened. I tried to deal with it by

..................... This is how the situation turned out: .....................
    In my present life, I tend to get double message from .................... about .................... I feel
.................... and try to deal with it by .................... I realise I may be giving double messages
to .................... about .................... I feel .................... about the double messages I get and
give now. I'd like to be able to resolve the situation so that ....................

Ben, who related strongly to the example of double messages about school performance, wrote:

*I felt that I just wasn't good enough when my parents praised my school report but focused on the one less-than-perfect mark. When I get a double message from my wife now, thanking me for doing some chore but also mentioning something I didn't do quite to her taste, I feel attacked. I act hurt because I am hurt and angry, just like with my parents. I'd like to tell my wife to separate out the complaints from the praise and concentrate on giving me more praise. That sounds demanding but I'm tired of double messages. I don't expect to get through to my parents but I have a chance with my wife.*

Clear, honest communication pointing out the discrepancies can cut through the protective confusion that conflicting messages produce. While you and the other person may feel uncomfortably vulnerable at first, if you communicate a caring, honest desire to understand, you have a good chance of clearing away the confusion and creating a stronger bond.

## EXERCISE

## BREAKING THE BARRIER OF HURTFUL SILENCE

If someone in your family simply stopped speaking and shut people out when he or she was hurt or angry, you have experienced how painful silence as a tactic can be. When any words you say to restore a dialogue are met with more silence, it can hurt as much as, or more than, angry words.

For example, if your mother suddenly stopped speaking to you, these are some of the feelings and thoughts you might have:

- **confusion** ('What did I do? I can't work it out!');
- **frustration** ('How can we solve this if she won't talk?');
- **anger** ('How dare she shut me out as if I didn't exist!');
- **hurt and sadness** ('I feel so lonely!');
- **guilt** ('I must have done something terrible.');
- **shame** ('I'm really worthless.');
- **panic** ('I can't stand this! I've got to get her back!').

If your mother would never address the reasons for her silence, you weren't able to resolve these feelings and thoughts directly with her and you may still be carrying some of the pain and self-doubt.

You may also have learned that working things out with each other in direct communication is too painful to risk, so you may find yourself repeating the pattern of silence with your current family members or friends. In this exercise, you can supply the words that you and the silent person from your past did not speak, a first step in breaking through the communication barrier.

A  Bring back a specific memory of being given the silent treatment by someone in your family.

B  Remember and write what happened before the silence and then put in writing the feelings you had when the silence began. What did you try to do in response? What did you say to yourself about the silence and what did you try to say to the other person? How long did the silence last and how did the other person begin talking to you again?

C  Imagine that you can get inside the mind of the silent person and write what he or she is saying internally about what is happening. By taking the other person's point of view in your imagination and writing his or her words, you may learn the motivations and feelings behind the silence, which will help you heal from the pain of not understanding why you were shut out.

D  Ask yourself how your childhood experience of being shut out by silence has affected your communication with others today. Do you do anything to avoid the silent treatment or do you resort to it in frustration when you are hurt and angry?

E  If you are still experiencing the effects of confusion, frustration, anger, sadness, guilt, shame or panic, write about those feelings as you experience them.

By giving voice to your feelings with written words the barriers that silence created can begin to come down. As those inner barriers no longer block your good feelings about yourself, you'll be strengthened to be more direct and expressive with others, breaking the chain of resorting to silence.

Kim wrote about her powerful father's lingering influence:

*When Daddy pressed his lips together and strode out of the room, his disapproval and disappointment just shouted at me. I would cry and plead with him to speak to us again, but he'd just go into his study and shut the door. Inside, I'd feel so guilty, saying, 'It's my fault. If I just got better marks or were more popular . . .' It might be days before he would walk in from work and say something normal, like, 'What's for dinner?' No explanation, no resolution.*

*When I tried to write what was in his mind, this is what I came up with: 'They simply don't realise how hard I work and they don't give me my due. How could she be so disrespectful? I need to be treated the way a hard-working professional who's an excellent provider for his family deserves to be treated. I refuse to have anything to do with such ingratitude.' When I wrote out his thoughts, I sensed that he was sensitive and easily hurt. It seems less like my fault now. I want to understand how this relates to my problems with my husband, a thoughtful man who sometimes just goes off into his own musings. Maybe I can differentiate better now between Daddy's silences and my husband's daydreams.*

As with Kim, seeing both the similarities and the differences between your past family communication experience and your communication problems in your current relationships can contribute to tearing down the barriers that family silences originally built inside you and between you and others.

## EXERCISE

### HEALING THE HURT OF WORDS USED AS WEAPONS

Belittling remarks – name-calling, negative labelling and hurtful uses of humour – occur often in families, although we don't like to remember how painful they were. While the examples below may seem extreme, you will probably find similar ones from your family once you write your own memories.

Low self-esteem is the cause of the belittling remarks we make to one another; one way to act superior when you feel shaky is to put someone else down. Using words as weapons is common between brothers and sisters who are competing for power, privileges or attention. If the adults in your family belittled each other or the children, they were unable to deal with their feelings and took them out on others. You may have learned to handle hurt either by lashing back with similar remarks, feeling bad because you believed them, or shutting off your feelings and acting as if you didn't care.

By re-opening the memories you may feel bad at first but you will be able to understand why others said what they did, recognise the tactics you used to deal with your hurt and be strengthened to redefine yourself in positive rather than belittling ways.

A  Put a tick by each of the following types of belittling communication you remember your family using during your childhood and adolescence.

- **name-calling** ('Eating again, Fatty?')
- **negative labels** ('What's wrong with you – no son of mine should be a coward.')
- **mean-spirited teasing** ('She's embarrassed again because she lisps – what'th the matter, thilly?')
- **sarcasm** ('If you weren't doing so many important things shut away in your room, you might actually make some friends at school.')
- **ridicule** ('Why should you buy a bra? What are you going to put in it, tissues?')

B  Choose the most vivid memory from among those that have surfaced and write it out fully, noting how you felt when the remarks were made.

C  Imagine that you can translate the remarks into another language that more accurately reflects what the speaker was thinking or feeling. For example, if a mother said, 'Eating again, Fatty?' she might be thinking 'How can I get her to stop overeating?' and feeling 'People will think I'm a terrible mother, having a fat child'.

D  Using what you have just learned about what was behind the remarks, write a message to the person who made them, telling how you felt then and how you feel now.

E Describe similar instances in your present relationships when words are used as weapons between you and someone else.

F Write what you discover and how you want that communication to be different.

A teacher in her late fifties wrote:

*It was very difficult to bring back memories of my sharp-tongued mother and aunts. 'Jean, that little bookworm of yours is going to get even more cross-eyed if she keeps reading all the time.' 'Your aunt is right, get your nose out of that book. How are you ever going to amount to anything when you can't do anything practical?'*

*My chest would hurt as I put down my book and went to do chores. I still feel that deep ache as I write. I think I became a teacher so no child would ever have to feel belittled for wanting to read and learn.*

*As I try to imagine what my mother was thinking and feeling, I realise that she was afraid of what her sisters thought. She was the youngest and weakest and she couldn't even stand up for herself, much less me. She imitated their sarcasm, just the way I see the weaker students do in my classes today.*

When you take the risk to confront the old hurt as this teacher did, you gain a clearer perspective on why your family used words as weapons. You can counteract the painful past messages with a fairer, fuller description of who you are, reinforcing positive views of yourself and healthy communication habits.

# ESTABLISHING NEW COMMUNICATION PATTERNS

While the memories you have reviewed in writing showed you some painful or blocked areas in your family style and habits, you can bring change to those areas now. The more you write about the thoughts and feelings that you couldn't express then, the more you can clear away your inner barriers to clear communication.

In addition, every family leaves a heritage of good communication skills and you have been building on them both consciously and unconsciously in your adult years. In this exercise, you can remind yourself of the communication strengths you have and make plans to build on them for the future.

## EXERCISE

## BUILDING ON YOUR COMMUNICATION STRENGTHS

You have broken new ground by writing about your family language style and habits, and you can build on what you've learned by planning for future awareness, assessment and change in your ability to communicate. You can profit by thinking back over what you discovered about your family's communication style – their approach to conflict, agreement and emotional honesty – and by reflecting on their communication responses, the balance of placating, blaming, computing, distracting and levelling that they modelled for you. You also can review your discoveries about harmful communication habits in your family – double messages, silent withdrawal and belittling words. Now you may want to expand your repertoire of new communication patterns.

To develop new strategies, write your responses to the following questions:

A **What would you like to become more aware of in the way you communicate from now on?**
Since change begins with increased awareness, you can select some area that you have observed in writing about communication and decide to notice it more frequently. For example, if you realise now that you give a lot of double messages, a habit you learned from your family, write about how you want to tune in to times when the words you're saying don't match how you feel.

Frances, the librarian profiled earlier, wrote:

*I am going to be more aware of how automatically I hide what I'm feeling. Saying, 'I'm fine,' when I feel terrible comes naturally to me because my family insisted we always put on a good front.*

B **What aspect of your communication style, responses or habits would you like to investigate and understand further?** Change proceeds from awareness to assessment. You can explore and evaluate further one of the communication patterns you wrote about earlier. By assessing the effects of the pattern through writing about it, thinking about it or discussing it with people you trust, you gather enough information to build on the strengths in the pattern and change the weak or limiting areas.

Kim, whose writing about her father's silent withdrawal appeared earlier, wrote:

*I need to assess how much of my reaction to my husband's quietness is due to reminders of my father's punishing silences and how much is due to annoyance at Charlie for being less talkative than I'd like him to be. I can write down what my thoughts and feelings are when I notice Charlie being quiet and that should help me work out how much the past with my father is getting in the way.*

C **What is one specific small change you would like to make in your communication patterns in the next year?** Keeping your plans for creating new patterns modest and reasonable is a good way to ensure that you will follow through on them. You can choose one area in which you have some communication success or one relationship in which you have some trust and look for ways to build on it. You can also go back to the metaphor you imagined for your family communication style earlier in the chapter and see whether it holds some clues for helping you to change.

For example, Tom, who described his family pattern of conflict and blaming earlier, wrote:

*I described my family as a time bomb ticking. Well, one thing about a time bomb is you've got time. You don't have to just wait for the explosion. One of my friends likes my argumentative style; she gets frustrated when I shut off my feelings. Maybe I can ask her to help me experiment by taking a break during a discussion when I start feeling my heart pound.*

By acknowledging that you will continue to develop your communication skills throughout your life, you can strengthen the life-enhancing aspects of your family's communication and clear away the confusing or destructive aspects that perpetuate your family's communication problems in your life now.

'Who am I?' is a question we ask and answer at all stages of our lives. The next chapter investigates how you grew to have your own sense of identity. Our earliest answers to the question of who we are come from our parents. Their attitudes and actions shaped your fundamental sense of self in relation to your body, your mind, your emotions and your spirit. The roots of confusion or problems you are having in any of those areas lie in your early family experiences. By writing about how your family taught you to view and define yourself, you can reaffirm the healthy messages and counter the harmful ones with new beliefs about who you are now and who you can become.

# CHAPTER 5

# YOUR FAMILY AND YOUR SENSE OF SELF

Your sense of self today is defined by how you imagine, experience and describe yourself as a person separate from others, with an identity uniquely your own. As with life stance and communication, you first learned about your sense of self from your family. A strong and healthy sense of self grows from a strong and healthy inner foundation of trust and from clear, directly communicated messages that you are a valuable, precious human being. Both the inner foundation of trust and the outer communication of value came from your first teachers – your parents and other family members.

The stronger your base of family encouragement towards knowing and developing your sense of self, the more fully you can express all the facets of your being. Yet most of us received a double message: be yourself *and* be who we want to be. In *The Dance of Intimacy* (Harper & Row, New York, 1989), Harriet Lerner writes that from birth on, 'family members encourage us to be our authentic selves, while they also unconsciously encourage us to express certain traits, qualities or behaviour patterns and to deny or inhibit others.'

For instance, in a highly competitive family, a child who loves to daydream may be pressured to focus, set goals, complete tasks and stop daydreaming. Both daydreaming and goal-setting are important creative acts but in this family, the child's sense of self may be less strong than if his or her parents could recognise the creative trance as part of the child's authentic talent. Further, the child may be less able to follow these daydreams through in his or her own time because the family has taught that you are either a daydreamer or an achiever.

One reason that your family did not encourage all aspects of your sense of self is that they had difficulty seeing you as separate from them. Separation is no less a task for the parents and other family members than for the growing child; parents have to let go of goals and dreams for their children that they may have been constructing since their birth.

Another reason why your family did not encourage all aspects of your sense of self is related to society's expectations. Cultural attitudes affect family values. The prevailing messages from social institutions such as schools, religious organisations and government influence what your family felt about the relative importance of developing and expressing various aspects physically, mentally, emotionally and spiritually.

If your parents were unable to let you develop an authentic sense of self, you may have these problems in adulthood:

- **confusion or guilt about your personal characteristics** ('Am I selfish?' 'Should I be more independent?' 'Is it unfair to want this for myself?')
- **automatic compliance with or rebellion against family needs and goals** ('My mother needs me; I can't move to Leeds.' 'I'll be damned if I'll let them tell me what to do.')
- **blockage or lack of development in one or more areas of personal growth – the physical, the mental, the emotional or the spiritual** ('I was the sickly one in our family.' 'My parents decided I wasn't as clever as my sister.' 'My family just doesn't express strong negative feelings.' 'We were taught not to question our religion.')

In addition, you may be experiencing difficulties in intimate or professional relationships that trace back to family circumstances that prevented development of a complete sense of self. In *The Dance of Intimacy*, Harriet Lerner emphasises that 'changing *any* relationship problem rests directly on our ability to work on bringing more of a *self* to that relationship. Without a clear, whole, and separate 'I', relationships do become overly intense, overly distant, or alternate between the two.' When you strengthen your own separate identity, you will be better able to differentiate your needs and wishes from those of others and to address the inevitable conflicts when those needs and wishes are at odds.

A key element in positive change, then, is to focus on and develop your personal identity, enhancing your sense of basic worth and strengthening areas of your selfhood that your early family experiences may have taught you to neglect or undervalue.

In this chapter, you will write about the roots of your sense of self in your family experiences. The four aspects of self – **body** (your sensing self), **mind** (your thinking self), **emotions** (your feeling self) and **spirit** (your longings, your essential self) – encompass the areas of personal identity that your family influenced. By surveying your memories and feelings about each area, you will discover where your sense of self is clear and solid and where it is confused and undeveloped. Understanding its roots will enable you to bring more clarity and perspective to the task of defining yourself as an individual and a family member.

In the first section, you will examine what you learned from your family about your **body**, your physical, sensing self. As an infant, you didn't even realise you had a body separate from your mother until you were about five or six months old. Your earliest physical sensations were of comfort (warmth, dryness, fullness and caring touch) or discomfort (cold, wetness, hunger and lack of caring touch). Your parents continued to hold primary responsibility for your physical needs as you grew – to comfort you and care for you in illness or injury, to provide nourishment, to keep in touch literally.

In their care of you, your family demonstrated the life stances they had towards the body, their attitudes and approaches towards the physical dimension of themselves and their children's selves.

These attitudes sprang from their own family background and affected how they treated themselves and you in relation to these topics, each of which is very important:

- **appearance and grooming;**
- **health and strength;**
- **nourishment;**
- **sensual and sexual pleasure.**

Through the writing exercises in this section, you can gather basic information about how you learned to value and care for the physical aspect of your sense of self. The long-range development of a stronger and more fulfilling sense of self can begin with linking your early memories to your present-day patterns.

If your family had a healthy life stance towards the body, you may have received messages that communicated these attitudes towards your physical self:

- **acknowledgement** ('It's no fun being ill, but you're a strong child, you'll be well soon.' 'It's natural to want to touch yourself there because it feels good, but it's a private part of your body and you can do that in your private place, your room.')
- **appreciation** ('You look wonderful!' 'I like the way you can choose your own clothes and get yourself ready.')
- **confidence** ('I'll help you stay healthy until you are big enough to take good care of yourself – which I know you can.' 'She'll learn to choose the right foods for herself, Mum.')
- **encouragement** ('Go ahead and have fun playing football – if you get in the team, fine; if not, you can still enjoy playing with your friends.')
- **delight** ('What a wonderful dance you made up – you're so graceful!' 'My goodness, you jumped off the high board!')

If you grew up surrounded by these healthy attitudes, you probably have a strong sense of self in the physical domain. You take good care of yourself, trust your health and strength and enjoy your body's vitality and capabilities.

On the other hand, if your family had an unhealthy or destructive life stance towards the physical aspect of self, you may have received messages that communicated these attitudes towards your physical self:

- **denial** ('Stop complaining and ignore your stomach ache. You can't pamper yourself; just keep going.');
- **criticism** ('Can't you stand up straight?' 'You have no willpower – stop stuffing yourself or you'll get even fatter.');
- **anxiety or fear** ('If you play outside, you might catch cold.' 'If you go out wearing those clothes, you'll get yourself in trouble.');

- **discouragement** ('You're too skinny to play football.' 'Girls shouldn't try to play sports like boys do; it's unfeminine.');
- **distaste** ('Oh, you smell, get away from me.' 'It upsets me to see you fat like this; you could be so pretty if you were thinner.').

If you grew up surrounded by these attitudes, you probably lack a strong and confident sense of your body and the whole physical domain. You may take poor care of yourself, neglect or fear for your health, doubt your strength and take little pleasure in your physical appearance, sensations and abilities.

Ultimately, it is the overall balance of these healthy versus destructive messages that determines how you grow up feeling about your physical self. The more negative the family attitudes and behaviour towards the body were, the more likely it is that you now feel bad about your physical self or have problems related to physical well-being. If you didn't receive adequate physical care and emotional soothing from your parents, you may have become addicted to food, alcohol, drugs, sexual relationships, work or other activities as substitute ways to fill an inner emptiness. If in childhood you were hurt and violated by physical or sexual abuse, your sense of self as related to the body has been severely traumatised and you may have learned to adapt by separating your intellect from your physical self. You may still be out of touch with your body as a result of the abuse and you may feel shame or guilt despite the fact that you were clearly victimised.

Whether you simply lack some confidence in your physical self or have more severe problems due to destructive family attitudes and behaviour, you can learn to adopt a healthier stance towards your body now and experience its strengths and pleasure more fully. The exercises in the body section will trace the roots of your physical sense of self to your family, explore the family attitudes and behaviour that affected you in positive and negative ways and offer strategies to improve your confidence in and care of your physical self today.

In the second section, you will investigate what you learned from your family about your **mind**, your thinking self. Your thinking abilities began developing in infancy and toddlerhood, when your mind responded to your environment through your senses (tasting and touching) and your movements (grasping, rolling, sitting, crawling, standing, walking and running). Once you could use language, your mind began to symbolise, to describe your experience through what you said. Your mental operations became more sophisticated: between 7 and 11, you learned to think about things in concrete ways, understanding cause and effect; between 11 and 15, you developed the ability for abstract thinking.

Throughout your mental growth, your family shaped your attitudes about your mind's abilities by their attitudes and behaviour. They demonstrated their life stances towards the mind, their approach to the mental dimension of themselves and their children's selves. Their mind-oriented life stance was a legacy from their own upbringings and influenced your development in regard to:

- **your view of your intelligence;**

- **your success at activities dependent on thinking skills;**
- **your use of your reasoning abilities;**
- **your use of your intuitive abilities.**

How intelligent you believe you are and how effectively you use your mental abilities today depend to a large extent on attitudes about your mind that your family communicated to you. You can enhance your mental development by recalling positive attitudes towards your mind from your family. You can also clear away blocks to fuller use of your mind's capabilities by identifying and calling into question any unhealthy family attitudes towards your thinking self.

Your family's life stance towards the mind was reflected in the following reactions to your mental achievements and creativity:

- **acknowledgement** ('It takes time to learn these things, but you will.') or **denial** ('Don't try to work things out in life; it's too complicated.')
- **appreciation** ('You have a good mind.') or **criticism** ('How could you be so stupid?')
- **confidence** ('I know you can think this out for yourself.') or **anxiety and fear** ('If you don't succeed at school, you won't succeed in life.')
- **encouragement** ('Go ahead – make a guess; it's okay to make mistakes while you're learning.') or **discouragement** ('Stick to what your teachers tell you; they know best.')
- **delight** ('It's exciting to see you be so thoughtful and creative!') or **distaste** ('You may be clever at school, but where will that get you?')

Each of these attitudes influenced how you viewed your intelligence, how successful you were at tasks that had to be thought through and how freely you developed your abilities to work things out rationally and to follow your creative hunches. If you feel at ease with mental tasks, you can trace some of your competence and success to your family's constructive attitudes and teachings. If, however, you feel blocked, anxious or ashamed about your mental abilities, your family probably passed on to you some of their unresolved feelings about their thinking selves by discouraging or criticising your intelligence and thought processes. You may avoid pushing what you feel are your mental limits; you may make decisions you later regret because you didn't feel capable of thinking them through or trusting your intuition.

No matter what your family taught you about your mind, you can develop a healthier stance towards your thinking self, valuing and enjoying your mind's abilities. By tracing the roots of your current view of your mind to your family's stance towards thinking, you can learn how to counteract negative attitudes that may be hampering your mental abilities, while building on those that are positive.

In the third section, you will discover what your family taught you about your **emotions**, your feeling self. Your emotions began developing at birth, when the only emotion you showed was a generalised excitement; by three months, you showed more specific emotions of distress and delight. By age 2, you had acquired a wider range of emotion, experiencing and expressing fear, disgust, anger, jealousy, affection, elation and joy. The development of these and all other human feelings was most strongly influenced by the bond you had with the people who took care of you the most. You watched your parents' faces and bodies to see how they responded to your feelings and what their feelings were. Your attachment to these special people meant that what they taught you about your feelings took on great importance.

Your family shaped your beliefs about your emotions as well as your actual experience of them by their stance towards their own feeling selves and their responses to the feelings you displayed. Your emotional development was strongly affected by your family's attitudes and behaviour in relation to:

- **how you acknowledge your feelings to yourself;**
- **how you express your feelings outwardly;**
- **how intensely you feel your emotions;**
- **how easily you respond to changes in your emotions.**

How you experience and express your emotions today is largely dependent on the attitudes about feelings that were passed on to you by your family. If your family was open and accepting about emotions, you probably learned to notice your feelings, express them freely, accept that intense feelings are part of life and adapt flexibly to your changing feelings.

If your family feared or denied emotion, you probably learned not to acknowledge what you felt to either yourself or others. You may be unaware or fearful of your emotional intensity and you may try to avoid changes in emotional states – for instance, staying angry in order not to be afraid.

Both healthy and harmful responses to your feelings were learned from famliy messages about emotions, including:

- **acknowledgement** ('Yes, I am sad; I'm missing your daddy while he's away, just like you are.') or **denial** ('I am *not* angry!')
- **appreciation** ('I like it when you tell me how you're feeling because I can't aways tell.') or **criticism** ('You shouldn't feel jealous of your sister; only bad little girls are jealous.')
- **confidence** ('It is frightening to go to a new school. It's natural to start off scared but then you learn how to feel less worried about it.') or **anxiety or fear** ('Don't get so angry – you might hurt somebody and then you'd be sorry.')
- **encouragement** ('I cry too when my feelings are hurt.') or **discouragement** ('It's better not to let those things upset you; it doesn't get you anywhere.')
- **delight** ('I love it when you stand up for yourself and show how you feel.') or **distaste** ('Only people with lack of self-control show their feelings.')

These attitudes about the value of experiencing and expressing feelings may have been directly communicated to you, in words, or indirectly, through family behaviour. If no one said anything negative about expressing sadness but everyone walked out of the room whenever your grandmother began to cry, they communicated fear or distaste about sad feelings without a word being said. You learned to shape your emotional expression to fit within a range that your family found acceptable, or you learned to take the consequences of their reactions if you went ahead and expressed what you felt despite their disapproval.

If you can easily acknowledge and freely express the full range of what you feel today, your family accepted the emotional aspect of your identity. If you have trouble knowing or showing what you feel, or if you are uncomfortable with intense or changeable feelings, your family legacy of negative responses to emotion may be holding you back from your full selfhood. You may become bogged down in your emotions or run away from them. Your emotional ups and downs may interfere with your well-being, your relationships and your activities. Whether your family helped or hampered your emotional development, you can make changes now in your stance towards your feelings and strengthen your emotional sense of self.

In the fourth section, you will explore what your family taught you about your **spirit**, the core of your self that connects you to deep longings, wonder, religion and mystery. Since this dimension of your sense of self is not an obvious physical reality like your body, you will need to define what it means for you as you write about spirit in this section. Definitions of what people mean by the core of their identity have included not only the word 'spirit' but also 'soul', 'values', 'the meaning of life', 'character', 'God', 'essence' and 'Self with a capital S'. The roots of the word 'spirit' come from the word for breath, so you might consider that the dimension of your spirit is whatever gives you vitality, as your breath is necessary to life.

No matter how you define this core aspect of self, your experience of other aspects of selfhood is changed by the involvement of that core spirit. When you run, dance, play a sport or musical instrument, or make love, your body and spirit often interact. Your physical experience expands into a fuller, more wondrous sense that psychologists call 'flow'. When you read, write, teach or discuss ideas that fascinate you, your mind and spirit often interact. Your mental experience becomes charged with the mystery and fascination of creativity. When you express your deepest feelings to someone you trust, your emotions and your spirit often interact. Your feelings become not just energy to discharge but a vehicle for healing and relating.

Your sense of what spirit means changes and develops throughout your life. As an infant and very young child, before you learned to use language, everything was wondrous to you; once you could understand and use language, you began to explore through questions about life and your family's beliefs and practices: 'Where do my dreams come from?' 'Why do we go to church?' 'Is God inside me?' 'Why do people do bad things?' 'Where do we go when we die?'

Throughout childhood, you formed your beliefs in this area in response to the authorities in your life: first your parents and family members, later your teachers or religious leaders. In adolescence, you may have begun to question some of your family's beliefs about spirituality, religion or faith, starting down the path of individual belief formation that continues throughout your life.

This individual quest for spirit is always in tension with the inherited and learned beliefs from your family past. Your family's stance towards the spiritual aspect of life reflected their own backgrounds and influenced your development in the areas of:

- **what you believe about your essential nature;**
- **what you believe about how people should act;**
- **what you believe about a divine being or force;**
- **what you believe is the meaning and purpose of life.**

The types of spiritual beliefs you hold and how you put them into practice are strongly connected to your family's attitudes and behaviour. As in all other areas of family influence, the determining factor in the growth of your spirit is your family's openness and trust. If you were encouraged to question and explore, you grew in your own understanding, using your family's beliefs as a foundation when you needed that stability, diverging from them as you became more aware of your deepest convictions. If you were told that only beliefs prescribed by family and religious authorities were acceptable, you had to either limit your spiritual growth to what the family would tolerate or risk losing family approval by exploring your own beliefs.

You can see your family's life stance towards the spiritual aspect of yourself by the way they treated the following:

- **acknowledgement** ('The feelings and ideas you have deep inside are really important.') or **denial** ('Nobody knows the meaning of life, so what's the point in asking those questions?')
- **appreciation** ('I like hearing what you believe about God.') or **criticism** ('Who are you to have opinions? Leave that to the priest.')
- **confidence** ('You will find your own faith as you grow up.') or **anxiety and fear** ('It's dangerous to stray from what the Bible says.')
- **encouragement** ('How do you imagine God – I'd really like to know.') or **discouragement** ('Don't both me about things you're too young to understand.')
- **delight** ('When I listen to that beautiful music, I feel I understand what life's about.') or **distaste** ('What's to get excited about? Life is hard and then you die, like the car sticker says.')

The range of your family's attitudes towards spiritual selfhood shaped how you developed in this area. If you can explore and express your spirit in how you live today, you owe some of your strong core and sense of meaning to family encouragement towards growing spiritually. If you feel blocked from exploring or expressing your spirit now, if it is an area of conflict for you, your healthy spiritual self-development may have been held back by your family's unresolved fears or the imposition of their beliefs and practices. By describing how you were affected by your family's stance towards the spirit, you can strengthen the positive aspects and heal and bring out the hurt, neglected or constricted aspects of your inner self.

In the final section, you will summarise the development and interaction of all four aspects of your sense of self. You can use this fresh perspective on how you grew into your present physical, mental, emotional and spiritual self to plan for new growth, building on family strength and healing family hurts. You can move from a new vision of your selfhood to fulfilling that vision through gradual change in your attitudes and actions.

# YOUR SELF, YOUR BODY AND YOUR FAMILY

Because you experience all aspects of your self through the thoughts, feelings and deep longings of your physical body, the body is a good place to start exploring your identity. In order to clarify your own stance towards your body and free yourself from unhealthy family patterns that relate to it, you need to separate out how you view the physical dimension of life and your body from the influence of your family's views.

In this section, you will define your family's stance towards the body and how that has affected your physical sense of identity. You will then focus in on one key memory that relates to your body and your family, communicating your feelings about it now. Finally, you will explore creative ways to strengthen a positive expression of your physical sense of self.

## EXERCISE

### BODY HISTORY: YOUR PHYSICAL SELF THEN AND NOW

*Body? What body? We didn't talk about bodies in our family*, one woman wrote. As a child, your family influenced your stance towards your physical self in many different ways, whether or not they ever talked about body matters.

Use the examples below to write an introductory passage about your family's view of the body then. You can draw on attitudes mentioned earlier in the chapter to spark your memories and guide your descriptions.

Your family's attitudes and actions towards the body may have reflected:

- **acknowledgement** or **denial**;
- **appreciation** or **criticism**;
- **confidence** or **anxiety and fear**;
- **encouragement** or **discouragement**;
- **delight** or **distaste**.

A Think back over your childhood and adolescence and write a description of the family messages you received about each of the following:

- **enjoying how you look;**
- **taking care of your health;**
- **feeling physically competent and strong;**
- **enjoying eating and drinking and nourishing yourself well;**
- **appreciating the pleasures of your senses and enjoying your sexuality.**

Elizabeth, a theatrical set designer in her mid-thirties, wrote:

*My family was obsessed with fears about health. I was born prematurely, the youngest of five children. They called me 'Bitsy' because I was tiny and frail and it seemed I never did what the others did. I was stuffed with food whether I was hungry or not; I was criticised for playing rough games with other children because I might hurt myself. I didn't want to absorb the anxiety and fear but I did. I grew up wanting to prove myself physically.*

As Elizabeth indicated, the establishment in childhood of attitudes and behaviour patterns related to your physical self shapes your body awareness and functioning when you grow up.

B Survey your life *now* – your health, your relationships, your work and your leisure activities – and see how various areas have been affected by your family's teachings about the body. List about five examples of how you see your family's body-stance attitudes and behaviour influencing you today, and describe how you feel about these effects.

Elizabeth reported:

*I had no trouble listing effects of my family's fear for my physical well-being. In my life now, I see that I:*

*1 don't ever want to acknowledge that I'm ill or hurt.*
*2 panic when my son has an allergic reaction.*
*3 chose set design as my work because it makes me feel big and strong to work on a huge scale with stage sets.*
*4 don't take good enough care of myself – I'm often out of touch with how I feel physically.*

*My family's influence on my attitude to health makes me anxious, angry and confused. I resent their anxiety but I've absorbed it, so I'm angry at myself as well as them.*

This focused recounting of a single memory will sharpen your perception of your family's shaping of your physical sense of self.

## EXERCISE

## BODY MEMORIES

Select a negative experience you might have had with your family's approach towards your physical self that especially stands out as uncomfortable or painful – teasing, punishment, rejection, hurt or criticism. As you bring the memory back through writing, you will be better equipped to remove some of its sting. Though bringing back the details may be hard, you get the experience out of your body and on to the paper and that itself eases the burden. You may be less preoccupied with the old hurt and more connected with positive opportunities for change.

A Examine what happened by writing about your experience in thorough detail – where it took place, who was there and how you felt.

Laura, a department store buyer, wrote:

*My mother, grandmother and aunt taught us not to feel or show anger. If we fought, 'Don't get angry with each other. Have a biscuit.' 'Don't think about that it if upsets you. Here's a doughnut.' Then one day I went shopping with all three of them and I couldn't fit into the dresses in the ordinary children's section. Suddenly, these three women were shrieking and carrying on because nothing would fit. I stood there red as a beetroot while my mother loudly asked the salewoman with her black glossy hair where there was a shop 'for fat children'. I cried as we walked down the cold street and asked them if they were cross with me. 'Of course not,' they said in angry voices, but when we stopped for lunch, we all ate huge portions in silence. I choked on anger and ice cream.*

B After you have described the memory, write a short letter to the child or adolescent that you were then, telling that young person what you would want him or her to know about interpreting the event from your adult perspective. Include your feelings as well as observations.

Laura wrote:

*Dear 10-year-old Laura, it wasn't fair or loving of them to humiliate you that way. They put you in an impossible position, telling you to eat instead of getting angry and then getting angry at you for the results of your eating. You need to know that you deserve to be treated kindly, that you can learn to stand up for yourself. Next time you feel angry, write down what you're feeling before you have something to eat. (That's not bad advice for 39-year-old Laura too.)*

Although the process of opening up any dimension of selfhood to fuller expression, particularly the physical, is a long, slow one, you can initiate some positive changes now.

## EXERCISE

## EXPANDING YOUR PHYSICAL CONFIDENCE AND WELL-BEING

You can build on whatever positive foundation of physical selfhood you now have.

A 1 Think back through the growing-up years and recall an instance or a pattern of constructive, helpful encouragement in some area related to your physical self. Perhaps your uncle told you that you were big and strong when you helped him build a fence, or your big sister taught you how to ski and encouraged you until you stopped falling all the time, or maybe your mother held you close and read to you at night before bed.

2 Write about this positive memory, detailing what your feelings were and how your body responded to the praise or comfort.

Elizabeth wrote:

*I had a kindergarten teacher who was a very tiny woman and she used to whisper to me, 'We small ones are more powerful than people realise'. I felt gratitude and happiness blowing up like a balloon in my chest.*

Laura wrote:

*When my daughter was born, the nurse put her in my arms, saying, 'You did it, Mother – here's your daughter!' I felt immensely proud of my body.*

B Now reflect on the current state of your physical, sensing self. What area needs encouragement, healing or further development most? First describe the situation as it is now; then write what you wish for, how you want it to develop.

Elizabeth wrote:

*I ignore my weak back and keep working until it goes into a muscle spasm. I'd like to be aware of how tense or strained my back is before it gets to that stage, then do something different to prevent it happening.*

Laura wrote:

*I've come to terms with my weight but I still don't feel comfortable with myself as a sensual or sexual person. I feel starved for affection and praise from my husband but I keep busy and push him away also. I wish I could tell him how much his praise means to me, then open my arms and reach out for him.*

C Use writing to get in touch with your inner wisdom about your body's needs. Of course, you are not really separate from your body's needs and wishes but you can find out more about them through a written dialogue. You can interact with your appearance, your health, your appetite or your sensual or sexual nature, as well as with any part of your body.

Elizabeth wrote:

*I wrote down, 'All right, lower back, I'm talking to you. Why do you knot up on me like you do?' My back replied, 'I go into spasms because you won't slow down otherwise.' I countered, 'But I try to do my back exercises.' It said, 'You don't really change your habits.' I asked, 'What could I do that would make it different?' It told me, 'Pay attention to my early signals. Don't make me your excuse to get some rest. You don't have to prove yourself.' I think that the next time I feel that first twinge, I'm going to remember those words: I don't have to prove myself.*

Laura wrote about feeling starved for affection:

*I realised that in both my happy memory of reaching for my newborn daughter and my wishful thinking about embracing my husband, I was using my arms and hands to reach out for something I loved. I wrote, 'Arms, what do you want?' They replied, 'To hold and be held, to feel the warmth of another human being'. I said, 'Hands, how about you?' They answered, 'We want to grasp and caress, but instead you use us to push others away'. 'Why do I do that?' I asked. 'Because if you push away first, you won't get hurt if you reach out and no one's there, like when you were little'. 'What would help me be less afraid and more able to reach out?' 'Fill yourself with the feeling you had after your daughter's birth. Keep doing that until you feel confident and ready to reach out to your husband. Start small; ask him to hold you as you're both going to sleep'. I found this dialogue helpful – and practical too. My body has more to tell me than I realised.*

The more you notice and write about the physical dimension of your experience, the more you will be able to liberate yourself from unproductive or painful family stances towards the body. As you experiment with improving your physical awareness and well-being and enhancing your bodily sense of self, you will find that there is positive momentum in paying attention and giving care to neglected parts of yourself. You can feel progressively more confident in and comfortable with your body.

# YOUR SELF, YOUR MIND AND YOUR FAMILY

You probably associate your mind with your intelligence, which you interpret to mean how clever you think you are and how well you did at school. While your thinking self does include this dimension of mental experience, such a definition is far too limited. Your thinking self includes two major dimensions: your left brain thinks logically and sequentially, processes information in a linear way and breaks things into parts to analyse them; your right brain thinks by associating things that are similar, processes many elements at once, using imagery and emotional response and brings parts together into wholes.

Your left brain functions by cause-and-effect reason; your right brain by flash-of-insight intuition. Both kinds of thinking are vital to problem-solving and creative living. If you are not accessing both, you are not valuing, using and enjoying all your mental skills. An eminent American brain researcher, Marilyn Ferguson, wrote:

Cut off from the fantasy, dreams, intuitions of the right brain, the left is sterile. And the right brain, cut off from integration with its organising partner, keeps recycling its emotional charge. . . . This fragmentation costs us our health and our capacity for intimacy.

You formed your mental sense of self in response to what your parents, other family members, teachers and peers told you about your mind. They transmitted to you their attitudes about the mind in general and their beliefs about your mind in particular, but those attitudes and beliefs may have been limited by their upbringing and experience. If so, they limited you. But by identifying how your family's input may have enhanced or blocked your mental development, you can take the first step in developing a more fully activated sense of selfhood to problem-solving and creativity.

In this section, you will first describe your family's stance towards the mind and how that has contributed to the formation of your mental sense of identity. Second, you will re-create in writing an influential incident that illustrates your attitudes towards your mind's abilities from your family past. Third, you will discover ways to make fuller use of your mental faculties, as you feel more confident and creative about your thinking self.

## EXERCISE

## MIND HISTORY: YOUR THINKING SELF THEN AND NOW

When asked what words their families used to describe having a good mind, students have come up with many answers, including 'intellectual', 'brilliant', 'logical', 'canny', 'brainy', 'genius', 'creative', 'egghead', 'clever', reasonable' and 'too clever for your own good'. Each answer reflects family attitudes about the value of mental talents and activities in relation to other skills and pursuits. You can find out more about your family's perspective on the mind by writing about it.

A Write a description of your family's spoken and unspoken messages about:

- how much they emphasised developing your mind;
- how clever they thought you were and how successful they expected you to be with thinking skills;

- how much they valued logic and reason and expected you to use that function of your mind;
- how much they valued intuition and expected you to use that function of your mind.

To evaluate whether your family's messages had more positive or more negative effects on your developing mental sense of self, examine these contrasting attitudes. Which of them did your family offer you:

- **acknowledgement** or **denial**;
- **appreciation** or **criticism**;
- **confidence** or **anxiety and fear**;
- **encouragement** or **discouragement**;
- **delight** or **distaste?**

Doug grew up as the second son in a family of two boys and two girls. He wrote:

*My whole family is very intelligent. They could all talk circles around me, even my younger brother and sister. I wanted to show them I was clever, but the things that came easy to me, like playing football and working with a group of people in a team, weren't important to them. Their denial of my abilities and their discouragement and criticism of my efforts made me feel stupid.*

B  After writing the summary above of your family's attitudes and beliefs in this area, list about five examples of ways you notice your family's mind-stance attitudes and behaviour affecting you now in the areas of general intelligence, success at tasks requiring well-developed thinking skills, logic and reasoning, and intuition and insight, and explain how you feel about this continuing family influence.

Doug went on:

*Here are some consequences of my family's attitude that I wasn't bright:*

*1  I became a teacher because I wanted to show them I could succeed in a school setting – and I have.*
*2  I still feel like the least intelligent person in any group, especially with the teachers at school.*
*3  I'm worried because the Head wants me to teach some new subjects and I'm afraid I won't be able to master them well enough to do a good job.*
*4  I am always pleasant and put myself out for people so they'll like me even though I'm no genius.*

*When I read over that list, I feel frustrated and resentful. Maybe I wasn't stupid, maybe I just wasn't clever in the way they wanted me to be, but I'll never get them to admit that.*

If you, like Doug, have internalised a negative family opinion of your abilities, you may be your own worst enemy in breaking out of the pattern because you are still under the spell of a harmful belief. By describing one particular incident or pattern from your past, you can often marshal the evidence of your feelings now about what happened to you then to help you change your mind – literally.

## EXERCISE

## THINKING STYLES

If your style of thinking was different from that of most of your family members, you might have negative memories of incidents in which your mental contribution was not understood or appreciated. For instance, if you got your best ideas in feelings or images while your family tended to concentrate on logic and argument, your creative mental abilities may not have been recognised and encouraged. Or you might feel that your family valued you only for your mind, as a clever child whose other interests and talents were overlooked while the good reports were celebrated.

A  Choose an uncomfortable or painful family event related to your mental abilities. Recount what happened in vivid detail, bringing back both the circumstances and your feelings at the time.

Peggy, a bookshop manager in her forties, wrote:

*My family thought things through carefully, in a very conventional, rational manner. I had these sudden, exciting hunches of how to do things, but my parents didn't understand and discouraged me. This one night, I was listening to my parents talking about how to pay for my sister to go to university. I could see it all like a flash: they needed to sell some shares my grandpa had left us. I babbled it all out, saying, 'This'll take care of it, I just know it!' My mother got angrier than I'd ever seen her and raised her voice. 'Peggy, your wild ideas are no good at all. Your father and I will come up with a sensible solution.' I rushed away from the table in tears, feeling like a rejected freak.*

B  After you have written out your memory, follow it with a short letter to the young person you were, telling this younger self what you now think might be helpful and how you feel about his or her situation.

Peggy wrote:

*Dear Peg, your intuition is a talent you can trust and develop. I know you didn't want to blame your parents for not appreciating your gut feelings as a valid form of intelligence, but you would have been better off back then if you had allowed yourself to get angry. As it was, you blamed yourself and refused to acknowledge a real gift.*

Peggy went on to write that even now she is reluctant to be as intuitive as she'd like with the man she's living with, whose more rational style reminds her of that of her family. In this close relationship, she is reminded of her family's rejection and fears experiencing it again.

Most of us are still struggling with vestiges of old family opinions about our abilities. In the next exercise, you can reinforce the mental strengths you already feel confident about and use them to explore new or blocked areas.

## EXERCISE

## ENHANCING YOUR MENTAL CONFIDENCE AND CREATIVE THINKING

Whether you have self-confidence or have doubts about your intellectual capability, you can learn to use more of your abilities by expanding strengths that you already use.

All of use have thinking skills that we take for granted. You can tap yours to help expand your mental resources. Think of several activities that come easily to you, that you may not even think require mental skills. They might be solving crossword puzzles, carpentry, planning gardens, working out how mysteries are going to end, playing tennis or chatting with a friend. A particular mental talent might emerge: language skills, skills to manipulate raw material and create a precise result, visualising skills, associative skills, mental strategy merged with physical effort or skills to recognise nuances of meaning and emotion in another's remarks.

A  Write down one or more activities that come easily to you and describe what your mind has to do to bring them off successfully. You may find it helpful to list the steps of how you perform an activity or you may prefer to describe your mind's action with an image or an analogy.

Doug wrote:

*I have fun making diagrams of football tactics. I think about a tough team we might face, then I imagine moves that might stop their attack. I play out the action like a film in my head. It's like pictures happening in order.*

Peggy wrote:

*I like forecasting book trends. I walk through the shop I manage before we open, looking at titles in each area. Then I start to feel pieces fall into a pattern and all of a sudden I see a need that some publisher's going to fill. Usually, I see a book that fills the gap in a catalogue some months later and I place an order. I knew it was coming by watching for the right pieces of the pattern.*

B  Once you have written in images and/or analysis how you do whatever comes easily, describe how you might apply the same mental process to some other situation that feels stuck or blocked. For instance, if you have identified that your bird-watching hobby means that you can sort things into categories well, you can apply that mental process to a completely unrelated problem – say, a tense relationship with your mother-in-law. You could list all the times you remember having difficult interactions with her and then see what common categories there are, such as conflicts over child-rearing, misunderstandings about holiday plans or differing needs for contact. Then you are better equipped to sort out which category is the most troublesome or the most easily addressed and to start thinking through in sequences or pictures what you would like to see happen.

Doug wrote:

*How can I apply my football-diagram talent to my anxiety about teaching these new subjects? Well, if my mental process is to create pictures in sequence, like a film, what sequence of pictures would help me learn new subjects? I can tell what my obstacles are going to be: getting started on the reading and research, asking some colleagues for help and advice, getting the children excited about the subject. I suppose that with each one, I could picture the obstacle, then picture what would help me get around it. If I took them one at a time, the way I plan football moves, I might not feel so overwhelmed.*

As you experiment with applying skills from your areas of mental strength to areas of inexperience or past difficulty, you will develop the unique attributes of your own mind. While your parents shaped your genetic inheritance and helped form your mind's habits, you can grow beyond these to new patterns of thought and action, enhancing yet another part of your whole self.

# YOUR SELF, YOUR EMOTIONS AND YOUR FAMILY

Your emotions are as fundamental to your sense of self and your experience of each day's events as the weather is to our human community. Your perspective on what is happening in your life is coloured by your feelings in the same way that a glorious, sunny day can lift people's spirit and a dark, drizzly one can depress them. Yet just as some people seem oblivious to the weather, forgetting to wear a coat when it's cold and not reacting to the beauty of a spring day, some of us are cut off from fully feeling or expressing our emotions.

If you don't know what you're feeling, you may be confused by what happens to you or think your life is out of control. If you can't express what you feel, you can't share a complete self in your relationships. If you withhold either acknowledgement or expression of your feelings, you may have physical pain or illnesses that flare up and block your full participation in life.

All of these problems go back to what you learned about feelings from your family. Your emotional self developed in response to your family's emotional environment, the weather of your particular family group. If you were allowed and encouraged to notice and express your feelings, your family environment contributed to the development of your emotional self in a positive way.

If you came from a family that was open in this way, you can build on the healthy start you received for your emotional development. Most of us, however, grew up in less comfortable emotional climates. Your parents' attitudes towards the feeling side of themselves and their children's selves may have been clouded by their upbringing and experience. Painful or repressive family backgrounds develop through the generations into healthy environments for the development and expression of feelings.

You can address many current problems in your life by tracing their connections to frozen or blocked emotional energy from your family past. In the process of linking past and present, you are also taking action to release and develop your feeling self more fully. In this section's first exercise, you will spell out your family's stance towards emotions and investigate how the influence of their approach to feelings has affected your own perceptions and experiences. In the second, you will re-create two emotionally charged memories that stand out strongly from your family past, one that blocked or hurt your emotional development and one that contributed to its growth. In the third, you will learn how to be more in touch with your emotions, making your feelings a more accessible and flexible part of your sense of self.

## EXERCISE

## EMOTIONAL HISTORY: YOUR FEELING SELF THEN AND NOW

Your family stance towards recognising and expressing feelings was as characteristic and distinctive as the high cheekbones that came from one side of the family and the slouchy walk that came from the other. The wide range of possible family stances towards emotions is indicated by two summaries: Elizabeth described her family's emotional stance as 'hysterical – all feelings expressed in extreme intensity', while Doug reported, 'Nobody talked about feelings, just the intellect, and emotional involvement meant you weren't being reasonable'.

A Write about what kind of family messages you received about feelings in your own growing-up years, using these aspects of emotional functioning as a guide:

- **inner acknowledgement** (having permission to know what you are feeling);
- **outer expressiveness** (having permission to show what you are feeling);
- **intensity** (having permission to express the true strength of your feelings rather than restraining yourself );
- **flexibility** (being taught that a wide range of feelings is healthy and normal).

Once again, you can use these contrasting attitudes and actions to describe how your family approached their feelings and yours, and how you may still be affected by past experiences of:

- **acknowledgement** or **denial**;
- **appreciation** or **criticism**;

- **confidence** or **anxiety and fear**;
- **encouragement** or **discouragement**;
- **delight** or **distaste**.

Laura wrote:

*My family acknowledged and appreciated only nice, pleasant, hopeful emotions. I was the angry one and did I get criticised for it! Mother said, 'Frown marks will ruin your pretty face'. We all ate, stuffing our bodies so there'd be no room for feelings. In the process, I never learned that feelings can change, that anger goes away.*

B  To amplify what you may have noticed about your family's continuing influence in your emotional life, list about five examples of different situations and relationships in your life now that your family's stance towards feelings most affected and describe your current reactions to them.

Laura's list included:

1  *Still eating automatically when tension heats up anywhere.*
2  *Not knowing that I'm angry until I'm so angry I can't speak.*
3  *Being a split personality – either sweet at work and raging at home or a dictator at work and Superwife/Mum at home.*
4  *Not knowing how to react to my children's anger. I give them double messages: Let it out! Oh, not that much, not now!*

*My family's pattern of forced pleasantry has left me emotionally blocked and limited. I want more freedom of expression, for myself and for my children.*

You can augment your discoveries about how your family's stance towards feelings affects you now by examining specific instances that harmed or helped the formation of your emotional self.

## EXERCISE

### FEELING MEMORIES

Feelings are always present in families, like an underground water source – sometimes hidden, sometimes breaking through. Because water takes so many forms, ice, steam, rain, rivers, it's a good source of imagery for your family's emotional life. Were feelings in your family like a dammed-up torrent, a violent storm, a quiet pool or a stagnant pond?

A  Use water imagery to describe two memories from your family past: an uncomfortable or painful memory in which feelings played a hurtful role, and a pleasurable or helpful memory in which they played a healing role.

Elizabeth wrote:

*My family's fearfulness about my health was just one expression of their emotional style. They reminded me of the ocean – wave after wave of intense emotion, everyone competing for attention. The worst day in my memory was Uncle Frederick's funeral. He was my father's brother, a relatively calm, peace-keeping type. His funeral, when I was seven, made a big impression on me. Everyone sobbed so loud they drowned out the minister. Back at home, the adults began to quarrel. Without Uncle Frederick, they got louder and wilder. The hysteria was like a huge storm, and I became seasick. I started to run upstairs, got dizzy, and passed out right there in the midst of them.*

Doug wrote:

*My family's motto was 'feelings aren't facts'. I knew I didn't fit in because I felt things deeply, although I learned not to show it. But when I was eight a boy named Jim moved in next door, and his family seemed from another planet – very expressive, even the men. Once, Jim invited me to go to a football match with his dad and grandpa. My feelings, which had been frozen in my family's icy atmosphere, thawed and spilled over. I was amazed that his dad and grandpa cried at the national anthem, and my own eyes burned a little. They shouted angrily when the referee was unfair and hugged each other and Jim and me when the home team won. I shouted and leaped and hugged back. Driving home in their big old car, I couldn't stop grinning.*

B When you have written out both a negative and a positive memory connected to your feelings, write a few lines in answer to these questions:

How have these formative experiences from the past affected your stance towards feelings today? Can you use some aspect of the positive memory to change a block or limitation in your emotional life now?

Elizabeth commented:

*My family's inability to contain their emotions led me to put distance between myself and others. My positive memory of the calmness I felt as a child visiting museums and churches is like a quiet pool of water inside me. I draw on the memory of those vast spaces when I am surrounded by upheaval at work. I want to try bringing my internalised calm to my next family visit.*

Doug wrote:

*I see sports as my way to relate to my feelings. I can allow myself to get worked up with my team, but I have a harder time expressing what I feel separate from my coaching role. I have to remind myself that I*

111

*don't live in that chilly family anymore and that I can warm up and even boil over without being criticised.*

Your emotional sense of self will become stronger and clearer as you identify what you feel in the present and heal the damage to your feelings from the past. You will learn to tune in to your emotions more frequently and precisely and to trust that what they have to teach you is necessary and good.

## EXERCISE

### EXPANDING YOUR EMOTIONAL CONFIDENCE

One reason that you may not feel entirely comfortable with acknowledging or expressing your deeper emotions may be that they stir you up physically – evoking tears with sadness, trembling with fear, pounding in your ears with anger, a sarcastic tone in your voice with jealousy. You may feel that if you express them you will go out of control. The physical sensations that go with feelings are part of healthy expression; by holding them in you hold yourself back from going through to the healing release on the other side. You can become more comfortable with these sensations through this exercise.

A 1  The next time you feel some emotion intensely, find a private place where you can write.

2  Start by writing for two or three minutes directly about your feelings, describing them in physical terms ('my heart is aching; my chest is heavy'), the reasons for the feelings or any connections to your family past.

3  Take a long, slow, deep breath. Relax as many muscles as you can while you breathe out.

4  You may find it helpful to repeat silently a phrase that has meaning for you as you exhale (such as 'Let go', 'One day at a time', or 'I am OK').

5  After a long, slow inhalation and exhalation, pay attention to your body and your feelings. In relaxing, your sensations and emotions have probably changed. Write down what you are feeling now.

6  Repeat this process of a deep breath, an inner survey, and writing it down several times, until you feel finished.

7  Read over your passages and note what you have learned. How did your feelings change with the pacing of breathing and writing?

Using this technique helped Laura modify intense emotion and clarify its meaning. Laura chose to write after a difficult phone call in which her mother tried to convince her that she should lose weight before a forthcoming family wedding. After going through the breathing/writing process, Laura commented:

*I was just amazed that the more I let the anger in, the more I craved food. I decided to repeat the phrase 'You don't have to do anything you don't want' to myself while I did the breathing, but another phrase, 'I've got to eat something!' kept intruding. So I had to find another phrase and I tried 'It's OK to be angry', which seemed to work really well. I just went round and round with the three phrases until I gradually got calmer and the hungry voice faded away.*

Your feelings are as necessary to your good health as water is to your survival. The more you acquaint yourself with all the aspects of your emotional self, the more deeply nourished you will feel, able to recognise and express feelings without holding on to them. Like water flowing through your hands, they cleanse you and pass on. As a river slowly smooths the roughness from a piece of granite, generations of family pain can be eased by your willingness to unblock emotional flow. Accepting your feeling side integrates a critical aspect of selfhood into your life.

# YOUR SELF, YOUR SPIRIT AND YOUR FAMILY

We all create a mental context of some kind for ourselves that gives meaning to our lives from childhood through our adult years. We explain feelings and events to ourselves in certain ways and experience hopes, wishes and longings that touch us deeply. You may call this context of meaning your values, your world view, your integrity, your spirituality or your principles. You may call these longings your idealism, your hopes for the future, your heart, your trust, your soul or your faith.

No matter what you believe about the existence of the soul, the presence or absence of some divine being or force, the value of private spirituality or organised faith communities or whatever you call this dimension of your life, your sense of self probably includes a belief in a personal essence or core that encompasses who you are more fully, deeply and truly than other descriptions of your roles or activities.

Your family's teachings about life's meaning and your own sense of personal value can be a great help or a great hindrance when facing difficulties. If you find your life meaningless and yourself without any core of value, your sense of self is incomplete, and the inevitable problems and pain of life can become overwhelming.

Your spirit, or your potential self, is always more powerful than the damage done to it, and you can help it overcome any damage by understanding and describing your family's influence on the development of the sense of spirit you now have.

In this section's exercises, you will begin by defining your family's stance towards the spirit and stating how their approach has affected the development of this aspect of yourself. You will then portray two childhood memories related either to your own experience of wonder and mystery or to your family's interpretation of spirituality. Finally, as part of the ongoing work of self-development, you will contrast some of your inherited attitudes and beliefs with your own current sense of worth and meaning.

## EXERCISE

## SPIRITUAL HISTORY: YOUR CORE SELF THEN AND NOW

Your family may have talked directly to you about spiritual matters and participated in family or organised religious community rituals or celebrations. On the other hand, they may have avoided conversation about spiritual subjects and participation in spiritual activities. In either case, you received family education about this dimension of life. You absorbed and responded to what your family valued and found meaningful. By describing your spiritual history with your family, you can trace how certain aspects of your current problems or strengths in this area may connect to your family's stance towards the spiritual side of your selfhood.

A Think back over your growing-up years and describe family attitudes, beliefs and practices concerning:

- **goodness and evil in human nature;**
- **spiritual or religious codes of behaviour;**
- **the existence and nature of divinity;**
- **the meaning and purpose of life.**

Since these are all abstract concepts and children learn from specific remarks and actions, you might refer to this list of people, places and practices to see what your upbringing contained: church services, grace at meals, religious holidays, studying holy writings, private or family prayer, catechism, Sunday school, revival meetings, Hebrew school, meditation, baptism, confirmation, bar or bar mitzvah, saints, priests, ministers, nuns, rabbis, religious symbols at home, occult or esoteric practices, feelings of deep knowing, experiencing nature as sacred, spiritual dreams, singing in the choir, religious retreats or camps, spiritual mentors or teachers, conversion experiences.

B From these or any other remembered sources, write what you learned, including attitudes of either:

- **acknowledgement** or **denial**;
- **appreciation** or **criticism**;
- **confidence** or **anxiety and fear**;
- **encouragement** or **discouragement**;
- **delight** or **distaste**.

Doug wrote:

*My parents worshipped reason and intellect and thought that people who were foolish enough to depend on religion were weak and deluded. Part of my fascination with my friend Jim's family was that they were Catholic and had this whole other part of their life that I knew nothing about. As an adult, I still feel attracted to learning something about religion but I don't want to be forced to believe things that don't make sense to me.*

Laura summarised her family's influence this way:

*I was taught to be a good little girl, so I associate religion with fake sweetness and light. Learn the catechism, obey the nuns, go to confession. I'm confused about spirituality today. I feel turned off to the Church because the emphasis on purity and sacrifice reminded me of my relatives' insistence that only positive emotions were acceptable. But I still yearn for some way to express what I feel deep inside.*

If you, like Doug, find few opportunities to talk easily about your deep longings or, like Laura, are confused about your spiritual self, you can more clearly pinpoint your family's spiritual heritage in the next exercise.

## EXERCISE

## SPIRITUAL MEMORIES

Families can strongly influence how children acquire 'a reverence for life'. As a child, when you became absorbed in the tiny world of an ant's nest or looked up at the night sky, you were participating in mystery. If the adults in your life recognised and encouraged your curiosity, caring and wonder, you were able to share that mystery with them and grow in a context of reverence for life. But the adults in your life may have been too busy, confused or unhappy with their own problems to nurture you in this area of the self.

A  Write out two memories from your childhood – one describing an experience with the spiritual or religious dimension that was upsetting, inhibiting or harmful to you and the other portraying an experience of wonder, mystery or joy that had a freeing, life-enhancing effect on you.

B  Note what role your family played in each memory.

Elizabeth wrote:

*My very dramatic family was extremely rigid about their religious beliefs. Ours was a fire-and-brimstone faith, with threats of punishment forever if you didn't do just what the Bible said. The memory that stands out was of a time when my friend Judy's mother left her husband. In church the next Sunday, the priest declared that Mrs. Baxter had left God's people and that we were to grieve for her as if she were dead, because she was now lost. At lunch my parents announced that I couldn't play with Judy anymore. I didn't rebel but inside I resolved that I would never believe in a God who was so mean he would split apart two little girls who liked each other.*

Peggy wrote:

*My family went to church in a very conventional way; it was the thing to do. I found it incredibly boring and meaningless. But when we moved to the country with a river at the bottom of the garden, I found out where I believed God lived. I heard voices in the babbling water; I lay for hours on the bank watching the insects dance on the surface and listening to the birds. My family thought I was strange – 'Peggy's down at the river again, talking to the birds!' my brothers would yell, and my parents chuckled. I felt alone but I had something magic of my own. I've found everything I ever needed spiritually through being out in nature.*

Whether you have diverged strongly from your family's spiritual attitudes and traditions, like Elizabeth and Peggy, or have forged your own combination of your family's stance towards the spirit with ideas and practices that are meaningful to you, you can benefit from clarifying what you do believe.

## EXERCISE

## CONNECTING MORE DEEPLY TO YOUR SPIRIT

As in the other three components of your sense of self, a sign of health and growth in the spiritual aspect of your identity is the ability to know what is right for you and to express your individuality, which is a blend of your family heritage and your own unique attributes. You can define more clearly what you believe by contrasting it with messages from your family past that do not match your sense of spirit.

A 1  On one side of a piece of paper, list some of the negative messages you heard about spirituality from your family or other early authorities in your life. These are sayings or beliefs that made you uncomfortable, or hurt or limited you.

2  On the other side of the paper, write a statement that is a positive, contrasting message that you now look to for guidance or wisdom. The act of defining helpful statements will connect you more deeply to your own core self.

The following responses, a mixture of Peggy's, Doug's, Laura's and Elizabeth's, illustrate how you can refine or change a family belief to make it meaningful for you:

*Ours is the one true faith.*

*Every person can find her own truth.*

*A mature person doesn't need religion.*

*Maturity is finding what helps you grow.*

*Obedience is the most spiritual value.*

*Without doubt there can be no faith.*

*Religion is part of belonging to your community.*

*Solitude and beauty nourish my spirit.*

B 1 After you have stated what matters to you, write a description of how you now see your own spirit, your core identity, your deep self. Think about 'the shining light of the spirit' and visualise and describe the worthy essence at the core of yourself. If you have difficulty attributing that value to yourself, describe that core in someone you know and admire.
  2 Underline parts of your description that you can imagine as true of yourself.
  3 Read whatever you have written aloud to yourself and end with the words 'This is about me'.

Here are four more sentences from the descriptions of the people whose stories and selves have been partly revealed in this chapter:

*I have a deeply loving nature that wants to reach out to people.*

*I can make a difference in others' lives by my efforts and caring.*

*I am a strong, fierce creative spirit.*

*I participate in creation by honouring the beauty of this world.*

Throughout your life, you continue to develop more fully in all aspects of your selfhood – body, mind, emotions and spirit. In the final section, you will examine how your current sense of identity is formed by the interaction of your personal physical, mental, emotional and spiritual selves with your family roots.

# STRENGTHENING YOUR SENSE OF SELF

Getting to know more about your sense of self has probably shown you aspects of your identity that are strongly developed and comfortable and aspects that are less well-developed or painful. Growth in any aspect of selfhood comes through a balancing act between the impulses and directions of the family you grew up with and the impulses and directions of the people who are central in your life now. The centre pole of the seesaw must be your own firmly anchored sense of individuality.

At any time, you can regain your balance by getting in touch with your body, mind, emotions and spirit. Your current bodily sensations, thoughts and attitudes, feelings, and beliefs and longings hold the best clues to what your growth requires. As you encourage undeveloped aspects of yourself and heal those damaged by your family past, you will not only strengthen your personal identity but also relate as a more complete person to the others who are important in your life.

In this final exercise, you can sum up your observations about your family's selfhood patterns and assess and plan action for your own individual development.

## EXERCISE

## YOUR SELF IN THE PROCESS OF BECOMING

Your family's patterns developed some aspects of your selfhood more than others. But you can now focus on the talents and resources of the more developed aspects of yourself to strengthen those that are less developed.

- A  Write a short passage describing how you now see the interaction of the four aspects of body, mind, emotions and spirit in your childhood family and how you see your current balance and development of selfhood.
- B  Describe how you might use the strengths of your more comfortable aspects to support the less comfortable growing edge of other aspects.

Doug wrote:

*My family chose to emphasise intellectual development. They ignored physical strengths and activities, played down emotions and dismissed spiritual concerns. I was shocked to realise that I have done pretty much the same thing in another area. I've developed the negative stereotype of me as a 'thickie' into a positive asset – I'm a successful coach and I know how to help others make the most of their physical potential. But my other areas are undeveloped. I worry about my intellectual abilities, I have trouble expressing my feelings away from the playing field and I just haven't taken the time to examine my spiritual needs. What I want to do is to focus on breaking my intellectual blocks by getting myself well-prepared for teaching new subjects. If I start there, I think I'll feel happy about myself and I'll be encouraged to be more expressive with my feelings and spirit.*

One student remarked that the best thing about the four aspects of yourself is that they will be around the rest of your life and you can keep working on them. The psychologist Florida Scott-Maxwell wrote very late in her life: 'Age puzzles me. I thought it was a quiet time. My seventies were interesting and fairly serene but my eighties are passionate. I grow more intense as I age.' You can look forward to continuing your journey of self-development throughout your life, always finding the intersections of your uniqueness with your family's patterns.

In the next chapter, you will explore how your sense of personal power developed in your family context. The ability to take initiative and follow through is a vital factor in any attempt to change and grow. Your skills today at feeling capable and independent and initiating and following through plans and goals are conditioned strongly by your early family experiences.

By describing what your family taught you about your capabilities, you will understand more clearly the connection between your current view of yourself as powerful or lacking in power and the messages and experiences of your family past. You can take advantage of strategies to develop and use your personal power more fully and wisely from now on.

# CHAPTER 6

# YOUR FAMILY AND YOUR SENSE OF PERSONAL POWER

Personal power comes from within, from a strong and healthy sense of self. Your personal power includes several components: your **self-esteem**, how good you feel about yourself; your **independence**, how well you can decide on your own what is right for you to do; and your **initiative**, how well you can take action and follow through. It consists of knowing what your individual talents and resources are and having the confidence to act on them.

As with your sense of self, your personal power develops from your family roots. Your family laid its foundation with their attitudes and actions. As your first answers to the question 'Who am I?' came from family members who reflected to you who they thought you were, your first answers to the question 'What can I do?' also came from your parents and other relatives who showed and told you what they thought about your capabilities.

Your identity and your personal power are always linked, because you express your sense of self in action and your actions reveal who you think you are. Just as your family may have pressured you to be who they wanted you to be, they may have pressured you to do what they wanted you to do. In defining yourself and choosing how to act on your self-defined identity, you were either helped or hampered by your family's willingness or reluctance to let you act independently.

We naturally grow up looking to parents and family members for the affirmation of abilities that gives us confidence. Your earliest achievements, such as standing and walking, took place in the family context and you looked to your parents for reassurance that what you were doing was good and admirable.

As a toddler, you experimented with separating from your parents, but you looked back to make sure they were still there as you bravely walked away. Each new stage of independence, from starting school to leaving home as a young adult, included a mixture of forward and backward pulls from within. You wanted to grow up but you were scared of the responsibility. Would you succeed on your own? Your ability to take initiative and move forward now is linked to your family's past record of encouraging this development of your personal power.

However, if your family had difficulty seeing you as separate from them, if they wanted your identity to serve their own selfhood needs, they may not have been able to help you develop the personal power characteristics of self-esteem, independence and initiative. All parents struggle with letting their children grow up and away from them, because children give parents' lives focus and meaning. As your emerging identity made your parents question who they were, your emerging abilities pointed out the areas of their lives that they may never have had the time, money, energy, courage, support or resources to develop. Any painful or unresolved issues of self-esteem, independence or initiative in your parents' own lives made it harder for them to encourage you.

To the degree that you are held back by the family messages, you internalised about your abilities, your sense of personal power is limited. If your family did not help you build strong self-esteem and discouraged your independence and initiative, you may find that you:

- **doubt your own abilities** ('I'm not bright enough to go on to university.');
- **have a strong need for control** ('If you would just do it the way I asked you to, things would work out fine.');
- **are never satisfied with your achievements** ('Yes, it was nice to get that award, but there are lots of people better than I am.');
- **feel that you always have to prove yourself** ('If the work's all done well, then I can relax.');
- **prefer being a follower to being a leader** ('Just tell me what to do and I'll be happy to do it.');
- **desire money and success as symbols of security** ('If I could just get that promotion and rise, I'd know I was doing well.');
- **refuse to take risks** ('If I do that, it might not work out and then I'd be in a worse position than I am now.');
- **set limits on what you believe you can do** ('I can probably get an article published in a local paper, but I'd never make it as a writer for a national magazine.');
- **have relationship problems related to power issues** ('If he would only let me do what I want, then I could . . .').

By becoming more aware of how your family addressed issues involving personal power and the effects of your family's approach to your current sense of power, you can discover the origins of many things that keep you from doing what you want or feeling satisfied with your actions. A more developed sense of personal power contributes to your individual growth and the health of your relationships.

Positive expression of personal power involves both independent initiative to take actions that are fulfilling for you and caring and responsibility in relation to others. This balance between considering your own *and* others' needs and wishes requires a high degree of awareness and flexibility. Without that balance, you can easily draw back from your personal power because it is risky to act on what you believe or hope for, or you can become overbearing by using your personal power without regard for its effect on others. Harriet Lerner writes:

In the name of either **protecting** or **asserting** the self, we may fail to take a position on something that matters or we may cut off from significant others, operate at their expense or behave as if we have the truth of the universe.

Your family experiences may have taught you that power is either something fearful to be avoided or something vital to be seized and controlled. The emotionally charged aspect of personal power extends to the word *power* itself. People have commented that their associations to the word reflect their mixed feelings. You might stop and reflect on your own associations; others have suggested these words: *struggle, money, conflict, status, oppression, tyranny, intimidation, selfishness* and *hierarchy*. The root of the word *power*, however, simply means 'to be able', so you might think of personal power as a confident, thoughtful use of your abilities.

In the first of the four sections that comprise this chapter, you will examine the relationship between your **self-esteem** level and your ease of access to your personal power. High self-esteem allows you to believe in your talents and your ability to make good use of them. Although your early childhood experiences created the foundation of how you view and value yourself, you can increase your feelings of self-worth at any time in your life.

Your self-esteem is based on your personal sense of confidence, an outgrowth of your family's attitudes about trust. In the first few years of your life, your family's life stance regarding trust determined how secure you felt. To the extent that their care was trustworthy and they showed you that the world was a safe place for you, you developed a confident, positive view of yourself and your surroundings. To the extent that they were unreliable or uncaring, or communicated mistrust, you lacked self-confidence and developed a fearful, negative or hopeless view of yourself and your surroundings.

If you didn't receive positive responses from your family and now have a low sense of self-esteem, you may have problems in relationships because you need so much approval from your partners or colleagues. You may not feel that you have the personal power to take independent, powerful actions, because you don't value your talents. By writing about your early experiences that affected your self-worth, you can communicate with the damaged, childlike part of yourself that still lives inside you, strengthening the foundation from which your personal power extends.

In the second section, you will investigate how your **independence** developed in the context of your family. The more you were permitted and encouraged to become independent, the more you will be able to put your personal power to use in action. On the other hand, the more you were encouraged to stay dependent on your family, the more trouble you will have acting as an autonomous or independent person.

The psychologist's model of human growth suggests that the earliest stage of trust versus mistrust is followed by a stage of autonomy versus shame and doubt. Your natural impulse as a toddler was to experiment with moving away from your parents, your most important human connection, by asserting your independence. You pulled away from your mother's hand, said 'No' a hundred times a day, refused to eat foods you didn't like and dared to walk out of your parents' sight. At other times, you showed your doubt of this new independence by becoming clingy and needy. You needed your parents and other family members not only to tolerate but also to encourage your alternately autonomous and doubting use of your personal power.

If your parents were strong and stable at this stage of your life, they reassured you of your worth and of the safety of separating and becoming more powerful. If instead they were discouraged, frightened and made you feel bad about your wish to be independent, you learned that separating and becoming more powerful might be too risky. You might have felt doubtful of your abilities or ashamed of developing your power.

By evaluating what you know about the development of your independence in your growing-up years, you will understand how past family experiences may be impeding your ability to stand on your own today. You can also clarify your current needs for independence and implement strategies to become more autonomous.

In the third section, you will explore the role of **initiative** in developing and exercising your personal power. Initiative means planning and following through in personal activities, work and relationships. As with self-esteem and independence, the motivation to initiate things and follow through is a skill you learned primarily from your family.

According to psychological theory, you first began to absorb family teachings about initiative when you were about four or five years old. At that time, you naturally became more assertive and active and your family's reactions to the choices you made were important in shaping your self-image. If they encouraged your efforts, applauding your successes and minimising your failures, you learned that when you took initiative and planned well you could carry out your intentions successfully. If they discouraged your initiative, ignoring what you did well or criticising or punishing you for what you did poorly, you learned that exercising your personal power was associated with pain and guilt.

The consequences for you as an adult if you absorbed negative teachings about initiative in childhood include indecision, hiding your talents, lack of direction and blaming yourself when things go wrong. To learn how to take initiative now, you must free your will by engaging your feelings. You can't know what you want to do until you know what you feel.

In the final section, you will sum up your discoveries about **personal power** in your family context. No matter how much your family circumstances either helped or hindered the development of your self-esteem, independence and initiative, you have a powerful inner spirit – the core self mentioned in the last chapter – that can be further released and empowered. As that spirit becomes freer, you will have a much greater range of creative responses to life.

# SELF-ESTEEM: THE FOUNDATION OF YOUR PERSONAL POWER

*P*aul is a social worker who tirelessly does good works; he is known as the person you go to when you want special help. Marge is a valuable member of a team of software designers who turn out products for a large division of an electronics firm; her ideas are sound but she constantly apologises for herself, undercutting her effectiveness. Craig is the manager of Marge's products division and his employees fear his sarcastic tongue and bullying manner. Nancy, a nurse in a large hospital, follows almost every remark with 'Is that OK?' Her husband complains that she comes home from work depressed and worried about her abilities and frequently asks for reassurance. Alison is a university professor who spends all her time teaching, researching and writing. She has no close friends and does not socialise among her colleagues, firmly discouraging those who try to form more personal ties with her. Nick is still single at 33, but not for lack of longing. He believes that there is one special woman out there who is the right one for him; the many women he dates say that he is romantic but has completely unrealistic expectations of a relationship.

Despite their many differences, these people share a common problem: they lack a clear, well-developed sense of personal power, and the root of their problem is low self-esteem. People with high self-esteem have the confidence necessary to bring independence and initiative to their daily lives; all of those profiled have undeveloped areas, dissatisfaction or conflict in their personal relationships or working lives.

The love that you received from your family as a child laid the foundation of worth and self-esteem from which you began to build independent, active, personal power. If your parents had difficulty feeling or expressing their love for you because of their own lack of self-love, you may have grown up with a weak sense of self-esteem. You may be trying to please, apologise and seek approval like Paul, Marge, and Nancy, or you may now need to control and dominate others like Craig, push them away like Alison, or long for someone else to make you feel real and whole like Nick.

In addition to its foundation of love, your self-esteem was shaped by your parents' responsiveness. Two important types of responses needed to develop self-esteem as a child are empathy and mirroring. **Empathy** is the form of responsiveness that understands your situation as if from inside you. When you were frightened or angry as a very small child, you needed to have your feelings noticed and validated ('You're scared of fireworks aren't you? Loud noises are very startling').

**Mirroring** is another form of responsiveness that communicates your worth and value by showing delight in your very existence. From cuddling you and babbling at you when you were an infant to admiring your sense of hmumour or your strong throwing arm when you were older, your parents had many opportunities to build your self-esteem by mirroring their delight in your unique self.

If your parents didn't show their delight in your existence and actions, you may have been affected negatively, as described by mental health professionals Howard and Margaret Baker:

Parental responses of indifference, hostility or excessive criticism reflect back low worth and consequently inhibit the child's assertiveness. The mirroring responses of the parent are concerned with the maintenance and development of self-esteem and self-assertive ambitions.

No matter how much empathy and mirroring you received as a child, you have continuing needs to strengthen and develop your self-esteem as an adult. Certain situations make you feel vulnerable – such as a job review, the loss of a friendship or troubled relationships with family members. These stresses deplete your self-esteem reserves. However, you can also learn to create or augment these reserves for yourself by offering yourself the understanding and appreciation you did not receive as a child. As you lay a solid foundation of caring for yourself and strengthen it, you build self-esteem, confidence and the sense of personal power necessary to grapple with life's problems more successfully.

The exercises in this section focus on three approaches to identifying the family roots of your self-esteem and strengthening that foundation in your life now. The first exercise explores the range of approving, conditionally approving and disapproving messages that you received about your worth from your family. The second allows you to interview the family members who most shaped your self-esteem in childhood and whose internalised opinions most shape your responses now. The third helps you contact your own self-esteem needs and longings at this time in your life and connect them to the child that you were. All of the exercises aim to increase your trust and self-esteem and to enable you find ways to put higher self-worth to work in service of your current goals and needs.

## EXERCISE

## WHO DID THEY SAY YOU WERE?

You can assess the variety of self-esteem messages that you received from different family members through the following survey:

A  Divide a sheet of paper into three vertical columns.

B  In the left column, headed APPROVING, write things your parents and other adults in the family said to or about you when you were little that showed appreciation for who you were and affirmation that you were special and important to them. ('What strong arms you have!' 'Timmy is the best grandson anyone ever had.')

C  In the middle column, headed CONDITIONALLY APPROVING, write family messages that affirmed your worth with conditions attached, such as your taking certain actions. ('I like it when you are good and quiet.' 'Your hair looks pretty when you let me comb it.' 'If you kept your room neater, I'd be really happy with you.')

D   In the right column, headed DISAPPROVING, write family messages that criticised or complained about who you were or lacked acknowledgement that you were special and important. ('Mummy won't love you if you're mean to your brother.' 'You're so slow and lazy that you'll never get anywhere on time.' 'Don't get big headed – what makes you think you're so special?')

E   After completing all three columns, answer the following questions:

- Which kinds of messages did you get the most of ?
- How did you feel when you heard these things? How do you feel now after writing the memory?
- How did the balance of messages from the three columns affect your overall sense of self-esteem?
- How do the effects of these messages continue in your attitudes and actions today?

Paul, the social worker, wrote:

*The column that was fullest for me was the CONDITIONALLY APPROVING one. I see that I lived in an 'If – then' family. IF you get a good report, THEN we'll buy you a bike. IF you are cheerful and helpful, THEN Mum will be less depressed. I felt tense when I heard these things as a child; I felt angry writing about them now. I only remember a couple of APPROVING messages without strings attached, and they made me feel ten feet tall. My grandma thought I had a great smile, so I smiled all the time around her. The DISAPPROVING messages came when I didn't do enough or the right thing. If they thought I was being selfish, I really heard about it. I felt frightened hearing that then but I feel a mixture of anger and doubt now. I keep my self-esteem high these days by my activities that bring me so much approval.*

Discovering the frequency and effects of different types of self-esteem family messages will put you more in touch with the feelings that underlie your current sense of worth. You can become more aware of how your past experiences and feelings influence you now by homing in on the person who has shaped your self-esteem the most.

## EXERCISE

## ASKING QUESTIONS OF YOUR MIRROR

Your parents and other adults in the family reflected an image of who they felt you were from the time you were an infant. If that mirrored image reflected their own needs and pain more than it did your worth and value, you may have a distorted picture of yourself that has negatively affected your self-esteem. You can learn much about the development of your self-esteem from tapping in on what you remember of this 'childhood mirror'.

A Decide who was the family member – probably one of your parents – who gave you the most positive self-esteem messages. If you're not sure who that person was, look over your survey in the previous section to see who was most often cited in the columns.

B Imagine that you are interviewing that person. You may still be close to that family member, in which case it will not be difficult to picture asking him or her questions. If you are in a tense or conflicted relationship or no longer communicate with the person, you can imagine that there has been a truce or thawing in the relationship that would allow you to talk. Or you can picture yourself as if you were a neutral figure, such as a reporter who interviews the family member for you.

C Start the dialogue by writing what you imagine would be the person's answer to this question: 'What did you most want .................... [your name] to know when he or she was little?'

D Keep asking the person all the questions you can think of: 'So how did you try to tell him/her that? What kind of behaviour from him/her made you feel you needed to tell him/her that? How did you feel about yourself during this time in your life?' Avoid explaining or arguing with your family member, as this exercise is designed to help you understand that person's point of view.

E When you feel you have received all the information you want, close the interview. In the next exercise, you will have a chance to respond from your perspective.

F Finish by writing a summary of what you learned from your family member and how you now see the past and present effects of this person's contributions to your self-esteem.

Nick, the romantic bachelor, chose to interview his mother and wrote this summary of the experience:

*I chose my mother because my dad was a salesman who was hardly ever around. Ma poured out so much love to me and sure enough, when I asked her what she most wanted me to know, she answered, 'That he is the most precious boy who ever lived and that he is Ma's brave and helpful little man'. I was proud to have her say that when I was small, because I felt important, like I could be the man of the house when Dad was away. But when I asked her what behaviour from me made her want to say that, she answered, 'When Nickie wanted to go out and play with the neighbourhood boys or wanted to do something too dangerous or grown up'. Plus, when I asked her how she felt at that time in her life, she responded, 'Lonely, always lonely. I just kept busy with my boy.' Putting those pieces together, I can see that I felt really important and special and needed but Ma got anxious when I was away from her. I got this message: 'You're a wonderful little boy if you keep Mother happy'. Maybe this message is connected to my relationship problems.*

Looking at the origins of your self-esteem through the perspective of the person who mirrored your selfhood to you helps you judge with your current perceptions how clear or distorted that view was. In the next exercise, you will focus on the perceptions of the child who heard those mirroring messages in order to connect what you longed to know about yourself then with the self-esteem healing you may need now.

## EXERCISE

## LIVING FROM A NEW BASE OF SELF-ESTEEM

Laying a new foundation of self-esteem is not as simple as mixing up a batch of concrete and pouring a strong, solid slab. It's more like piecing together a mosaic floor, each little chip contributing to the beauty and strength of the whole. You build on your foundation of worth throughout your life. Now you can find self-esteem pieces to add by contacting the child within you.

A  Imagine you are interviewing yourself as a child. Because children don't think abstractly about concepts like self-esteem, you need to ask concrete questions.

B  For the responses, try this writing technique to gain access to your more intuitive, childlike self. Have the child self respond by writing with your nondominant hand, the hand you don't usually write with. Take your time to imagine that you are little again and don't worry about messiness.

C  Ask your child self to name four or five things he or she really needs from his or her family to help build his or her self-esteem. Your child might find it easy to answer by starting: 'I want . . .', 'I like it when . . .', 'I need . . .', 'I feel good when . . .', or 'I wish. . . .'

D  Read over what your child has told you and, as your current, adult self, write your responses to these questions:

• What did this younger version of you need to know about itself to build up its self-esteem?
• Do you still long for that today?
• If so, how are you trying to get it?

Is the approach you are taking to enhance your self-esteem working? If not, identify what people, places or activities might help you feel good about yourself.

E  Review your resources! How can you strengthen your relationship with them? How might you find those attributes somewhere else? Is there something you need to remind yourself to reinforce a new base of self-value? Since the process of strengthening self-esteem is lifelong, how might you keep these reminders going?

Nancy, the nurse who seeks reassurance from her husband and colleagues, wrote:

*My child self's list included: 'I want Mummy and Daddy to notice me. I like it when they tell me I am a big help. I wish they wouldn't drink beer and fall asleep at night before I go to bed.' I felt so sad that I cried as I wrote these things. I helped in ways that I shouldn't have had to so young.*

*I still want to be noticed and praised. I do work really hard, but no matter how much people tell me I'm doing well, I don't feel comforted for long.*

*My patients are my biggest resource to boost my self-esteem and I really like the notes they sometimes write after they leave the hospital. Maybe I could save them and reread them. Somehow when something good about me is written down, I believe it more than when it's just said in passing.*

*How could I build on that? Well, my supervisor reviews my performance in writing and I could ask her to let me have a copy. I'd feel silly asking my husband to write to me, but I can keep writing to my child self and maybe someday I'll have the courage to ask other people who are close to me to write me some messages of praise.*

Like Nancy, lacking a firm sense of our personal power, we bolster our self-esteem by actions designed to prove to others and to ourselves that we are worthy. But while you cannot go back to your family roots and receive the treasuring that might have helped you feel better about yourself then, you can consistently show your caring for yourself by identifying what would contribute to healthy self-esteem now. Then you can focus on finding resources to meet those needs and fulfil them in a variety of ways. By seeking affirmation of your worth both from outer sources and from the inner wisdom you can tap in writing, you will increase your own personal power and your confidence in it.

# INDEPENDENCE: THE ENERGY THAT FUELS YOUR PERSONAL POWER

An independent spirit, based on healthy self-esteem, leads to the feeling of capability necessary to take initiative. If you can confidently think for yourself, without being fearful of the feelings and thoughts of others, you will feel free to take action. Thus independence provides the fuel to express your personal power.

Mature independence includes both the ability to stand on your own and the interdependent ability to work with others. But your journey towards independence began at ages two and three as a zigzag dance between dependent neediness (when you clung to your parent) and clumsy, insistent attempts at autonomy (when you screamed to get your own way). When you were in this contradictory stage, your parents' ability to support your growth by tolerating your extremes was crucial to your later independence.

If your parents couldn't let you go, you may have translated their clinging to you as 'You can't make it independently on your own' or 'I need *you* to take care of me.' If your parents didn't allow you to regress to clinging, you may have translated their push for your independence as rejection: 'You're on your own, now' or 'I won't be there for you.'

As an adult, your unresolved childhood difficulties with independence may show up in doubting your abilities, as it did with Marge, who apologises, or Nancy, who asks for reassurance. You may feel, like Paul, that you always have to prove yourself in order to earn your independent status. Like Marge, you may prefer to be a follower rather than a leader; conversely, like Craig, you may prefer to have control over others, needing the trappings of power, such as money and prestige, to make you feel independent.

A key factor in your family's support for your independence was the degree of involvement that family members had in each other's lives. This involvement can be described in terms of **family boundaries** – the separations between parent and child, brother and sister and grandparent and grandchild. In families, the closeness of living together and sharing blood ties can create two types of boundary problems.

Families who have **enmeshed boundaries** live as if their selves were overlapping circles; they identify with each other to the extent that they are not independent selves but are overinvolved in each other's lives. 'Everything you do is a reflection on me' is a fairly enmeshed parental statement. Families who have **walled boundaries** live as if their lives were circles with quite separate orbits; parents stay out of their children's lives to the extent that the latter may feel isolated or lonely. 'I learned to keep everything to myself' someone who grew up in a walled family might say.

Becoming your own person requires discovering your boundaries: knowing what you think, what you want, how you feel and what your interests, needs and talents are. Becoming independent in this way is a vital adult task but your family past may have interfered with your ability to set boundaries clearly.

If your family boundaries were enmeshed, you may be excessively dependent on others and lacking a clear sense of selfhood in relationships. If your boundaries were walled, you may act so independent that people cannot get close to you. In either case, if your independence was not well-supported by your family, you may suffer from self-doubt or fail to achieve what you otherwise could because you are ashamed not to be perfect.

Either way, your family's boundary characteristics contributed to your sense of independence or lack of it in adulthood. In an overinvolved family, characterised as having enmeshed boundaries, the members are more dependent than independent, impairing their personal power. As an example of what happens with these overlapping boundaries, Nick grew up very enmeshed with his mother and now his energies in adulthood focus on finding that one true love who will make him feel complete. He needs someone else in order to feel comfortable.

In contrast, in the underinvolved family, characterised as having walled boundaries, the members show more 'pseudoindependence'. Alison illustrates a pseudoindependent stance very well: she appears to need no one and to be very self-reliant. However, her emotional and psychological walls are up all the time, because she grew up in a family who kept one another at a distance and she does not know how to be close.

In the following exercises, you will describe the evolution of your independence as it was supported or blocked by your family's needs and characteristics. The first exercise connects that family history with your ability to be independent now, while the second focuses on physical and emotional boundaries in your past and present experience. In the third exercise, you will look for ways to encourage the growth of your independent spirit now and in the future.

## EXERCISE

## LEARNING TO STAND ON YOUR OWN TWO FEET

Your parents and other family members had many opportunities to encourage your developing independence and you can trace how your personal power was shaped by their actions and reactions.

A   Listed below are a number of experiences related to independence; circle those in which your family freed you to participate, and put an X through those in which they discouraged you from participating.

| | | |
|---|---|---|
| playing outside | crossing the road | going to a friend's house |
| choosing clothes | doing homework | spending money |
| going to camp | staying home alone | having a job |
| learning to drive | starting to date | handling problems |
| planning the future | thinking for yourself | expressing feelings |
| leaving home | | |

B   Write what you notice about how the balance of circles and Xs portrays your family's attitude towards your independence.

C   Look for patterns or connections between how your family treated you then and what role they or other influential people have in your life now. Describe how your independence level now relates to your family past.

Nick wrote:

*I've lived alone since I was 23. I make a decent living as a manager at the car factory. I vote according to my conscience. I look for what I want in a special lady to share my life. But when I looked at the circles and Xs on that list, I saw that my parents didn't often encourage me. Dad just wasn't around; he taught me to drive one Sunday in the supermarket car park and that's all I remember of his encouraging my independence. With every step I've taken towards independence, Mum has tried to act brave but cried or worried. I tell her that once I find the right girl and give her some grandchildren she'll be on top of the world but she shakes her head and says, 'Nickie, there aren't many good girls out there.' I wonder if I'm not getting married because I don't want to make Mum unhappy by choosing the wrong person.*

You may find, like Nick, that you are holding yourself back from independence now because of long-ago unspoken agreements between you and your parents. On the other hand, perhaps your family pushed you too hard to be independent. Someone like Craig, who is forceful and domineering as an adult, may have been given the message that he had better get what he could for himself, because there wouldn't be any help from the family. As with Nick, the good, attentive son, and Craig, the self-made man, your degree of independence may have been schooled to meet your family's needs even when it has worked against what would be natural or helpful for you.

## EXERCISE

## FAMILY BOUNDARIES: TOO CLOSE, TOO DISTANT, JUST RIGHT

Closely related to your family's reactions to your dependence or independence are the types of psychological boundaries and degree of separateness they established. When a family's boundaries are too close for the healthy development of independence, they may express this in physical intrusiveness (excessive worry about health or safety, lack of privacy or inappropriate touching), in mental merging (insistence on agreement, discouragement of divergent opinion or feelings), or in emotional overinvolvement (indirectly asking the children to take care of the parents' needs, being unable to let the children form their own relationships outside from the family).

A family whose boundaries are too rigid for the healthy development of independence may express this in physical isolation (not playing with or holding the children), in mental detachment (not showing interest in or support for the children's ideas) and in emotional underinvolvement (subtly abandoning the children by not demonstrating caring and empathy).

Somewhere in the middle of these two extremes, a healthy family respects privacy, encourages thinking for oneself and pours out attention and caring but can step back and let the children move away to develop their personal power when they are ready, even if the parents aren't.

You can discover how your family dealt with boundaries in the exercise that follows:

A  Create in writing an image that would portray your family's boundaries. This might be a fortress with stone walls, a bunch of puppies tumbling over each other, planets orbiting around a central sun, different colours juxtaposed in a painting or blobs of liquid paint being stirred to create one colour. Describe what you imagine in detail, noting why the various features remind you of your family and how the image reflects the daily reality of your household as you were growing up.

B  Write in answer to these questions: How have your early experiences with family boundaries affected your adult abilities to set and maintain comfortable, workable boundaries? If you could have more closeness or more distance in your life now, which would help you feel more independent?

One woman described her family as encased in suits of armour; they got up from the table after dinner, went to their individual rooms and did not talk again until breakfast. A man imagined his large, intrusive family as a group trapped on a treeless desert island; he said he couldn't even change clothes without at least one person barging in. Alison spoke up without her usual crispness and read:

*The image that came to my mind was of a strong, high fence with one gate, remote-controlled by my father. All the windows of the house behind the fence had bars; all the doors inside had locks. It was the ultimate in security. Similarly, in my family everyone had his place and kept to it. My father directed our efforts, planned our lives, and if we fulfilled his expectations, we left the family stronghold directed and independent. So I thought. But maybe I have erected my own fence and controlled gate. Would a really independent person need all that protection? A very worrying question.*

No one solution fits everyone concerning family boundaries. What feels just right for one family may feel too distant for another and what felt just right for you when you were ten may feel too contricting now that you are forty. The word *boundary* originally meant a path between fields. As an adult you can now determine the shape and size of your own path, creating a defined space between your private selfhood and the rest of the world, including your family. Clear and well-maintained boundaries promote contented and productive independence.

## EXERCISE

## DEVELOPING YOUR INDEPENDENT SPIRIT

As you remember how you grew towards independence in your family, you may make connections between your childhood home environment, your parents' attitudes then and your present circumstances. Similarly, defining your family's boundaries gives you valuable information about how you keep others close or at a distance today. You can decide what your needs for independence are and come up with ideas to adapt your present pattern towards a fuller use of this important source of your personal power.

A  Reviewing the previous exercise, describe how independent you now think you are. Use imagery to describe your style of expressing your independence: if you imagined your independent spirit as a flame of energy, what would it look like? If it's a bonfire almost out of control in some area of your life, what might you do to reassure yourself that you can give out light and heat without scorching yourself and other people? If it's a spark on damp wood, what can you do to fan the flames and provide the proper fuel?

B  Describe small, practical attitude changes or actions that you have a good chance of translating to your daily life now.

Marge, who introduced herself to the class as wanting 'to understand why I can never blow my own horn', wrote:

*Once I wrote about being one of the youngest in a really big family, I saw more clearly how we all tended to blend in together. In town, it was always, 'Oh, you're a Kelsey, which one are you?' I always feel I'm such a part of the whole that I can't stand out. When I do, I immediately apologise just in case something I did doesn't work out for the rest of the people.*

*I visualise my independent spirit as this cosy little fire burning inside a wood-burning stove. The heat comes out nicely but you never see the fire. I'm tending it well, adding enough fuel, but I'd like to be able to open the door and enjoy the light and the dancing flames. I feel more comfortable writing out my ideas than presenting them in a meeting. I don't apologise when I write; it sounds wishy-washy. Maybe a way to open the door on my independence a little would be to volunteer to write up some of our group's findings on our recent project.*

Your level of independence will always vary with your circumstances. In times of stress, it's natural and helpful to depend on your family and friends more heavily, although it can be hard to ask for support when you feel vulnerable. In times of prosperity and success, you will feel more confident about exercising your personal power by thinking and acting on your own. Self-esteem and independence result in feeling free to think and act – the third component of personal power, **initiative**.

# INITIATIVE: THE EXPRESSION OF YOUR PERSONAL POWER

The final expression of your personal power is your ability to initiate and take action. You can have high self-esteem yet lack independence. And you can have both high self-esteem and an independent spirit but not take action to express yourself and make your mark. Full personal power includes the hopeful confidence of self-esteem, the dynamic vitality of independence and the initiative to plan what you want and take action.

It was your initiative that pushed you to roll over and sit up as a baby and learn to walk as a toddler. According to developmental theorist Erik Erikson, you began focusing intensively on initiative when you were four and five years old. Children that age are often 'reined in' by their parents because their urge for action makes them challenge all limits.

Erikson described the intensity of childhood initiative by stressing that 'initiative adds to autonomy the quality of undertaking, planning and attacking a task for the sake of being active and on the move.' If your parents dealt with your drive to be 'on the move' by proving guidelines while encouraging your efforts, you developed the courage to try out new things, to pursue satisfying your curiosity and putting your dreams into action. The strength of your initiative today is related to your parents' encouragement of this drive.

If your parents reacted to this urge to be 'on the move' with alarm, anger, discouragement or disinterest, your ability to take initiative did not have a clear field in which to develop. If they were excessively alarmed by your enegy and drive, you may have learned to hold back on your impulses and plans out of fear. If they were extremely upset and angry at your wild and out-of-bounds behaviour and attempted to control it, you may have acquired a strong sense of guilt. If your parents consistently discouraged you from trying something different, you may have learned that the status quo was more important than new actions and ideas. If they rarely showed interest in your actions, you may have learned that your efforts would not bring you recognition and approval.

If you have carried negative family teachings about initiative into adulthood, you may struggle with problems related to this area. Like Marge, you may set limits on what you believe you can do out of old fears. You may have a strong need for control, wanting to shut out others, like Alison did, or dominate them, like Craig. Like Nick, you may have trouble moving out of the status quo even though you think you know what you want. You may seek approval somewhat compulsively, like Nancy, looking for evidence of others' interest and praise.

In all these circumstances, your difficulties now related to taking initiative may be due to your feelings about your family's reactions to your efforts. These feelings may still be painfully held inside you, a frozen pattern of blocked energy, caused by stored unhappiness. Because you avoid taking action that would stir up those painful feelings, you have 'a disabled will' impairing your personal power at the source. Breaking out of the frozen pattern and claiming your natural initiative requires confronting any feelings of fear, anger or sadness from your famly past.

This section's exercises encourage you to look for the patterns of reaction to initiative in your family past and to discover new patterns you can set in motion. The first exercise takes inventory of your family members' styles of initiative, sorting out the helpful and harmful qualities you have inherited from them. In the second exercise, you will break down the steps of will and action to survey where your own current style of initiative needs to be adapted or changed. The third exercise prompts you to consider positive, practical applications to initiate your personal power in your family and work life now.

## EXERCISE

## TAKING STOCK OF YOUR FAMILY'S DRIVE

Families, with their need for harmony, tend to value mid-range expressions of initiative and drive, sometimes calling the very active one 'controlling' or 'ruthless' or the very inactive ones 'timid' or 'lazy'. These labels, whether placed on you or someone else in the family, affected your willingness to take initiative. Changing your own approach to initiative now will mean that old labels and roles get shaken up – first inside you, then in the family's interactions. You can be better prepared to meet these reactions by writing about who followed and who led in your family.

A Listed below are a number of descriptions of qualities related to initiative. Circle those that fit a family member in the past and put the person's name by them.

| | | |
|---|---|---|
| go-getter | passive | lazy |
| scared rabbit | hyperactive | bossy |
| wilful | follower | selfish |
| leader | dictator | obedient |
| headstrong | hesitant | ambitious |
| inventive | dutiful | creative |

B When you have finished, look at the variety of roles played and write your responses to these questions:

- Which of these qualities and roles did you inherit, unwittingly adopt or consciously copy?
- Which qualities best describe your approach to taking initiative in your life now?
- Are there qualities you need to play down or adopt now?
- What small action could you take towards doing so?

Marge wrote:

*I could identify all the qualities I circled either with my mother or with my father. Mum used to take-charge, doling out chores, punishment and rewards to us all with a lot of energy. My father, on the other hand, was more passive, a follower. She bossed him around as if he was one of the children sometimes, and he dutifully complied with her orders. Her big word was* co-operation. *Do what you do for the good of the whole group; otherwise, you're being selfish.*

*I realise now that I'm a confused mix of my parents' qualities. I can't help taking some leadership in a group because I know how to organise things after growing up in a family of twelve. But then I feel apologetic, as if maybe I'm hogging the spotlight. My colleagues encourage my leadership, so I don't think I really am too bossy.*

If you remove the critical labels your family placed on the qualities related to initiative, you can see that all those qualities are useful for different purposes. The quality of being able to focus on yourself, which some families label *selfish*, can allow you to use your resources wisely. The quality of being a *follower* of someone else's well-thought-out plan can save energy to fulfil goals you believe in. The quality of passionate commitment, which some families label *ambitious*, is necessary to see big projects through to completion.

In developing your initiative now, what matters is your commitment to a balanced perspective on taking action, appreciating the qualities of reserve and drive that you learned about in your family. You can also identify parts of the cycle of initiative where you might have trouble and learn how to work with them more effectively.

## EXERCISE

## EVALUATING YOUR CYCLE OF INITIATIVE

Initiative takes shape in a circular sequence of stages. The planning you do at first is followed by initial action, which requires follow-through. Crucial to your action's continuation through time is assessment, which gives rise to further planning, after which the cycle begins again.

Each of us has especially strong talents and skills for particular parts of the cycle. We also tend to neglect or undervalue other parts that are uncomfortable or difficult for us. For example, Nick loves to plan but has trouble taking initial action. Craig likes to initiate action and have the people who work for him do all the follow-through, which doesn't interest him. Paul is so busy that he doesn't stop for assessment, which might help him use his energy more efficiently.

You can discover how well you do with different parts of the cycle of initiative by recalling several significant actions you have taken or projects and plans you have carried out. You can include personal items, such as a romantic relationship or a creative hobby, as well as family patterns, such as celebrating holidays, and professional concerns, such as career planning. For each endeavour, look at how you moved through each of the stages: planning; initial action; follow-through; assessment; further planning.

1  Write about your areas of natural ability and comfort, as well as those of difficulty and discomfort.
2  Choose one minor action that you could take to make a difficult area more comfortable, such as setting aside one evening every few months to assess how well your plans are going, including some of your favourite things (a good dinner, a bubble bath or going to bed early with a book, for example) as a reward for developing your assessment skills.

Nancy wrote:

*I get stuck after I take that initial action. I ask other people what they think or if what I did was all right rather than using my own observations and intuition. Once I get feedback from others, I use it to assess how I'm doing and plan what to do next. I suspect that my parents' drinking meant that they didn't notice a lot of actions I initiated. I'm still trying to get enough attention to feel secure about pursuing what I start.*

*Maybe I could plan both the initial action and some things I might do for follow-through. Then when I got to that time in the cycle I'd already have committed myself to the next step. If I have some ideas stored up ahead, I'll be more likely to follow through. That seems like an awfully little step, but it is likely to work, so maybe it's better to start small.*

Whatever part of the initiation cycle you feel you need to strengthen, you can increase your chances of success by building on your strengths, as Nancy did through her reliance on the planning she does well, in order to sustain your efforts through the more challenging stages of the cycle.

**EXERCISE**

## TAKING THE INITIATIVE: FULFILLING YOUR DREAMS

The last lines of Mary Oliver's poem 'The Summer Day' ask: 'Tell me, what is it you plan to do with your one wild and precious life?' You may not have received the encouragement from your family to try to fulfil your dreams. If not, you can begin to take steps to realise them now by exploring the poet's question.

1 Start by finishing this sentence: 'If I were really as creative as I could dream of being, this is what I would do . . .'
2 Imagine taking initiative in the ways you would need to in order to fulfil these dreams and write about what would happen.
3 Look at your dream with an eye to current reality. Are there elements that are already present in some small way in your life now? Are there elements that you could bring into your life fairly easily? How would you take action to do so, thinking through the stages in the cycle of initiative?
4 Sometimes you can tell in advance where your dream may run into old blocks or limits related to your family teachings; acknowledge that possibility and explore ways to get yourself unstuck if that happens. Remember: dream big – take small steps.

Paul wrote:

*I dream of working out a better way for social programmes to serve people in the community. I volunteer for about eight different voluntary organisations, and they all reinvent the wheel each time there's a new head of staff or a new set of regulations. They waste their energies trying to find individual solutions when they have more in common with each other than they realise.*

*By writing down what I've learned about the duplication of effort, I might be able to dream up some sort of central clearinghouse for pooling resources and solving problems. I have that knowledge already in my head but I'll have to make time to get it out. If I cut back on the activities that don't relate to my particular dream, maybe I'd make enough time to take some initiative on this clearinghouse idea. I can feel excitement bubbling around in me and I think this might actually be a better use of my energy.*

As you learn to bypass family patterns that block your initiative, you will feel a greater sense of purpose behind everything you do. This meaning will keep you connected to your family roots but directed towards your personal dreams. It is these dreams that fuel the strength of your personal power.

# PERSONAL POWER PAST, PRESENT AND FUTURE: ROOTS AND WINGS

You may have a more positive set of associations to the word *power* after exploring its components in this chapter's exercises. One group of students contributed the words *vitality, potential, responsible leadership, passion* and *following my heart*. You might take a moment to jot down your own revised impressions of what personal power is as well as those you noted at the beginning of the chapter that still seem accurate.

You have discovered that your personal power has been formed in the feelings and memories that are rooted in your family experiences of self-esteem, independence and initiative. From reviewing those feelings and memories, you now have a clearer sense of the foundation of your personal power.

Your personal power is at work in your life in the present, reflecting both your connections to your family and your divergence from their influence. Every day, you are in the process of drawing on your confidence, defining your independent perspective and expressing your viewpoint in your behaviour.

In this final exercise, you can sum up what you have discovered about the role of personal power in your family past, your life now and your imagined future.

## EXERCISE

### ENVISIONING YOUR PERSONAL POWER THROUGH TIME

For this exercise, you can use both words and images to describe the roots of your personal power in your family past, the trunk and branchings of that power in the present and the changing skyscape of your imagined personal power in the future. As a child, you probably often drew trees with roots, trunks, branches, birds, clouds and sky. Now you can play with words to portray these symbols of your personal power, draw what you imagine, or do both. Often students draw what they see in their minds' eyes first, then write in words, phrases or sentences on top of the drawing or in the white spaces.

A 1   Try to recall signs of strength and health in your family roots. Perhaps your grandmother contributed to your self-esteem, your father encouraged your independence and your older brother modelled how to take initiative.

2  Write or draw what you want to keep in conscious memory from your family's teachings about power.

B  Look for signs of strength and health in the personal power that you feel today. Your co-workers may have taught you to trust your professional instincts, increasing your self-worth. You may have demonstrated your independence by ending a relationship that was draining your energy. Your children may be pushing you to take initiatve, encouraging you directly by their belief in you. Write or draw what you want to keep in your present awareness about your personal power.

C 1  Imagine the distant future, visualising signs of the personal power you want to have. You may picture increased self-esteem as a sky with only a few nonthreatening clouds. You may dream that you will someday be able to heal your broken places and take wing as a more independent spirit. Or perhaps you see the continuity of your creative ideas as a flock of migrating birds, always returning to your home ground.

2  Write or draw what you want to have in the future as imagined fulfilment of your personal power.

D  When you have finished, write any additional comments that will help you remember the meaning of what you have described in writing or drawing.

E  It is especially important to keep pieces of creative work like this that integrate dimensions of your identity and purpose, so store this piece of writing for future reference.

Marge summed up her personal power portrait:

*The roots part of my drawing was very full, almost more than I could integrate, all packed together. By describing my present state of personal power, I could see that my trunk and branches brought up some of those helpful attributes from the roots but needed to grow farther out. Finally, at 36, I am beginning to develop my independence, and it's exciting. I don't want to fill up my future with many projected ideas or images now. I only drew a few drifting birds to symbolise their power to look down from a distance and see the whole picture. I want to feel uncrowded in my future, to build slowly towards future expressions of creativity. That to me will be the essence of my personal power – space and time to express my identity in ways that will echo my heritage and be stamped with my uniqueness.*

As with your sense of self, your sense of strength accompanies you throughout your life, continuing to develop from its family roots. While it is natural to feel powerless in the face of some of your problems, you can draw on what you have learned in this chapter to determine where family patterns cut off this power. When this happens, you now have ways to get in touch with and mobilise your resources from the components of self-esteem, independence and initiative. As you do so, you will develop and gain increased access to your personal power.

In the next chapter, you will investigate the stories, secrets and silences that are at the heart of every family. You have dipped into the memories of your past partly to solve the mystery of what your family experience meant and how your past and present fit together. Getting to the roots of your family truth is not a once-and-for-all endeavour, for your recollections and interpretations shift and change as you mature and gain new wisdom and perspective. However, you can understand yourself and your family better by consciously choosing to focus on and investigate your family mythology. In a clearer, fuller portrayal of the truth of your family experience, there is healing potential and promise for future change.

# CHAPTER 7

# THE TRUTH OF YOUR FAMILY EXPERIENCE

Your desire to understand the patterns of your family past in order to see where you are repeating unhealthy patterns in your life now has been one of the driving forces in the reading and writing you have done so far with this book. In the preceding chapters, as you clarified how your family shaped your communication styles, your sense of self and your personal power, you cleared the road back in time, perceiving more fully the influence of the past. You also opened up the road into the future by discovering what choices and changes you wanted to make.

However, when you deal with particularly persistent and painful family patterns, your awareness of where they came from and your wishes and plans to change them may not be enough to keep the road clear. Completely facing the painful truth of your family experience can become a roadblock. When you approach a newly realised truth about your family, you may not want to acknowledge or act on it for one or more of these reasons:

- It may hurt someone.
- It's too painful for you.
- You have been told not to explore that area.
- It may make someone angry.
- It feels frightening or dangerous.
- You doubt whether you have the real truth.
- You might lose something or someone.
- You might have to change.

All of these are powerful reasons for being reluctant to tackle a painful truth. All are also valid possibilities that you may have to face. However, they are excellent clues to how your family dealt with their problems.

The more your family wanted to avoid thinking or talking about their painful truths or acting to change them, the more they reacted with reasons such as those above. If your parents communicated these reasons for avoidance either directly or indirectly, you probably internalised their reluctance and the family status quo was preserved. In Chapter 3, you examined the effect of the family trance – your shared view of reality – on your ability to write your observations, memories and feelings. You will look more deeply in this chapter at the truth of your family experience. In seeking your individual truth, you will find clarity and healing potential.

The issue of truth in families is generally complex because it is almost impossible to come to one truth that everyone in the family perceives similarly and accepts equally. The simpler issue is to find *your own truth* of your family experience; it may not be the same as the generally accepted family version but it is your most reliable guide to change that works and lasts. The first important principle for dealing with the painful truths in your family experience is: **all members of a family perceive truth differently.**

A young woman named Jenny wrote that everyone in her family agrees that her father drinks too much. However, each person describes that fact so differently that their responses taken together sound more like disagreement:

*My father himself feels ashamed and says he's weak. My mother always insists that it's just that my dad has a poor tolerance for alcohol, while my younger sister calls him a falling-down drunk. My older brother says that my nagging mother drove him to drink and my little brother thinks that if he hadn't been born, my father wouldn't have felt the economic pressure of four children that made him drink. Me? I'm confused. I defend everybody and don't know what I think.*

We also interpret painful family truths based on our positions within the family and the pressures we feel from within and from family members. A second principle states: **all versions of the truth in a family stem from attempts to adapt.**

In Jenny's family, the motivations behind the varying interpretations might break down like this: her father's view of himself as weak keeps him stuck in his alcoholism because he doesn't believe he's strong enough to change. Her mother's rationalisation about alcohol tolerance is her attempt to present an acceptable façade because if she acknowledges her pain she will become overwhelmed. Her older brother is afraid to get stuck in his father's role as head of the household and he thinks he can break free by blaming his mother. Her younger sister is angry enough to blurt out the darkest view of her father's drinking and her anger keeps her from recognising how sad and abandoned she feels. Her younger brother feels as though his father's drinking is his fault; by taking blame on himself, he can keep trying to fix the problem by being good. Jenny has tried to take care of everyone and abandon no one but in the process she has abandoned herself. Her confusion is a signal from within that she must find her own truth.

All of these family members' interpretations of the truth are attempts to adapt to painful circumstances. You, as well as Jenny and her family members, may have constructed a view of painful family realities, your role in them and your feelings about them that was the safest or most workable perspective for that time in the past.

Unfortunately, your life now may be hampered by old versions of painful truth. If you are ruled by these outdated, unexamined or unchallenged perspectives on these family truths, your problems may now include:

- **confusion and a lack of sense of control over your life.** Jenny's reaction to her family's varying views is an example of confusion; another student describes his family's agreement that the family business has to come first in everyone's life as a controlling constraint.
- **protecting others to the detriment of your well-being.** Members of a family in which the wife unexpectedly died protect one another from their feelings by idealising her memory, when she was actually a very difficult person; Jenny's mother's making excuses for her alcoholic husband is another example of destructive protection.
- **a chronic high level of anxiety and worry.** One family worries over every detail of daily functioning, such as mealtimes and chores; anxieties about the real, larger problems don't get addressed.
- **being cut off from your feelings.** In one family in which both parents are depressed much of the time, the children learn to act cheery or comical, no matter how they feel; in another family, a raging husband and father so frightens his wife and children that they seldom feel their own anger.
- **repeating destructive behaviour without understanding why.** A woman who idealised her father, unable to reconcile the family story that he was a romantic hero with her true feelings of disappointment in him, repeatedly seeks the impossible from her relationships with men, then finds herself alone.

If you feel confusion, protection, anxiety, numbness and self-destructiveness when you think about painful family truths, you may be out of touch with your own truth. However, if you uncover and work through your feelings, you will be more likely to understand why things happened as they did and change your course successfully in the future. To adapt a classic saying, **your own truth will set you free**.

Hidden within the labyrinth of family 'truth' and myth is your own story, your own truth. You can move towards uncovering more of that truth through the exercises in this chapter. In the first section, you will look at the **stories**, **secrets** and **silences** that went into your family's version of painful truths. You may have grown up comforted, entertained, mystified, angered or frightened by these family stories and myths, but you probably have not examined them from any distance.

Stories, secrets and silences become family myth – and the word *myth* reflects not a lie but a deep layer of truth, an explanation for why things happen as they do, an imaginative perspective shared by those who believe in the myth.

Family **stories** recount remarkable moments in a family's history or illustrate family characteristics in a larger-than-life, legendary fashion. They can convey any emotional tone – humorous (the Christmas when everyone spilled, dropped and broke things), defiant (the time Dad stood up to the unethical landlord), sad (the death of the family's favourite dog) or proud (the way Grandma and Grandpa kept their shop going through the Depression).

Family stories create a sense of shared identity and solidarity: this is who we are; this is how we feel. Their effects vary depending on the helpful or harmful qualities that are being held up as family characteristics. You can examine your family stories for initial clues about your family's version of the truth.

Family **silences** cover painful truths about the family that are kept unspoken. You and your family members may all have known that Mother couldn't handle any mention of her dead brother or that politics was a forbidden topic because an election argument had split apart two branches of the family, or that your younger sister was slightly retarded. You all may have known the truth, but if you kept silent about it, you shared a potent myth whose power derived from its hiddenness. Looking at what sort of material your family keeps silence about is an excellent way to understand undercurrents of the family truth that may still be affecting you without your knowledge.

Family **secrets** concern material that is kept hidden and that not everyone knows or whose explanation has been lost over time. You may have wondered all your life why your parents eloped when all the other siblings had church weddings, or why Uncle Jim's grave is in Brighton when Aunt Rachel says he died at home, or why you and your brother were sent to live with your grandmother for a year when you were very young. Family secrets can cover both material that has little significance to you and events that have had great influence on you. As with family stories and silences, you can begin to shape your own truth by calrifying the meanings in your family's secrets.

In the second section, you will focus on your growing-up years with your family and examine the **facts** (concrete details you clearly remember or know) and the **myths** (the generally accepted family version behind painful truths). You can sort out what you need to know to fashion your own version of the truth, comparing the explanations that you were given with the feelings and hunches you now have in response to family myth. You can discover what you need to know now by paying attention to the intensity of your curiosity and your physical reactions as you investigate family themes and stories. For example, Cathy commented:

*My curiosity was certainly most intensely focused on why my parents divorced when I was seven. However, when I started writing out the few memories I have from that time, I began having strong physical reactions – my stomach tightened, it was hard to breathe and I felt afraid. I decided to stop writing and wait but I woke up next morning with a memory of my parents' arguing about something my mother found in my dad's wallet. I think he was having an affair.*

As Cathy did, you can follow your instincts to explore what family themes or stories seem to hold the most importance for you at this time, knowing that you need not and can never arrive at a final conclusion. Your version of the truth of painful family experience will change throughout your life. Your perspective will encompass more emotions as well as more facts; your level of understanding will broaden and deepen. Gathering information, acknowledging emotions and anchoring new versions of your truth by writing them down or sharing them with others forms a blueprint for the ongoing cycle of truth-seeking.

Writing of the constructive nature of the truth-seeking process, psychologist Carl Rogers asserts:

**The facts are friendly. . . .** Every bit of evidence that one can acquire, in any area, leads one that much closer to what is true.

In the third section, you will continue the truth-seeking process by writing about both the **hurt** and the **healing** that come with discovering your own version of your family's painful truths. At first, as you discover more about the painful events and relationships, as well as how you really felt about them, you will probably be more aware of the pain they caused you. Psychiatrist Alice Miller states: 'The truth always causes much pain before giving us a new sphere of freedom.'

Your pain comes from releasing perceptions and emotions that you had blocked or ignored. It is like the tingling and ache of an arm or leg that has been 'asleep' and is now being restored to full circulation. Cathy referred to the initially painful impact of remembering hints of her father's affair and her hope for healing in keeping more truth in her awareness:

*The hurt came tumbling out with a cascade of tiny memories, hints and clues that I pushed down and ignored before. I think I even saw the woman he was having an affair with once, but that memory's not ready to come – or I'm not ready for it. What I do see is how much this has affected me, how suspicious I have been of my boyfriends, how strongly I react to infidelity of any kind. Perhaps some healing can come along with the pain.*

In the final section, you will put some of that healing to work in your own life by summing up your progress in seeking your truth of painful family experiences. Psychologists David Feinstein and Stanley Krippner describe three stages of uncovering this individual version of the truth, which they call 'personal mythology', your inner story. The first stage is **your guiding myth** – the story that has formed and directed your life in the past. In the context of your roots, your guiding myth is your family's version of the story. The second stage is your **counter-myth**, an alternative version of family myths that acknowledges parts of the story that may have been left out of the guiding myth. Since your counter-myth usually releases blocked emotions, it does not have the clarity and distance that comes with time and further seeking. The third stage involves what Feinstein and Krippner call a **unifying mythic vision**, a version of the story that encompasses past and present views while looking towards your future.

Describing her own changing versions of the truth, Cathy stated:

*My guiding myth was that my parents divorced for unknown reasons and that I wasn't particularly affected. My counter-myth was that my father was an adulterous traitor and that my mother hurt me by refusing to acknowledge the truth. My new truth goes something like this: My dad had some character flaws and did some things that hurt me badly. My mother couldn't face up to her pain and that hurt me too. I still feel angry and sad. But I survived the hurt, and I am determined that my own relationships will be better the more I can heal from that early betrayal.*

Cathy not only summed up her past in a new way but she also stated how her present life has been affected. Finally, she articulated her determination to heal, and her decision will help her choose future actions that continue the healing process. You too can sum up your version of the truth at this point in your life and decide how to put your truths into action every day.

Psychologist Rollo May writes: 'It seems that there are potentialities within us for health that are not released until we make a conscious decision.' By making a conscious decision to write about painful family truths, you release healthy potential and live more fully in touch with your own reality.

# YOUR FAMILY'S STORIES, SILENCES AND SECRETS

When someone asks you where you grew up, your answer is probably along the lines of 'in a flat in Chiswick' or 'on a farm in Sussex'. While that answer is true, you also grew up in the shelter of your family's stories. Your family's explanations of why things happened as they did – their family myths – were the structure of your inner reality. All families' story structures have both bright, open spaces and places no one likes to talk about, dark corners no one visits.

Family therapist Emily Marlin writes of the drama of a family's story structure:

Truth is stranger than fiction, and your family history is rich in tales of love and war, mystery and adventure. What makes this drama so interesting is that we're players in it. Deeply ingrained in all of us are rules of human standards of social interaction, belief systems and certain expectations. These have been passed down to us in 'scripts' from our predecessors. Families have different scripts and in any one family there may be several sets of directions. Usually these scripts strengthen family life. They cast our families in a very appealing light; they make them brave, passionate and successful. But sometimes they portray a dark or sinister view of family life, full of anger, suspicions and resentment.

When you focus on your family's story structure with some clarity and distance, you will notice how your parents and other adults in your childhood family emphasised certain qualities and events concerning family truths and played down others that they preferred not to have associated with the family image. Keeping in mind the principle that all versions of a family's story are attempts to adapt to the family's circumstances, you will discover two mechanisms that re-shape family stories: **denial** and **distortion**.

Denial is a refusal to acknowledge pieces of your reality, a helpful tool when that truth would otherwise be intolerable but a hindrance when you need to break out of a limiting approach to life. In writing about family versions of the truth of her father's alcoholism, Jenny observed that her mother's mother, who often stayed with the family, completely denied her son-in-law's disease. She would retreat to the guest room when Jenny's father was drunk, and changed the subject when anyone brought up the problem. Jenny remembers her grandmother saying flatly to her sister, who spoke most directly about his drinking, 'You are imagining bad things'. Jenny also noticed that her grandmother's denial influenced her mother's distortion.

Distortion alters the facts of a truth to make them more palatable to the person doing the distorting or to others sharing difficult circumstances. Jenny's mother's habit of saying her husband had little tolerance for alcohol was one form of distortion. During her own mother's visits, Jenny's mother distorted even more, saying that her husband was 'resting' when he was passed out and phoning his boss with excuses of illness when he coulnd't make it to work.

In your own family, both denial and distortion probably provided a defence for you to use at times against painful aspects of family circumstances, giving you a version of the truth that you could more easily live with. In the long run, of course, both denial and distortion hamper your ability to know your own truth and to live fully. Each of the following exercises allows you to sort through your family's versions of truths, clarifying how you have been affected by their story structures and beginning to formulate your own truth.

## EXERCISE

## YOUR FAMILY'S STORIES

Family life has an inherently dramatic quality, with each family's conversations, attitudes and behaviour like a self-enclosed stage portrayal of a version of reality, played out on constructed sets and in costumes chosen to enhance the themes of the drama. You can begin to acquire an observer's perspective on your family versions of the truth by examining their stories in the context of a stage portrayal.

A Think back over your shared family life as if it were some kind of drama and your life inside the family home were the setting of a theatrical production.

B Write a description of the following:

- What kind of drama was your family portraying through the stories that they told about their life together?
- What sort of setting would be appropriate for your family's stories?
- What role did you have in the drama?
- Looking at your family's stories from the audience now, how did the mechanisms of distortion or denial shape their version of the family drama?
- How have you been affected through the years and how are you still affected by your participation in the presentation of your family's stories?

John, a salesman and aspiring writer in his mid-thirties, wrote:

*The image that came immediately was of a Hollywood film set – spacious building fronts on a tree-lined street – but they're only false fronts. Behind each of the cardboard house fronts are wooden supports, an earth floor, cables and miscellaneous equipment. My family had one mode of presentation to the outside world and another totally different reality behind the front door. At home, my parents squabbled a lot and paid very little attention to us kids. There was distortion of our qualities and achievements in our parents' stories about us to outsiders and complete denial of any of the less-flattering aspects. As a child, I took pleasure in blurting out the wrong thing in public; as an adolescent, I was constantly shooting my mouth off about the hypocrisy. My parents were delighted when I lied about my age and left home to join the Army. I've been left with a lingering fascination as well as repulsion for the difference between the hype and the reality. I run up against that as a salesman, having to present our products in a certain light, and I long to be a writer who just speaks truth with no compromises.*

As with John, you probably have a mixture of feelings about your family's stories. Some of the ways you and the others shaped your version of the truth were so clever or so well-suited to your needs at the time that you have to admire your family's ingenuity and spirit in stubbornly persisting in the chosen patterns of their drama. The more that you can view your family's stories as if from a balcony seat, the more you can gain the perspective to become a more effective witness of your own version of the painful family truths. You can also use an observer's ear to listen for the silences in your family stories.

## EXERCISE

## YOUR FAMILY'S SILENCES

In every family, some things are so painful they are never discussed. Unlike the material in family secrets, the subjects of family silences may be right out in the open but no one is supposed to notice them or talk about them. Family members live by the assumption that it is forbidden, dangerous or disloyal to mention these truths.

A  Make a list of some unspoken truths in your family, including:

- the impolite ('We weren't supposed to comment on Grandma's bad breath.');
- the eccentric ('Mother found the colour orange disgusting, so we never ate orange foods.');
- the judgemental ('We considered ourselves better than other people.');
- the destructive ('Our parents teased our youngest brother terribly about his clumsiness and slowness to learn and we were punished if we commented or defended him.').

B  After you have made your list, write some reflections, considering these questions: What were the consequences of these family silences? How is your present life still affected by this unspoken hidden material that was under the surface?

A young man named Andy expanded on the major item on his list:

*We just didn't talk about people's mistakes and failures – anyone's, but particularly those in our family. When my younger sister was less than two years old, my mother accidentally overturned a pan of boiling hot soup in the kitchen. My sister was playing on the floor and her left hand and arm were severely burned. Although she has had plastic surgery, her hand is still disfigured and partly disabled. She always wears long sleeves to cover her arm and she rarely uses that hand. We have never, ever talked about that horrible accident and we closed ranks as a family to protect Mum and Tina. If a stranger asked about it, we refused to answer. If a new acquaintance asked me about it, that person did not become my friend. I remember feeling torn when I brought my fiancée home to meet the family and she asked me about it. When I muttered, 'Childhood accident', I felt such guilt – but also a kind of release. Keeping silence has been a burden that has definitely caused me problems at work and in close relationships.*

As in Andy's case, the more that a family puts emotional energy into keeping silence about something, the more that fact or event takes on the characteristics of a family secret. The layers of distortion and denial that build up around a family secret force you to proceed slowly and patiently in investigating it, but you can begin to understand your family's truth more fully only by looking into the hidden areas.

## EXERCISE

## YOUR FAMILY'S SECRETS

Secrets usually cover truths associated with guilt and shame. If Andy's family hadn't had the evidence of Tina's scarred hand in front of them, they probably would have made that childhood accident into a family secret, because the mother felt an intolerable weight of guilt about it. Her guilt about the incident was mixed with shame about her very worthiness as a mother and a person. The others supported that distortion by maintaining silence. In the same way, a family can keep a secret directly by covering up and distorting truths they want to keep hidden; they can keep one secret indirectly by avoiding the hidden area, denying the existence of these painful truths.

A Write a list of small and large hidden family truths that you are aware of or suspect were kept secret in your family. Some may seem minor ('My dad changed our family name'); some may be only fragments of a possible secret ('There was something wrong in my parents' marriage'); and others may concern a skeleton in the cupboard ('My dad cheated on our income tax and never got caught') or a black-sheep family member ('My Uncle Daniel spent time in prison for fraud').

B  Notice which of these family secrets intrigues or bothers you the most now and write for five to ten minutes about it, letting all your thoughts, feelings and speculations flow out in a random fashion.

C  Although you don't have to resolve them, keep these questions in mind as you write: Does this secret affect my life today? What does this hidden area in my family have to tell me at this time? You may find that your musings lead you to some guesses or conclusions; if so, write them down as part of telling the story in your own way.

Julia, who described herself as 'the family confidante, the one everyone talked to', wrote:

*The fact that my mother was addicted to various prescription medications for most of my childhood is still the hidden area with the most power for me. My mother's brother was a pharmacist, and she got pill samples from him, sometimes directly, sometimes behind his back. He was terrified of being ruined professionally, so we all covered up for her. The worst secret, the one she said she told no one but me, was that she wished none of us kids had ever been born. When I first told my husband that two years ago, I cried for several days and frightened myself. I've been getting some counselling and I understand more about how painfully affected I was by what seemed to be a denial of my existence. I covered over for years, telling myself that was just the drugs talking, but I was hurt all the same.*

Like, Julia, you may find that family secrets peel back like the layers of an onion, with another truth beneath each layer. However, you can get to the core of the secret with the most meaning for you. You will find that recalling and writing what you have long held on to will allow you to begin to let go. In the next section, you can assess what more you need to explore or clarify about the truth of your family experience.

# WHAT DO YOU NEED TO KNOW NOW?

You have several excellent internal gauges to help you discover what you need to know about your family truths so that you can resolve present problems and grow in new ways in the future. The first gauge is your **thoughts**; the second is your **bodily sensations**; and the third is your **feelings**.

Focusing on what preoccupies your mind and fills your thoughts when you consider painful family truths is a gauge of direction. Perhaps you can't stop thinking about why you've never been close to your brother or wondering why you are so anxious when you're with your aunt. By writing such thoughts, you allow them to develop more fully and find out more of what you need to know and why you need to know it.

Because they are not always under your conscious control, your physical sensations are also excellent gauges of when you are getting close an important truth. Muscle tension, headaches, stomach butterflies and dizziness are just a few of your internal signals that something significant and powerful is at hand. Before you could understand things in words or decode the language your parents used, you took in what happened to you through your physical sensations and they can still be reliable guides to family truths.

The strength of your feelings also provides vital clues to the truths in your family past. If you can glibly explain why things happened as they did without much emotional response, you may be relating the family version rather than your authentic experience. But trying to explain why some aspect of an old family story upsets you is an excellent gauge that you are getting close to a family truth. Your feelings can be relied on to lead you further as you acknowledge them and write them.

Two specific feelings are also clues that can help you discover family truths: **confusion** and **disenchantment**. Paradoxically, you can find out what you need to know by noticing what confuses you the most. To adapt to the family version of the truth, you may have narrowed your perceptions and restricted your thoughts to what would fit with the family view. Thus anything that didn't fit was confusing, and you might have simply dismissed the confusing aspects and stuck to what you felt secure in knowing. The more some family myth confuses you now or creates confusing feelings you can't explain, the more likely a painful truth lies underneath the confusion.

A final guide to seeking your personal truth comes when you experience disenchantment with your old family view of reality.

When you start searching for your own truth as distinct from your family's version of your experience, you can expect to hear the clamour of old enchantments – expectations, obligations and fears – competing with the voice of your instincts. However, as you come out from the old spell by describing just what you need and want to know in the present, you will become more finely tuned to the sound of your own story. The following two exercises will teach you how to use your own perceptions to advance your version of your family truth.

## EXERCISE

## WRITING ABOUT CONFUSION AND CONFLICTING VIEWS

Rather than trying to eliminate the sources of your confusion or your internalised views of old family truths, you can clarify the confusion and differentiate others' views from your own by putting them down in words. The first part of this exercise focuses on confusion as a signal that you can uncover more of your truth; the second part helps you sort out your conflicting views.

A 1  Search within for any vague feelings of discomfort and confusion you have about some problem in your current life or some person or period from your past.

2  Home in what the confusion feels like and describe it in words. For instance, if you vaguely know you are having trouble at work because you get confused and uncomfortable when your boss gives you orders, imagine yourself at your workplace. Visualise your boss walking towards your desk or office. Start writing what you see, hear, smell, taste, touch, feel, guess or decide as he or

she approaches. It might be his face coming towards you, a sick lurch in your stomach at the smell of her perfume, a buzzing in your ears or an idea you will fail. Try to describe the most intense physical and emotional reaction you feel towards this triggering situation.

3  Describe other times you may have experienced this same feeling.

4  Draw any comparisons or conclusions you come to about this feeling of discomfort or confusion. Then you can let the feeling rest for now. In writing about it, you have signalled your inner self, the guardian of your defences, that you are open to discovering the truth behind the discomfort or confusion. Something will become clear in time once you have started this process.

A legal secretary named Kristin, who had recently become engaged, wrote:

*I have been feeling uncomfortable and confused since my fiancé took me to meet his family last month. Recalling my feelings when I met them at a restaurant there, I remember feeling nervous but happy at first. There's a blurry buzz of introductions but something starts to bother me – it's a sound, the sound of someone's voice. Oh, it's his Uncle Keith talking to me. He's a handsome, polite man, but something about his voice makes my hands go cold and my stomach get tight. I hadn't realised that. His voice seems to remind me of someone. Oh yes! He talks like Bill, my mother's boyfriend when I was little. Just thinking of him makes me really uncomfortable and the sound of his voice definitely scares me. Well, I don't want to go into that any more now, but I do see how something unpleasant from my past was stirred up by meeting Uncle Keith and the discomfort and confusion was the result.*

If you are troubled by conflicting views when you try to sort out family myths, you can clarify your perceptions by examining who in the family helped conceal the underlying myths. Try this exercise:

B 1  Choose an area of your family past that still affects you in the present, one in which you want to define your version of the truth more clearly. For instance, a student named Patricia wanted to investigate a pattern of distant and cold relationships between husbands and wives that she had noticed in her parents' and grandparents' generations and that she was afraid was starting to happen with her husband.

2  Divide a piece of paper in half vertically.

3  In the left column, write what you think, feel, and observe about this area of your past and present. State what *you* believe to be true, while watching for conflicting views and voices from within.

4  As soon as you start to argue with yourself, doubt yourself or hear a commenting voice, describe that interruption on the other side of the page.

5  Come back to what you believe and continue until you again are distracted by a conflicting view.

6  When you have finished writing what you believe to be true, you may have at least as many interruptions as statements of your own opinion. Now go through and see whether you can

identify who from your past might be offering these conflicting views; write those persons' names beside their comments.

7  Alternatively, analyse the conflicting views according to their effects: for each one, note whether it causes you confusion, attempts to protect others, makes you anxious, cuts you off from your feelings or sabotages your best interests.

8  When you have done one or both of these steps, write your reflections about getting closer to the truth by sorting out your own views from the competing ones that get in your way.

Patricia noted:

*I had plenty of interruptions and the significant thing I learned was that they were all from my female relatives. I started by stating how much I value closeness with my husband and want that to be preserved, despite the troubles we're having right now. Almost immediately some doubting, fearful and resentful comments started intruding – 'You can't expect that initial passion to last' – 'He's going to hurt you later' – 'Women have to do all the work in relationships'. They were the voices of my mother, my Grandmother Clark and my Aunt May. My mother's voice is sadly doubtful and resigned; Grandmother's sounds hurt and frightened; Aunt May's is downright bitter. I can see that these voices within me want to protect me but they make me expect the worst. I'll sabotage my intentions if I listen to them too much.*

Another effective means of discovering what you need to know to define your own truth about painful family truths is to break the power of old spells and enchantments from your family past. This advances your current level of awareness about what is true for you now – and what is no longer true.

## EXERCISE

## THE SPELL IS BROKEN

Recognising the value of old views of reality is an important part of being ready for a more expanded view of your truth.

If you can identify that a spell has been in existence, you have begun to break free of it to arrive at the truth, even if you don't yet feel that way. Perhaps the spell was like Andy's family's belief that his mother had to be protected from her guilt about Tina's burned hand. Or maybe the enchantment was that everyone in the family was happy (although you weren't), that your family didn't have enough money (although you didn't feel poor) or that your parents were models of virtue (when your mother slapped you and your father ignored you).

Write about a family spell you feel has started to break for you. Include your responses to these questions:

- What was the function of the old spell?
- What has brought you out of the spell?
- Are there parts of the spell that were positive and that you want to incorporate into a new version of your truth?

Cathy, who realised that her parents' divorce when she was seven was due to her father's affair, wrote:

*The old spell was that mummy and daddy and I were happy together for seven years, then he went away, but mummy and I were still happy. Nothing bad had happened; he just went away and we were fine. My father died in another country several years later. It was just like he had gone even farther away but I still wasn't affected. The spell continued; up until recently, I wasn't even aware of it. People would say, 'Don't you wish you had known your father better?' and I'd say, 'No, he was a nice man, but he died.' As if the divorce had never happened. The function of the old spell was to protect me from the hurt and anger – my own, my mother's, and even my father's, now that I think of it. What began bringing me out of the spell was my terrible jealous tendencies with my boyfriends. If there was anything positive about the old spell, it was that I felt really safe growing up with my mother. I trust women very profoundly and I'll always do so. But I want to be able to trust a man someday.*

As you become more aware of what you need to know to shape a current, workable version of the truth of your family experience, you may come face-to-face with areas of uncertainty where you have been hurt in your search for this truth in the past. Can you trust people? Can you say exactly what is true for you right now? Can you tell your friends the truth? Will you need to speak the truth to your family somehow? This next section will help you identify the areas where you were hurt and harness the power of expression to heal them – freeing you to define the truth more clearly.

# HURT AND HEALING IN YOUR FAMILY STORIES

Since all versions of family truths are attempts to adapt to its circumstances, you may be experiencing conflicting pulls anytime you dig deeper into what is true for you now. One pull tries to preserve your status quo with one set of facts and a single viewpoint on the truth; another pull tries to open you to more facts and to enlarge your viewpoint on painful family truths.

The best strategy is to become familiar with these conflicting pulls and to tap the wisdom in both of them. You can learn from the pull that tells you not to rock the boat as well as from the one that tells you that you're already in the water and had better start swimming. Both pulls are responses to anxiety about change, with the backward pull expressing fear of past hurt or reaction to hurt and the forward pull expressing the desire for future healing.

When Kristin thought about her mother's boyfriend from her past, she chose to respond to a backward pull at that time, stating, 'I don't want to go into that any more now.' Pressed slightly, she explained, 'I know something happened to me with that man when I was really little, because I get flashes of memory now and then or have nightmares that hint at it. But I haven't been ready to deal with that and I don't know if I am now'. In this response, Kristin could hear both the backward pull that had protected her for years from a traumatic experience and the forward pull that acknowledged that she is now undecided about exploring further. The former shied away from using more specific words than 'something happened' to describe the memories; the latter allowed her to speak clearly and directly instead of avoiding the issue.

Both forward and backward pulls are natural ways of reacting to hurt and trying to move towards a healing change. At some times, you want everything to go back to the way it was before: at others, you want everything to be fixed in the present. However, as natural and necessary as these responses are, the following guidelines will help you act wisely on your quest for your family truth.

**Ask questions**. You can hold dialogues with parts of yourself or with members of your family in writing or you can talk to your relatives directly, trying to come to your own truth by expanding your information base. In *The Dance of Intimacy*, Harriet Lerner writes, 'Questions enlarge our capacity for reflection and for seeing a problem in its broader context'. Patricia decided that she could ask her mother and aunt lots of questions about their memories of early marriage without dictating how they ought to feel.

**Set priorities and work on manageable chunks.** You can investigate one area of family experience or one relationship or period in your life to come to a greater understanding of the truth. Deciding to do it all at once is a sure way to trigger the backward pull. Andy decided that he was on the right track to want to talk to his sister about the accident that burned her. He made plans to share a few of his thoughts and feelings with her later, in the context of their routine visits.

**Pay attention to your resistance.** You are no less worthy a person for wanting to avoid painful past memories or difficult present problems. Giving your resistance full voice in a written monologue is a good way to respond to it. Then just notice how, whether and when it changes. Kristin discovered that her resistance to uncovering her memories changed when she first allowed herself to write the words 'I don't want to be afraid anymore.'

**Express your feelings.** An upsurge of emotion is always a valuable clue that what you are thinking about, remembering or doing is important. Your feelings connect you most reliably to your family past. Even if you, like Kristin, never allowed yourself to feel the fear of a past trauma, you still carry the emotion in your body's memory. Cathy found that after writing and talking about her anger at her father for his affair that caused the divorce, she became overwhelmingly sad. Her reaction to those losses – first divorce, then death – had only been delayed. She hated the grief at first, then found moments of healing release when the sadness would pass.

**Be gentle with yourself.** When you begin to define the truth of your family experience, you are separating yourself from views of reality that provided adequate shelter for a time. The stress of leaving the shelter of that version of truth is a necessary part of growing into a stronger individual, more able to connect fully to family and friends. Under that stress, you may ricochet between blaming others, blaming yourself, wanting to forgive the hurts, wanting to avenge wrongs and wanting to forget everything. If you can accept yourself in the truth of each day's thoughts, feelings and actions, you are on the road to healing.

These guidelines are helpful at all stages of truth-seeking – confusion, forward and backward pulls, strong emotion and clear definition. You can refer back to them as you assess in this section's two exercises what kinds of responses you want to make now to past family versions of truth.

## EXERCISE

### YOUR LOSSES AND GAINS WITH NEW TRUTH

The old family views of truth serve you as well as limit you. They provide comfortable adaptations that shield you from painful realities, as well as prevent you from understanding yourself and the world completely. You will be more likely to build on the positive qualities that developed from your past adaptations if you take note of them:

A List some benefits and advantages of your family's views from the past. (Andy: 'We didn't treat Tina as if she was disabled.' Patricia: 'I got the message that women were strong and capable.' Julia: 'I learned to trust my own judgement at a very early age.' John: 'I became fearless about speaking up in any situation.')

B List some benefits and advantages in leaving the family views of the past behind and choosing new definitions of what is true for you. (Andy: 'I want to let my mother know it wasn't her fault, and I can learn that it wasn't mine either.' Patricia: 'I can get closer to my husband, who I really do love.' Julia: 'I hope to forgive myself for not being able to save my mother.' John: 'I can find a social manner that's genuine, neither the phony salesman nor the cynical hermit.')

C Finally, list some potential obstacles or disadvantages to a more encompassing viewpoint. You will become more comfortable with and successful at the lifelong process of seeking truth if you are able to acknowledge that even positive changes have some difficult consequences. (Andy: 'I am afraid of being rejected by my mother if she doesn't like me breaking the silence about Tina's accident.' Patricia: 'I may find out that I'm not very good at this intimacy stuff.' Julia: 'If I stop taking care of everybody in my family, I might find out that I need more help than I think I do.' John: 'I may have to give up some angry and rebellious behaviour that covers up my real feelings.')

157

D Write any additional reflections that come to you about the losses and gains of your truth-seeking process.

Julia wrote:

*I always thought I was a courageous kid, keeping my family going while my mother wallowed in her drugs dependency. But now I see that it will take just as much courage for me to let go of my dependency on taking care of others.*

Because healing comes through the power of expression, like Julia, you will be freer for having written about your family truths. In the next exercise, you will go further and discover what your own personal truths are by imagining a series of severe life circumstances.

## EXERCISE

## THE TRUTH THAT MATTERS NOW

In times of shared crisis or disaster, people are much more likely to focus on what matters right here and now. When they nearly lose their lives in an accident, or when the area where they live is devastated by a flood or an earthquake, people find that the truth that matters comes quickly to mind. You can tap that same wisdom with your imagination.

A Imagine you only had a few hours to live in which you could tell the truth, find out facts, confront, blame, forgive, repair damage in relationships, communicate love or ask for what you wanted. What would you do?

B Write down at least three things.

C Imagine that you had only six months to live. What truths would you act on then?

D If you had one year to live: what truths then?

E In light of these imaginary responses, are there any real truths that matter to you now that you want to move towards?

Kristin wrote:

*If I only had a few hours, I would forget about whatever happened with my mother's boyfriend and concentrate on one thing – telling and showing my fiancé how much I love him. If I had six months to live, it would be different. I'd want to travel with my fiancé, but I'd want to spend time with my mother and sister, to let bygones be bygones. If I had a year to live, I think I would want to know more about that blocked-out time in my childhood and whatever happened with her boyfriend. I'd get some professional help; I'd ask for my fiancé's support; I might even talk to my mother and sister about it. I hope I'd die feeling more peaceful and whole. When I read over what I wrote, I felt a tightening in my stomach. Something inside me said, 'So, what's stopping you from feeling more peaceful and whole now?' The answer is my fear. Yet that missing piece is a truth that matters to me now, and I will move towards it slowly. Very slowly.*

Kristin is giving herself good advice regarding difficult areas of truth-seeking. As Harriet Lerner stresses in *The Dance of Intimacy*: 'The more intense the issue . . . *the more slowly one moves.*' But finding your truth is a healing process, and no matter what your pace, you will find that seeking what genuinely matters to you will make you feel stronger and more whole. In the next section, you can make your truth-seeking an ongoing process by writing your own truth.

# WRITING YOUR OWN TRUTH

All your life, your own truth has been intertwined with your family's stories. As exasperating, confusing or limiting as your family's versions of the truth may have been to you, you cannot leave them behind completely, any more than you can block out your whole childhood. Part of the richness and complexity of your individual personality comes from the influence of your family's perspective. But you probably have gained new perspectives and new healing from exploring your family's version of the truth through writing about how their stories have shaped your life.

Just as you grow in selfhood and personal power throughout your life, you grow in your ability to understand, interpret and act on your own truth. As you compare and contrast your guiding myths of the past and the counter-myths of the present, you move towards creating a unified mythic vision, a broad-scope version of your story that you want to make come true.

Your effectiveness at realising that vision in your life will be greatest if you can build on the family roots of your past and present. You need connection to what has been influential and meaningful – truth-filled – in your family experiences. For you have learned by those meanings, and truths carry pain or trauma. Writing about present truth in the light of those past truths can bring a feeling of completion to your search and provide an important foundation for new beginnings.

Psychologist James Pennebaker, who has specialised in studying the effects of writing about painful past truths, states:

Why does writing about upsetting experiences produce improvements in physical and psychological health? One important answer is cognitive: people think differently after writing about traumas. In translating experiences into language, people begin to organise and structure the seemingly infinite facets of overwhelming events. Once organised, the events are smaller and easier to deal with. Particularly important is that writing moves us to a resolution. Even if there is no meaning to an event, it becomes psychologically complete.

As you discover and articulate the truths of your famly, you pass through many attitudes, feelings and versions of the truth, each of which helps you feel more 'psychologically complete'. As Julia wrote, 'I will find more potential and vitality in allowing the Rescuer within me to go into semi-permanent retirement'.

In this final exercise, you can call on the roles that you and family members have played in your version of the truth to help you play the role you want to assume in the future by creating a positive, empowering myth of your own.

## EXERCISE

## THE BEGINNING OF A NEW STORY

Scholar of myth and story Joseph Campbell wrote: 'I don't think there is any such thing as an ordinary mortal. Everybody has his own possibility of rapture in the experience of life. All he has to do is recognise it and get going with it.' The process of seeking the truth and bringing it into your daily life is more demanding than Campbell's remark indicates – if awareness were all that we needed, we would have no more problems – but in writing out your longings for a new myth that is joyful and reflects your own truth, you begin to gather insight and courage for the actions that will move you towards it.

A  Write one statement that is true for you right now and that you want to build on in the future. For example, John chose, 'I am a person with a mask and a real face, from a family of masked people with real faces'. Kristin chose, 'I have one area of my past that is hidden by many curtains and veils. I can find people to help me decide when I am ready to remove a layer and move towards what is hidden.' And Julia chose, 'The heroine of the family has decided to go on a quest for some things she needs – lost parts of herself. She may have to ask for help along the way instead of always being the helper.'

B  Use that statement as the beginning of a story, starting with the facts and bringing in images of mythic elements to make the story more vivid and descriptive. You can incorporate people from your past, as well as friends and allies from the present and fantasy helpers from your timeless imagination. The story can be as short as a paragraph, summing up your situation now at the start of a new phase of your true story. Or you can write a longer myth, reaching back into the past and projecting forward into an imagined future in which you live your truth with more joy and freedom.

C  When you finish, look your story over for clues to any actions you can take to bring new truth into your daily life now.

Andy began his story:

*The young hero needs to learn that he can make mistakes and not be crippled by them. His greatest ally is a wounded woman who teaches him about living with your faults right out in the open. Together they can take the blinkers off a family that has been restricting their vision out of fear. He can't wear his old armour, but the wounded woman tells him that he will find protection along the way. . . . I want to get to know my sister Tina better, because I do believe she can help me, but I want to try hearing what she tells me about herself as a message about my own wounded side, the part of me that hides my scars.*

Patricia began her story:

*The heroine wants to learn how to let her beloved into her heart, which has walls of ice around it. She wants to look for some magic person to melt the ice, but then she discovers she has to take this cranky old dragon named Aunt May along with her. It turns out that it's the fire from that cranky old dragon's breath that will help her melt the ice. . . . I'd like to leave those negative females behind, but it's true that there's a part of me that's as bitter and cranky as Aunt May. I may try writing some more dialogues with her.*

Whatever version of your story you are writing now, the healing power of expression will carry you forward, easing pressure and pain around the tangles of your family roots and opening the way for your individual search for truth to continue.

You have used the healing power of expression to explore your family's patterns as they affected you in the past and as they linger in the present. To continue the work you have begun with these exercises, you need to review and reflect on what you have learned through the writing you have done about your family. Your insights alone have healing effects; you have also learned how to plan and carry out actions to build on the helpful aspects of your family's patterns and to change the hurtful ones. In the last chapter, you will sum up and integrate what you have learned and mobilise your healing resources for future goals and the ongoing task of living from your roots.

# CHAPTER 8

# LIVING FROM YOUR ROOTS

*I*n previous chapters you saw how the origins of the problems that confuse and block you now lie in the psychological root system of your family past. Your experiences with the family you grew up with shaped the person you are today. Defining the truth of your family experiences through writing has brought your past into clearer focus and created possible blueprints for solving your problems now and establishing healthier patterns in the future. To gain the greatest benefit from these discoveries, you can survey the learning and healing that has come from your writing and prepare yourself for the ongoing process of living from your roots.

Living from your roots means building on the history of your family past, emphasising the character strengths and healthy habits while changing the discouraging messages and destructive patterns. You cannot undo the past, but you can benefit from the clarity of new perspectives and the psychological completion of translating feelings into words. As you heal from the hurts that are an inevitable legacy of childhood and adolescence, you will be freed to express your unique individuality more fully.

By writing and living the truth of your family experiences, you have gathered a great deal of information and tapped a powerful pipeline of emotions and memories. You may be having a variety of reactions to the accumulated impressions, recollections and feelings generated by the discoveries you have made. You may be feeling:

- **vulnerable, longing for more healing** ('I notice the effects of bringing back memories of conflict; it's really painful.');
- **exhilarated, seeing the potential for change** ('Understanding why I am the way I am is exciting, and I'm full of energy to put what I've learned into action.');
- **disoriented, needing direction** ('Past and present are all mixed up for me now; I need to focus inward and find out where I am now.');
- **overwhelmed, confused by so much input** ('How can I ever put all this together? The information is really valuable but it's all jumbled in my mind.');
- **doubtful, wondering whether change is possible** ('I've enjoyed this process but I'm anxious about falling back into automatic destructive patterns.');

- **purposeful, wanting to know what's next** ('How do I put this to work once I finish all the exercises? I don't want to lose the positive momentum.').

Each of these reactions is a natural response to stirring up many memories and calling into question both your past assumptions and your current situation with family relationships and other aspects of your life. The process of living from your roots will bring up these reactions again and again as you question your past, work out your present and plan your future.

When you feel one or more of these reactions very strongly, you know you need to pause and discover what will help you settle into and integrate what you have learned. You are also being challenged to find out what you need to do next in response to the information and feelings that have emerged from your writing. By discovering the reasons for what you are feeling, you can decide on a direction for further exploration.

The first two reactions – **vulnerability** and **exhilaration** – represent opposite responses to opening up new levels of emotional honesty and expression about your family. In the past, you may have kept from feeling vulnerable by not probing into family matters that could stir up feelings and threaten you or your family's stability. Now you are more aware about feelings and unfamiliar amounts of anger, sadness, or even positive emotions such as love and joy can make you feel exposed and on edge. On the other hand, the new types and intensities of feelings may fill you with exhilaration. In the past, you may have held your emotions in check to avoid rocking the family boat. Now, you are excited to discover that you know yourself better by acknowledging what you feel.

Both vulnerability and exhilaration tell you that your emotional self is alive in new ways. Although vulnerability is uncomfortable and exhilaration is exciting, the two responses are similar – they make you feel more alive. Getting more in touch with your feelings enlivens your physical self and stimulates your mind to imagine new ideas based on a greater emotional range. Whether you feel fearful or excited, you can benefit from redefining yourself and your family in light of what you now know and feel.

The next two sections – feeling **disoriented** or **overwhelmed** – are common responses to a temporary overabundance of information to integrate. You were accustomed to thinking about your family members in certain ways and now you see them from different perspectives that make the old attitudes incomplete or outdated. You defined yourself in relation to your family in certain ways and now you know more about how and why your identity developed as it did in response to family influences. Both disorientation and overstimulation hold potential for personal growth and positive changes in your family patterns once you take time to sort through what you have learned and make sense of it gradually. Integrating what you have learned is the key to stability and direction when you are living from your roots.

The last two sections – **doubt** and **purposeful intention** – represent opposite responses to the ongoing work on your family patterns. When you doubt that you can maintain the clarity achieved through your writing, you demonstrate a natural anxiety about the long-term effects of change. When you feel purposeful about reinforcing your new attitudes and actions, you demonstrate an equally natural urge to guard your gains and build on them. In both cases, you will benefit from a definite plan to mobilise your healing resources.

The three sections in this chapter address the tasks mentioned above: **redefining your family, integrating what you have learned, and mobilising your healing resources**. In the first section, you will develop a new and fuller definition of your family circle, including people with whom you experienced pain or conflict and others who were a source of strength and comfort to you. To encourage your continued emotional growth, you need to acknowledge the people and the environments that gave you freedom. Two of the necessary conditions for our healthy development are a stable foundation of responsible, caring adults and an environment where it is safe for children to discover and express themselves.

To the extent that your family met these conditions, they gave you what Virginia Satir, in *Making Contact*, called 'the five freedoms':

**The freedom to see and hear what is here**, instead of what should be, was, or will be.
**The freedom to say what one feels and thinks**, instead of what one should.
**The freedom to feel what one feels**, instead of what one ought.
**The freedom to ask for what one wants**, instead of always waiting for permission.
**The freedom to take risks on one's own behalf**, instead of choosing to be only 'secure' and not rocking the boat.

All of these freedoms create a sense of permission to be who you really are. You can give these freedoms to yourself now as an adult, by living from your roots. But as a child you were dependent on your family members as primary sources of stability and safety.

Because we are born dependent on the adults who care for us for our survival, each of us has a strong need to belong, to feel safe, included and important. Any family members who recognised both your needs for belonging and your needs for becoming your own separate self gave you great gifts of freedom. When your father trusted you with the family car, your grandmother brought you out of your shyness, your uncle gave you your first job, your older sister asked your advice – all these family actions supported your individual development and created strong bonds of family community. By writing about the family members who supplied those needed conditions of responsible stability and a liberating environment, you redefine your family to include and recognise those who nurtured you in a positive way.

In addition to the positive influences from family members, you also benefited from the helpful influence of caring adults outside your family who guided and protected you. Anthropologists use the term *fictive kin* to describe people who are not blood relatives but who act towards you as family members ideally do. This term suggests that it is in the sharing of our stories, the created fictions of our human journeys, that we find deep and meaningful family ties. The neighbour who taught you to grow vegetables, the teacher who convinced your parents to let you go away to college, the family friend who listened to the adolescent longings you couldn't tell your parents – all these are fictive kin. By writing about the elders, mentors, advocates and friends of your past and present, you can redefine your family as those who love you and whom you love by choice.

Your redefined family can also include the environments in which you felt most at home. As you wrote the stories of your family past, you remembered not only the people but also the places that held meaning for you. The houses or flats in which you lived, as well as the neighbourhoods and regions in which you grew up, were your familiar surroundings. As a child, you absorbed the sights, smells, sounds, textures and tastes of your environment that became part of your memories of family and home. The smell of wet asphalt after rain, the red and gold leaves in autumn, traffic noises at night, soft spring grass that tickled your bare feet, aromas of familiar food cooking that met you at the door – sensory memories such as these formed your sense of place within a family circle. For many children, the world outdoors becomes a second home, a place to dream, reflect, play and be comforted. By writing about your childhood environments, you redefine your family to include the nurturing effects of the places that have sheltered you.

As you redefine your family to include the people and places that encouraged your freedom and growth, you call on sources of strength from your past. The memories of these sources offer emotional protection when you feel vulnerable in the face of painful memories from the past or difficult problems in the present.

In the second section, you will focus on **integrating what you have learned** about your family's influence on your growth in childhood and adolescence and on the developments of your adult life. Another condition necessary for your health and well-being as a child was a combination of love and guidance from your parents and other important adults in the family. The nurturing love that you received helped you know yourself and feel secure; the consistent direction of attentive guidance shaped your decisions about behaviour and relationships.

In writing about the events of your family past, you learned more about what you received from your parents and what you failed to receive. Your writings evoked many feelings about the gifts and the gaps in your parents' care of you. You may now appreciate the gifts of their love more fully; you may now mourn what you missed more fully also.

In either case, you probably have a greater understanding of the complex forces at work in your family's life in the past and the passage of both gifts and failures of care through the generations. Parents and other adults who hurt or neglect children do so because they themselves suffered wounds or gaps in their own upbringing. The failures of love and guidance become a painful legacy difficult to avoid passing on. You have probably also found, however, that learning about the past is part of the healing process. Your writing is a tool for further integration and you can continue to heal your family's failures and build on their gifts.

As part of the integration process, you can re-examine what you learned in each of the preceding chapters to define more clearly where you stand now. You will reflect on the basic information gathered in Chapter 2 about your family members and their interactions through the years of your childhood and adolescence. You will review your family's approach to life that you wrote about in Chapter 3, including how your own life stance has developed from the family base. You will return to your family's communication patterns as explored in Chapter 4, seeking ways to heighten the clarity and directness of your inherited conversational style. You will redefine your identity as surveyed in Chapter 5, exploring your family's influence on your developing sense of self in the areas of body, mind, emotions and spirit. You will revisit your family's teachings about personal power as described in Chapter 6, including how your self-esteem, your independence and your initiative grew from the family foundation. Finally, you will restate the truth of your family experience, as just defined in Chapter 7, emphasising what best sums up your perspective on your family's history.

By travelling briefly back through the material you have written about, you will become less overwhelmed, disoriented and confused. The integration of your discoveries about your family will proceed more quickly and smoothly. Reviewing what you have thought and felt fixes your insights more firmly in your memory and strengthens your ability to make changes in your life now and to plan for long-range alteration of destructive family patterns.

In the third section, you will discover how to **mobilise your resources** to continue the work of learning and healing after you finish this book. *Breaking Free From Your Past* has presented you with a new process for examining patterns in your life. You can use the techniques and strategies in future explorations of your family and work relationships, problems, goals and dreams.

The process of writing from your roots has involved you deeply in the three stages of growth as outlined in the first chapter: **awareness**, **assessment** and **change**. As you have found, you can be actively pursuing each stage of growth in different areas of your life – for example, increasing your awareness in a current relationship, assessing the effects of an old family pattern and making plans to change another established but destructive habit.

In order to make the most of all three stages' positive effects, you will review the tasks involved in each one. The task of increasing your awareness is exploration. Because this task requires expanding your horizons, it can be called **journeying**. When you go on a mental and emotional journey by writing whatever comes to mind, you explore thoughts and feelings of which you have not previously been aware, some new personal territory of consciousness. Your individual territory is always intertwined with that of your family. The more you deliberately choose to be a journeyer by examining what you think and feel, the more you will come to know and understand both yourself and your family. Your awareness will teach and heal you.

The task of assessment requires the ability to identify your thoughts and feelings and to express them in clear and precise language. This task of description can be called **naming**. As you become a more conscious journeyer, your awareness accumulates until you understand something so well that it bursts forth into language, describing and naming it more fully than you have done before. 'I have always allowed my parents to dominate my life', 'It is not good for me to rely on my brother the way I do; I need to learn to stand on my own', 'I have talents I haven't begun to use yet because I'm stuck in the past with my alcoholic mother' – all these are powerful naming statements. When you can clearly identify your own life patterns as shaped by your family, you have made a significant leap in growth. Your acts of assessment and naming will teach and heal you.

The task of enacting changes involves moving past old blocks and limits and fulfilling your individual abilities and potential. Because this task brings you back to the essence of yourself, it can be called **homecoming**. Once you assess and name your experience with clarity and distance, you are no longer controlled by it and you no longer react automatically in old ways. When you can understand an attitude or pattern of interaction well and describe it thoroughly, you have the power to change it. You move from a doubtful stance to a purposeful one. If opening up new awareness is like beginning a journey, taking action for healthy change is like coming home. The deepest form of homecoming is finding and expressing your own truth through courageous acts of change. One student wrote: 'My real home is inside now. I carry it with me wherever I go. I stand safe within that home even as I do things that I never dreamed I could do.' You will find, as she did, that your acts of change will teach and heal you.

As you redefine your family, integrate what you have learned from your writing and mobilise your healing resources, you will become more separate and independent as an individual. In addition, you will forge more conscious, loving and clear links to your family. You can strengthen yourself without having to reject family ties. You can immerse yourself in and enjoy the nurturing aspects of your family. You can also plan how to protect yourself from those destructive aspects of your family that you cannot change. Finally, you can create strategies to take action in those areas where your efforts will free you and others.

# REDEFINING YOUR FAMILY

Living from your roots requires a commitment to continuing redefinitions of yourself and your family members. You can strengthen your commitment to understanding your family from all sides by focusing specifically on family members' constructive and caring actions that helped you in the past or that support you now. If you are feeling sad or vulnerable about your family, you will find courage in recalling positive influences and support. If you are feeling excited about change, you can use your positive experiences to reinforce your new actions. Your family helpers modelled advice and problem-solving skills that you can call on now.

In addition, you can broaden your family circle by recalling and writing about people who fall into the definition of fictive kin. Anyone who was important in some portion of your life story can be fictive kin: your favourite babysitter, your tennis coach, the elderly neighbour you ran errands for, your older brother's best friend who defended you against teasing or criticism, or your mother's old school friend who visited once a year and brightened your life. There is something extraordinarily precious about being cared for by someone who has no obligation even to take notice of you. As one student wrote, 'My chosen family loves me just for me alone and I am fiercely loyal and loving in return.'

The following exercise will help you include all the people who have been sources of strength and comfort in your life in your definition of *family*. Whether they were family members or fictive kin, their attentive care nourished you in the past and continues to support you.

## EXERCISE

## RECEIVING LOVE WITH NO STRINGS ATTACHED

Unconditional love is a powerful force for healthy development and healing of hurts. The people who helped you the most may have had expectations of you, as a good teacher would, or demanded certain actions from you, as would a good employer. But if they also cared about you purely because they found you a delightful human being, you blossomed from their unconditional love and you probably did everything you could to keep their high regard. You may not have stopped to thank them then, and you may not have thought about them in years. Nevertheless, their love is still strong in your memory and you can reactivate its positive force, which can vitalise the roots of your life.

Those who encouraged you with no strings attached were your advocates. Sometimes they drew out your full self, having seen in you potential that others missed. Sometimes they spoke up for you to others, offering you safety. Four types of advocates include elders, protectors, mentors and friends. One advocate may have played some or all of these roles for you at different times, but the base of the bond was attentive care.

**Elders** offered you the wisdom of their age and experience. They took the time to listen, to offer advice from a broader perspective, to point out what you might have missed in your youth and hurry. **Protectors** offered you sanctuary. Perhaps it was the physical refuge of a home where no one yelled at you or the intervention of an adult who saw you getting hurt and took action; perhaps it was emotional protection, countering an environment that was lacking, numbing or hurtful with messages of love and hope. **Mentors** gave guidance in areas of expertise, such as how to make biscuits, how to cut through wood, how to deal with peer pressure or how to persuade other adults that you could be trusted. **Friends** treated you, a child or adolescent, as their equal. Adults often talk awkwardly to young people, as if they were another species. Those who spoke to you with respect, honesty and humour were your friends, no matter what their age or yours.

A Divide a piece of paper into four columns, heading each with one of the types of advocates: elders, protectors, mentors and friends.

B In each column, list the names of family members and others who gave you unconditional love at some time in your past. You may be surprised when a family member whose influence has seemed primarily negative in your writings throughout the book appears as an advocate here. When this happens, you can take note of it to create a more balanced picture of your family past. Few family members had a completely negative influence. You may also be surprised to remember people you had long forgotten – perhaps a piano teacher, or a nurse who tended you when you were in hospital. Continue listing as many advocates as you can recall in each column until you feel finished.

C From the four columns, choose the advocate whose positive influence was greatest and write a letter to that person. It does not matter whether he or she is alive or whether you ever expect to see him or her again. Simply write from your heart to convey to that person what his or her influence or intervention meant to you in the past. Include your reflections on how the person's contribution has changed you or continues to help you.

D In the light of your list-making and letter-writing, describe how you would broaden your definition of your family to include these people and their effects on you.

Hilary commented:

*I wrote a letter to my Uncle Barry. He was my dad's army friend, not my real uncle, but he stayed with us several times a year. He never asked about my school reports or what prizes I'd won or what I wanted to be when I grew up. He was a protector in that he'd tell my father right to his face to stop criticising me – and no one in our family talked to Dad that way. I realised that my nicest memories of Dad are when Uncle Barry was with us. He died suddenly in the first few weeks that I was away at college and I never really thanked him or said goodbye. Now I have, and I feel as if he's more alive than ever.*

You can also expand your definition of family to include the places where you lived and played as you grew up. It may seem odd to include nonhuman elements such as houses, woods, animals and streets in your family, but your child self viewed home as everything around you. As an infant, you first felt safest and most comfortable in your mother's presence but later you learned to feel comforted by everything your senses told you was familiar, such as your favourite blanket, your room, your dog, your garden and your neighbourhood. The best way to unblock your writing at any time is to re-enter childhood memories of home, pets or outdoor experiences, as those memories live within you in all their sensory dimensions and hold great emotional power.

Those timeless moments with places that comforted you and stimulated your imagination still live within you. Claiming them as part of your heritage – your family context – will anchor your memories of the past and remind you of a firm foundation that you can draw on for support. As you bring these places and experiences back in the following exercise, you will be including more of the healing presences from your past in a new definition of your family.

# EXERCISE

## EXPANDING YOUR FAMILY CIRCLE

Just as certain family members and fictive kin supported you with caring as you grew up, certain places that you remember were part of your circle of shelter and pleasure. In the intervening years, you may have left those places behind. However, their past influence is still important and they provide an ongoing source of support along with that of caring relatives and friends. Each section of this exercise takes you back to your roots, your sense of place or home ground.

A  Write your answer to the question **Where are you from**? Perhaps the answer will be 'London' or 'third generation Irish!' This indicates that you are proud to be rooted in one place and like mentioning your deep family connections. Write your usual response to that question and some reflections on why you answer as you do.

B  Reflecting on the places you lived as a child, select one memorable location about which you have strong positive feelings, for example, sitting in the garden, flying a kite on the beach or playing on the floor and listening to the customers talking while you sat under the counter in your father's shop.

C  Re-enter that location and write about it from a child's point of view, using the present tense, direct, descriptive words and simple sentences. Include objects, animals, colours and smells that are part of the life of your remembered location. If you felt especially safe or protected there, describe those feelings.

D  If describing one place memory brought a cascade of others, you can jot these down in a list for future writing possibilities; for example, 'my cat Tibby', 'sliding on the icy pavement', 'the place where no one could find me', 'the window seat where I read' and 'swimming in the river in summer'. Each of these memory locations carries power to transport you back to the past. Living from you roots means including memory locations as well as caring relatives and advocates in your definition of family.

E  Realising that your definition will change as constantly as you do, write a definition of your family that incorporates the people, places and things that gave you comfort and strength.

Peter wrote:

*Where am I from? Hard to say, we moved so much. It's nature that I remember most, because I felt most at home outside. The flat golden fields around the towns we lived in and the flat stretches of soft wet sand near our houses on the coast were my lands of adventure. I loved to dig down under the surfaces, to find worms in the ground, crabs and shells in the sand. I had no brothers and sisters, and my dad worked long hours and was short-tempered and tired when he was home. My mum was quiet and inactive; now I think she might have been depressed. I played outdoors at every opportunity.*

*Here's one favourite place: in the middle of a green grove of trees is the old well. The wood of the well-cover is crumbly at the edges. If I rub a little piece of it off, it falls way down into the water and I hear a soft splash. I can sit on the edge of the platform around the well and play with the toadstools that grow up in the cool, damp grass. Through the trees I see the bright yellow field behind our property. I can slither through the wire fence and crawl along in the wheat, pretending to be a soldier. Or I can stay hidden away by the well, where no one sees me.*

*Writing about that one special place of protection and imagination made me realise how rich my childhood was in many ways. I imagined hundreds of stories with me as the hero, the one everyone looked up to and liked. Sometime I want to write about these other memories – the first time I dug for worms, trying to make friends with Mr. Thornhill's horse, slipping out at night in the thunderstorm.*

*My teachers were always mentors and advocates; they were like family to me with their encouragement. I'm sure that's why I became a teacher myself. And with my love of nature, it's not surprising I went into biology. Writing about these people and places gives me a different perspective, less bitter about what I didn't get, more grateful for some of those rich moments. Here's a new definition of my family:*

*My family includes my relatives who did the best they could, my teachers, students and colleagues, who encouraged me and shared my excitement and nature, my true family home.*

Whatever memories surfaced for you in recalling and writing about the people and places who were part of your growing-up years, you can draw strength from the caring, beauty and comfort they represented. John Bradshaw's remark about the way we carry our family realities inside us even after we leave home is as true of the bright and clear memories as of the dark and painful ones. The continuing challenges of your life will be eased by living from a definition of your family that calls on your familiar allies from old times. Some of them, such as earth and sky, are just outside your door now. Some of them are as close as a letter or a phone call. All of them can come to life again through your written words.

# INTEGRATING WHAT YOU HAVE LEARNED

Writing about your family in the exercises in this book has undoubtedly changed your viewpoint and taught you many things. With the clarity and distance that comes with recalling memories, patterns and feelings, you are no longer immersed in the patterns of your family past in the same way. However, you may be overwhelmed by the sheer volume of memories, each with its own insights.

You may be confused about how to apply all this new information to living from your roots. You can create some order in your crowded impressions and thoughts by reviewing what you have already learned. Reviewing the themes you explored and the conclusions you made will accelerate the integration of the information and the feelings, a necessary part of long-lasting change.

Integration is always the last step in a process of change that involves **separation**, **transition** and **incorporation**. Times of change begin with **separation**, moving away from the old ways that no longer seem to work. Beginning to write about your family required a kind of separateness from your family experience that was probably new for you. In the second stage of change, **transition**, your accustomed perspective no longer holds true but you have not yet established a new one. You are probably still in transition with the thoughts, feelings, wishes, hopes and plans that have come up in relation to your family as a result of all the writing you have done. In the third stage, **incorporation**, you take the new information in thoroughly enough that it becomes coherent and integrated. Incorporation means integrating your new learnings about your family into all aspects of your self – physical sensings, mental attitudes, emotional reactions and spiritual longings.

The cycle of change will repeat every time you move to a new level of understanding yourself and your family. The key questions of how your family provided love and guidance and how you were affected by what they did and did not provide will be asked and answered in new ways every time you redefine these important relationships. Because each new level of understanding demands courage and flexibility, you will probably feel disrupted and uncomfortable at first.

In *The Dance of Anger*, Harriet Lerner writes of this process:

Is learning more about our family truly a daring and courageous act? Yes, it is. It is not easy to give up the fixed notions that we have about our family. Whether we rage against one family member or place another on a pedestal (two sides of the same coin), we don't want the 'stuck-togetherness' of our family to be befuddled by the facts about **real people**.

The disruption and discomfort of 'giving up fixed notions' was described by Paul, a man in his late thirties, when he said:

*I'm feeling that disorientation you mentioned, as if I can't tell the difference between past and present. I was the older of two sons, the one who had all the fights with my strict parents. I now have two sons myself. The older boy is just turned twelve and we fight about stupid things. He always seems to be pushing for more privileges and I'm likely to shout, 'I'm so much easier on you than my parents were on me. You don't know how good you have it.' I thought that if I was warmer and more understanding to my boys than my parents were, the family pattern would be changed and my sons wouldn't move away to escape from family the way I did. I go nuts when my son acts as if he hates me; I can see that I'm all mixed up in the past and the present.*

In Lerner's term, Paul is experiencing 'stuck-togetherness' in which he has difficulty separating his own childhood experience from his son's current rebellion. Family patterns can be most disorienting at times of major transition, because your own memories and feelings will get mixed up with the stress of a current family situation. If you, like Paul, have a child moving into adolescence, or any other major life transition in progress, you will need to pause and integrate what you have learned about your past so that you can see your present more clearly.

You can also simply get overwhelmed by a large amount of new information and the impact of strong feelings about your family, even though the information may be welcome and the feelings may bring you relief. 'I know everything I have found out is of great value,' remarked Lisa, 'but I feel swamped by it all. I can't think coherently about what it means.'

Lisa had come to the class because she and her husband were in conflict about bringing up their two daughters. She coulnd't work out why these clashes reminded her of her family when she didn't remember her parents fighting over child-rearing. Through writing, she identified a deep estrangement between her parents, a family secret involving her grandmother who lived with them, and her own low self-esteem, which made her constantly doubt her abilities. She spoke about the impact of all these discoveries: 'I can now see that my anger about the clashes with my husband come partly from believing that I would have a harmonious family life once I got away from my parents and grandmother. However, there's so much to try to understand and put to use. It's like a kaleidoscope constantly changing, and I just want to close my eyes until things calm down.'

If the information gathered about your family through your writing has had complex and far-reaching implications, you may feel overwhelmed and unsure about how to proceed. In those circumstances, you will find it helpful to take plenty of time to reflect on and review everything you have learned and to be cautious about taking action before you have a more solid sense of direction. You have to stay with the truths that you have uncovered long enough to know how you were affected in the past, how you feel now and what would be a wise and healthy response for you and your family members. The last section of the chapter will help you gather your resources to continue living from your roots but first you will review the information and insights from Chapters 2 to 7.

## EXERCISE

## RETRACING YOUR PATH THROUGH THE FAMILY MAZE

To review the family territory that you have explored in your writing, you will consider each chapter in turn. After reading through the summary of a chapter's issues and themes, reflect on what you learned from your writing in that area of family patterns. You may want to reread what you have written for that chapter's exercises; if you want to review more quickly, jot down whatever comes to mind by thinking back over the material.

In addition to considering what you learned in each area, ask yourself how you can apply your new insights now and in the immediate future. Make your ideas for practical applications of your new understandings as specific as possible. If you know you need to do more mental integration, you can state, 'Think and write more about . . .' If you have in mind a series of actions to take, you can list them: 'First, I will . . . Then I can . . . When I get that clear, I will go on to . . .' Write your responses in short form – condensed notes about the themes and listed items for future work – or in a more lengthy reflective fashion. In either case, you are clarifying and restating your insights about the influence of your family's patterns on your character and behaviour. You are priming yourself to plan and carry out further healthy changes.

For each of the following chapters, write your answer to these two questions:

What have I learned about my family's influence on my life that will help me now and in the future?

How, specifically, am I going to apply this information to build on my current areas of strength and to plan positive change?

## Chapter 2: Surveying your family system

In this chapter you described your family as you would have at different ages in the past and present, identified what your role was in your family and clarified who lived with you and made up your family through your childhood and adolescence. You described interaction patterns in your family, exploring how open or closed your family system was in regard to self-worth, rules, linking to others beyond the family and reacting to change. You examined your parents' relationship and its effects on you.

## Chapter 3: Your family's life stance

You learned that your family had a shared approach to their life together that shaped their attitudes and behaviour. This family life stance had the impact of a shared trance, which you needed to break in order to distance yourself from your family's patterns and understand their influence on you. You defined your family's life stance in terms of mottoes, attitudes and behaviour. You explored your family's ability to trust, which created a more open or a more closed life stance, oriented towards permission and encouragement or towards fear and control. You wrote about your family's relationship to hope and action, recognising how a more optimistic outlook and a more active stance enables growth and change.

## Chapter 4: Communication in your family

You learned that clear, direct, specific communication is a strong measure of health. Your family taught you about communication even before you understood their words, so their language habits may be contributing to problems you have now. You surveyed your family's communication style – their tolerance of conflict, their need for agreement and their ability to be emotionally honest. You questioned your family's use of the five communication responses of placating, blaming, computing, distracting and levelling, and the harmful communication habits of double messages, hurtful silence and belittling words. You decided how to establish new communication patterns reflecting clarity, honesty and respect.

## Chapter 5: Your family and your sense of self

You learned that your identity, or sense of self, grows from a strong and healthy foundation of trust and your family's communication of your value. You examined how your identity development was shaped by your family's attitudes and behaviour in four areas of selfhood: your body, your mind, your emotions and your spirit. You surveyed your history with your family in each area and looked for ways to expand your physical confidence and well-being, enhance your mental abilities and creativity, strengthen your emotional functioning, and connect more deeply to the longings of your spirit, your personal essence.

## Chapter 6: Your family and your sense of personal power

You learned that your personal power – your ability to feel good about yourself and to fulfil your dreams and goals – is shaped by your family's support of your growth in three areas: self-esteem, independence and initiative. To assess the growth of your self-esteem, you brought back memories of how your family defined you, mirrored your qualities and understood you with empathy. To understand your family's influence on your independence, you examined how involved or detached they were and how they supported or blocked you as you moved away from them. To evaluate your ability to take initiative, you listed family messages about action and achievement; and finally, you envisioned ways to develop your personal power more fully.

## Chapter 7: The truth of your family experience

You discovered how you might be blocked in pursuing your findings about your family because of the need to protect yourself or your family members. You might hold yourself back from full exploration and expression of your family's history and its impact on you because you fear hurt, anger, loss, or the responsibility to take action and make changes. By choosing to seek the truth of your own experience, not anyone else's, you will proceed at your own pace to acknowledge the pain and conflict and to move towards healing changes. You wrote about your family's stories, silences and secrets, and your written memories and dialogues helped you break the spell of destructive or outdated family truths. You assessed how to write about and plan your life course to work through the pain in your family past and to direct you towards greater freedom and health.

In discussing this exercise, Paul stated that reviewing Chapter 3, on family life stance, helped him the most to integrate what he had learned about the family pattern of conflict with older sons. He wrote:

*My family's stance of distrust had a major impact on my upbringing. Recalling their family sayings – 'Anything that can go wrong, will' and 'What has that child done now?' – showed me how pervasive their pessimism has been. Also, my own need for control stems from my family experiences in which my parents overreacted to whatever I did by cracking down on me. I want to stop treating my son as my parents treated me, and here are some specific plans: 1. List and write about his good qualities; he does have them! 2. Praise him warmly whenever I can. 3. Stop myself from reacting automatically*

175

*when he asks for the moon; I can say, 'I'll have to take some time to think about that, and I'll tell you tomorrow morning.'*

In turn, Lisa described the material in Chapter 4 on family communication and in Chapter 6 on personal power as the most fruitful for review and integration. She wrote:

*The many double messages that my parents and grandmother gave me – 'Everything's fine with our family' vs. 'There's something really wrong but don't ask about it' – were connected with my low self-worth. I decided that there was something wrong with me for feeling uncomfortable about the family rather than that there was something wrong with the family. Then I got scared that I could make it worse and lose their love. That connection between harmful communication patterns and feeling bad about myself still causes me problems. Now I don't want to address difficult situations with raising the girls. Then, when my husband confronts me about it, I feel like such a failure. I think I could really benefit from counselling help with this, because it's so complicated. Besides that specific idea, I want to keep writing and stay focused on my feelings. Trying to understand everything now will only make me feel incompetent. I'll understand it better in time.*

You can refer back to your writings from past exercises at any time as you continue to integrate what you have learned. The stages of separation, transition and incorporation cycle repeatedly, so you can benefit from reminding yourself, as Lisa did, that expecting full understanding and radical change will only lead you back into old painful patterns.

The more you continue to use the process of reflective exploration and written expression, the more you will incorporate what you have learned and make new discoveries. These discoveries will enable you to continue changing patterns that keep you from fulfilment. The final section will show you ways to sustain the healing effects of creative expression.

# MOBILISING YOUR HEALING RESOURCES

*B*reaking Free From Your Past has given you a new blueprint for a process of change. To prepare yourself to continue the work after finishing this book, you have redefined your family to call on sources of strength from your past. You have reviewed the issues and themes about which you have written to see what you have gained and what lies ahead. Now you can mobilise your healing resources to make the long-term adjustments required for lasting change.

Writing of the disrupting effects of changing long-established family patterns, Virginia Satir states:

Whenever change occurs, the old order is disturbed and a period of upheaval follows. During this chaos, it may be hard to see what has been gained. One other stumbling block to rapid progress arises when people try to accomplish new goals using an old process. It takes time to learn a new process.

As you have recognised how old patterns affected you and others in your family in destructive ways, you have probably wanted to change them quickly and completely. The work of change is measured in months and years, not days and weeks. The flashes of insight or courageous statements of truth that are the necessary prelude to the changes you want are dramatic and stand out in your memory. However, each one is followed by long periods of adjustment in which all the implications of the change must be dealt with on a daily basis. Steady commitment to living from your roots is at the centre of your change process.

You may be feeling doubtful about sustaining the momentum created by new insights. 'I'm past forty and pretty set in my ways', declared a man named Keith. 'I'm really afraid that I'll go back in my shell and get depressed rather than work on the changes I've planned. How do I keep in mind what I've learned and move forward?'

Sometimes slipping back into old habits seems like an easier alternative than continuing with the process of change. Doubting your ability to succeed can be a protective defence against your fear that you might fail. You can take care of some of your doubts by eliminating the application of the terms 'success' and 'failure' to your change process. A certain amount of doubt and anxiety is a healthy motivator but you don't want to immobilise yourself with excessive amounts. Reviewing ways to free up your emotional expression in Chapter 5 will expand your confidence and help you to accept the uncertainties of change more easily.

On the other hand, you may be feeling purposeful as you come to the end of the book, ready to go further with what you have learned. Rebecca described herself this way:

*I'm absolutely determined to use what I've learned here. I'm at least ten years older than Keith and I'd like to challenge him to consider that he's got that much more time than me, so he shouldn't lose the courage of his convictions. I'm going to make the rest of my life happier, but tell me – What's the key to knowing what to do when? I'm so intent on action that I may blunder off in all directions at once.*

The key to knowing what to do when is to understand that subjective immersion always precedes objective planning. You must first immerse youself in your memories and feelings about a particular issue in order to understand how your family past affected you in this area. Then you can use the clarity and distance gained from writing to plan how to avoid repeating the pain and malfunction of the past. A healing change process includes a three-part sequence of creative strategies: **reliving the past, restructuring the present** and **envisioning the future**. If you need guidelines to translate feelings of purposefulness into wise action, you can review the initiative section of Chapter 6.

The healing change of the living-from-your-roots process also includes several tasks that you can explore more fully by mobilising your resources. In Chapter 1, these tasks were identified as **awareness, assessment** and **change**. In this chapter, the task of exploration involved in increasing your awareness of family patterns is called **journeying**. All healing starts with a step into the unfamiliar, a journey into the unknown areas of your own mind and heart.

By declaring to yourself or others that you want to know more about yourself and your family past, you immediately jostle your established attitudes and shake loose some held-in feelings. These inner shifts in awareness will make you want to continue on the journey of discovery. First you tune in to what family patterns you deeply want to change; then you survey what healing resources are available to you. Your sensory recall is a great tool, for you can reflect and write about what your five senses – sight, hearing, touch, smell and taste – tell you about your memories and your current reality.

You can gather information and increase awareness with other healing resources as well, such as art, meditation, music, dreamwork, dance and movement. Rebecca found that she became more aware and progressed on her journey by doing small sketches of family scenes. She took delight in drawing as a child would, with stick figures, bold lines and exaggerated proportions. Keith noticed that his dreams tended to play out scenes that shed light on the reasons for his anxiety; by writing them, he became more aware of the role of doubt in his change process.

Once your awareness expands to include enough information and perceptions, you will become involved in the second task, **naming**. The assessment stage of the change process requires that you identify, or name, what is working well and what is working against you. To assign a name to something makes it more accessible to awareness and available for change. 'I think I might have a bit of a problem with drinking' represents one stage of naming; 'I am a recovering alcoholic' is another.

You can exercise care not to judge or limit yourself or others by the naming process. All types of assessment can be helpful as long as you recognise that you will never arrive at a final assessment that will completely name all the problems and point to a total solution. Instead, you are striving to name the truth of the moment, such as 'I feel envious that my kids are getting love that I didn't get', 'I am still hoping to be the centre of attention' or 'I will fall apart if I don't get some help with the problem'. All of these naming assessments set the stage for taking action.

Your two main healing resources for the naming stage are **clarity** and **courage**. Throughout the book, you have worked on developing focused vision to identify your assets and liabilities clearly. Your writings in each chapter's final section probably contain the clearest and most developed statements on each subject and you can refer back to them to mobilise your healing resource of clarity. In Chapter 7, you exercised determination and took risks to home in on the truths of your family experience; you can reread the guidelines for protection and encouragement in that chapter to mobilise your healing resource of courage.

As you assess your circumstances and your truth of the moment, you become involved in the third task, **homecoming**. Your progress to this point has swept away some of the clutter that keeps you from knowing what you want to do and expressing who you are in powerful ways. If your family did not model ways for you to make a good life and to cope with difficulties, your struggles to cope without a model have probably alienated you from your own true qualities and talents.

Taking action for positive change in your life is a form of homecoming because it restores you to yourself. Rebecca remarked, 'It took me until age fifty-four to realise that I'm not the capable-but-dull plodder of my family reputation. But at least I did discover that I'm a sparkler rather than a wet blanket, and I have a tender sense of protectiveness about my new sense of self.' As you feel more at home with yourself, you will be more at peace with your family past and more capable of continuing to choose healthy self-expression and change.

In the last two exercises, you will use your writing to create a bridge to greater healing of painful memories and relationships and further personal and family development and change.

## EXERCISE

## CREATIVE STRATEGIES FOR LIVING FROM YOUR ROOTS

You can use the three tasks of the change process – awareness or journeying, assessment or naming and action for change or homecoming – as a blueprint for future reflection and writing. For now, your integration of the book's material will be enhanced by examining each of the tasks in light of where you are with your family pattern and where you believe you are headed. First, you can most easily mobilise your resources for awareness and journeying if you know which one serves you best.

A 1  List five modes of expression, practical strategies or outer resources that you find most helpful.
   2  If you have trouble taking advantage of any of them for some reason, write a few comments on how you can clear the way to more regular use of these resources.

Keith's list included:

*1. Writing out my dreams. 2. Keeping track of my moods in writing so I can understand my tendency to depression better. 3. Playing football with some men friends after work. 4. Visiting my dad next summer to hear some of his life stories. 5. Digging in my garden – my deep thinking time.*

B 1  Think about all the names you have been called in your life – the name on your birth certificate, what your parents called you and any nicknames, endearments or critical labels.
   2  Describe how these names have helped you or held you back. Do they reflect who you know yourself to be now after all this writing?
C 1  The task of redefining yourself as an individual and as a family member is an ongoing one and you can answer the following naming question now as well as anytime you come to a crossroads: **If you could name yourself now – with a variation of your actual name, a new name or a title that describes your talents and aspirations – what would you call yourself ?**
   2  Write a short passage including this chosen name and your reasons for it.

Rebecca wrote:

*My mother said she named me Rebecca Ruth because even as a baby I looked like a solid traditionalist, a nice ordinary Jewish girl. She missed a valuable part of the real me, the part that likes to be seen, to be excited and exciting. From now on, I'm not going to name myself as an older woman who has to be dignified. I want those I care about to see more of my 'sparkler' self – giving off light and energy and noise!*

Finally, to mobilise your resources for the tasks of homecoming or putting change into action, you can use the following adapted version of Virginia Satir's five freedoms as a guide to writing about the core of your own current needs and plans. Each of the listed items directs you to a strategy for translating clear and authentic written expression of your current experience into action. Responding to simple questions can bring you to your home truths.

D    Ask yourself and respond in writing to any or all of these questions:

- What do I need to notice and reflect on right now?
- What am I feeling?
- Is there some thought or emotion that I need to act on?
- Is there something I want to ask for now?
- Is there some risk I need to take for future gain?

Keith wrote:

*I want to ask for some support from my friend Dave. He's someone I can really relax with but he also challenges me to grow. I want to ask him to have dinner twice a month. If I keep talking to him about what I've found out about my family, I hope to feel better and more at home with myself.*

These practical strategies will help you set your course for continued exploration of family themes using all the sources of support around you. The most important source, however, is within you, and this last exercise reminds you of and connects you to your own reserves of healing and insight.

## EXERCISE

### HEALING FOR THE PAST, COURAGE FOR THE PRESENT

One of the valuable aspects of writing from your roots is that you recontact yourself at earlier ages. Your child self absorbed a wealth of experience and still carries it within you; you can never go wrong when confused or blocked if you write a dialogue with your child self.

A  1  Choose the childhood image of yourself that seems to call to you at this time. Recall the writing you have done about your childhood and notice whether you fix on a particular image of yourself – you at your fifth birthday party, for example, or on the day your father left, or when you let your hair grow at fourteen.

2  Open a dialogue with that self by writing your child self's responses to the following questions: 'What bothers you?' 'Where do you hurt?'

3  Ask more questions if needed to understand your problems better.

It's your turn to use what you have learned through your writing to offer some perspective and hope of healing for your child self's personal and family dilemmas.

B  1  Write a message of healing and hope to the child that you were then.

2  Read what you have written aloud to yourself.

3  Do you have a similar message for yourself at the age you are now? If so, write it also, and read it aloud.

Store these messages and mark on your calendar to take them out and read them six months from now. Or you can give them to a friend who will be sure to remember to post them to you in six months. You can surprise yourself in the future with some wisdom from the present.

Rebecca wrote to 'my sad-faced, olive-skinned and droopy-eyed ten-year-old self':

*Dear Becky, someday you will look forward to each day because you have exciting things to do and people who love the real you. You will wear bright clothes and make your friends laugh. . . . Reading that aloud had a powerful impact. The phrase 'people who love the real you' was the one that made my throat catch. I still wish my parents had seen and acknowledged the real me, and now they're gone. My message for myself now is 'Go ahead and be sad. When you let yourself be sad all the way through, then your feelings will change.'*

With acknowledgement and expression, feelings do change. The purpose of writing about your family past is to tap the roots of memory and experience so that your unexpressed feelings no longer burden you. You understand how you got to be the person you are today. Knowledge of your psychological root system and expression of the full range of your family heritage can help you in two ways: you can strengthen the life-enhancing behaviour patterns that are learned from your family and you can change the limiting and defeating behaviour patterns from your past.

Writing and living from your roots is not just a workbook technique; it can be a way to mobilise your healing resources at any time. Writing about your family past puts you in touch with the inner strength that brought you through painful times. The act of writing also accesses the whole range of your creativity, broadening your perspective and opening you up to change. As you write, you capture your thoughts and feelings in the moment. That immediacy sets your current impulses and longings into the larger context of your growth so that you have the best perspective on what to do.

By remembering the past, questioning the present and writing your reflections, your expanded perspective will lead to an increasing sense of trust. The losses and lacks of the past remain, but you can trust what you are building now. Your own identity becomes stronger and clearer, while you also feel closer to others. You can discern when to wait and when to act, when you can do things alone and when you need advice and assistance. Your positive changes will affect your family, friends, and colleagues, presenting them with a different model that may help them as well.

Living from your roots answers a call to health and wholeness that has been inside you all your life. By staying in touch with the family roots that profoundly affected your development, you make an ongoing commitment to understand where you came from, where you are now, and where you hope to go. The process of writing and living from your roots will guide and support you in moving towards the health and wholeness that are your birthright.

# ACKNOWLEDGEMENTS

*My deep appreciation to these people for their love and wisdom:*

To my parents, **Jean and Corwin Johnson**, who gave me my sense of family.

To my husband's parents, **Dorothy and Ed Foster**, who welcomed me into their family.

To my grandmother, **Muriel Gearhart**, who linked me to my roots with storytelling, and to all my relatives, who make a family tree worth many stories.

To my pastors and friends, **Paula Kelso**, who helped me become Real, and **John Kelso**, who reminds me that words are sacred.

To the late **Don Whitney**, who helped me find my voice.

To my counselling centre colleagues and long-time friends, **Mary Alice Collins** and **Connie Pearson**, for all we've shared.

To **Madeleine L'Engle**, for being my writing mentor, and to **Pam Wolfson**, for being my writing companion.

To **Dr. Amal Winter**, for her strong and caring guidance.

To these special friends, each of whom has enriched my life and supported my work: **Barbara Gleichman, Gina Gordon, Claudia Hamm, Margot LaBeau, Dixie Mills, Miriam Rowan**, and **Karen Scott**.

To my colleagues and students at **California Institute of Integral Studies, Writers Connection, University of California Extension, Santa Cruz**, and **West Valley College Community Development**.

*My grateful thanks to these gifted professionals who shaped both me and this book through their dedication and support:*

To **Meera Lester**, co-founder of Writers Connection and visionary friend, for urging me forward in my writing and teaching and for helping this book find a home.

To my editor, **Hank Stine**, who saw the potential and championed the book at every stage.

To my agent, **Candice Fuhrman**, for her professional guidance and nonstop encouragement.

To **Jeremy Tarcher**, for giving me this chance to share the ideas from my workshops and courses with a wider audience.